ROMANS

VOLUME 2
CHAPTERS 6 - 11

THE

TEACHER'S

OUTLINE & STUDY

BIBLE™

ROMANS

VOLUME 2
CHAPTERS 6 - 11

THE

TEACHER'S

OUTLINE & STUDY

BIBLE™

NEW TESTAMENT

KING JAMES VERSION

Leadership Ministries Worldwide
PO Box 21310
Chattanooga, TN 37424-0310

May our Lord bless us all as we live, preach, teach, and write for Him, fulfilling His
great commission to live righteous and godly lives and to make disciples of all nations.

Please address all requests for information or permission to:
Leadership Ministries Worldwide
PO Box 21310
Chattanooga TN 37424-0310
Ph.# (423) 855-2181   FAX (423) 855-8616   E-Mail outlinebible@compuserve.com
http://www.outlinebible.org

Library of Congress Catalog Card Number: 94-073070
International Standard Book Number: 1-57407-053-3

PRINTED IN THE U.S.A.

PUBLISHED BY LEADERSHIP MINISTRIES WORLDWIDE

H O W   T O   U S E

THE TEACHER'S OUTLINE AND STUDY BIBLE™
(TOSB)

To gain maximum benefit, here is all you do. Follow these easy steps, using the sample outline below.

1 STUDY TITLE

2 MAJOR POINTS

3 SUB-POINTS

**4 COMMENTARY, QUES-
TIONS, APPLICATION,
ILLUSTRATIONS**
(Follows Scripture)

	B. The Steps to Peace (Part II): Prayer & Positive Thinking, 4:6-9
1. Peace comes through prayer	6 Be careful for
a. The charge: Do not worry or be anxious	nothing; but in every thing by prayer and supplication with thanksgiving
b. The remedy: Prayer	
1) About everything	let your requests be
2) With requests	made known unto
3) With thanksgiving	God.
c. The promise: Peace	7 And the peace of
1) Peace that passes all understanding	God, which passeth all understanding, shall
2) Peace that keeps our hearts & minds	keep your hearts and minds through Christ Jesus.
2. Peace comes through positive thinking	8 Finally, brethren, whatsoever things are
a. The charge: Think & practice things that are...	true, whatsoever things are honest, whatsoever things are
1) True	just, whatsoever
2) Honest	things are pure,
3) Just	whatsoever things
4) Pure	are lovely, what-

1. First: Read the **Study Title** two or three times so that the subject sinks in.
2. Then: Read the **Study Title** and the **Major Points** (Pts.1,2,3) together quickly. Do this several times and you will quickly grasp the overall subject.
3. Now: Read both the **Major Points** and **Sub-Points**. Do this slower than Step 2. Note how the points are beside the applicable verse, and simply state what the Scripture is saying—in Outline form.
4. Read the **Commentary**. As you read and re-read, pray that the Holy Spirit will bring to your attention exactly what you should study and teach. It's all there, outlined and fully developed, just waiting for you to study and teach.

<u>TEACHERS, PLEASE NOTE</u>:

⇒ Cover the **Scripture** and the **Major Points** with your students. Drive the **Scripture** and **Major Points** into their hearts and minds.

(Please continue on next page)

⇒ Cover *only some of the commentary* with your students, not all (unless of course you have plenty of time). Cover only as much commentary as is needed to get the major points across.

⇒ Do NOT feel that you must...
- cover all the commentary under each point
- share every illustration
- ask all the questions

An abundance of commentary is given so you can find just what you need for...
- your own style of teaching
- your own emphasis
- your own class needs

PLEASE NOTE: It is of utmost importance that you (and your study group) grasp the Scripture, the Study Title, and Major Points. It is this that the Holy Spirit will make alive to your heart and that you will more likely remember and use day by day.

MAJOR POINTS include:

APPLICATIONS:
Use these to show how the Scripture applies to everyday life.

ILLUSTRATIONS:
Simply a window that allows enough light in the lesson so a point can be more clearly seen. A suggestion: Do not just "read" through an illustration if the illustration is a story, but learn it and make it your own. Then give the illustration life by communicating it with *excitement & energy*.

QUESTIONS:
These are designed to stimulate thought and discussion.

A CLOSER LOOK:
In some of the studies, you will see a portion boxed in and entitled: "A Closer Look." This discussion will be a closer study on a particular point. It is generally too detailed for a Sunday School class session, but more adaptable for personal study or an indepth Bible Study class.

PERSONAL JOURNAL:
At the close of every lesson there is space for you to record brief thoughts regarding the impact of the lesson on your life. As you study through the Bible, you will find these comments invaluable as you look back upon them.

Now, may our wonderful Lord bless you mightily as you study and teach His Holy Word. And may our Lord grant you much fruit: many who will become greater servants and witnesses for Him.

REMEMBER!

The Teacher's Outline & Study Bible™ is the only study material that actually outlines the Bible verse by verse for you right beside the Scripture. As you accumulate the various books of The Teacher's Outline & Study Bible™ for your study and teaching, you will have the Bible outlined book by book, passage by passage, and verse by verse.

The outlines alone makes saving every book a must! (Also encourage your students, if you are teaching, to keep their student edition. They also have the unique verse by verse outline of Scripture in their version.)

Just think for a moment. Over the course of your life, you will have your very own personalized commentary of the Bible. No other book besides the Bible will mean as much to you because it will contain your insights, your struggles, your victories, and your recorded moments with the Lord.

> **"Study to show thyself approved unto God, a workman that needeth not to be ashamed, rightly dividing the word of truth" (2 Tim.2:15).**

> **"All scripture is given by inspiration of God, and is profitable for doctrine, for reproof, for correction, for instruction in righteousness: that the man of God may be perfect, throughly furnished unto all good works" (2 Tim.3:16-17).**

*** All direct quotes are followed by a Superscript Footnote number. The credit information for each Footnote is listed at the bottom of the page.

MISCELLANEOUS ABBREVIATIONS

&	=	And
Bckgrd.	=	Background
Bc.	=	Because
Circ.	=	Circumstance
Concl.	=	Conclusion
Cp.	=	Compare
Ct.	=	Contrast
Dif.	=	Different
e.g.	=	For example
Et.	=	Eternal
Govt.	=	Government
Id.	=	Identity or Identification
Illust.	=	Illustration
K.	=	Kingdom
No.	=	Number
N.T.	=	New Testament
O.T.	=	Old Testament
Pt.	=	Point
Quest.	=	Question
Rel.	=	Religion
Resp.	=	Responsibility
Rev.	=	Revelation
Rgt.	=	Righteousness
Thru	=	Through
V.	=	Verse
Vs.	=	Verses

Publisher &
Distributor

DEDICATED:

To all the men and women of the world
who preach and teach the Gospel of our
Lord Jesus Christ
and
To the Mercy and Grace of God.

———————— ℰ ————————

- Demonstrated to us in Christ Jesus our Lord.

  "In whom we have redemption through His
  blood, the forgiveness of sins, according to the
  riches of His grace." (Eph. 1:7)

- Out of the mercy and grace of God His Word has
  flowed. Let every person know that God will have
  mercy upon him, forgiving and using him to fulfill
  His glorious plan of salvation.

  "For God so loved the world, that he gave his only
  begotten Son, that whosoever believeth in him should
  not perish, but have everlasting life. For God sent not
  his Son into the world to condemn the world; but that
  the world through him might be saved." (Jn 3:16-17)

  "For this is good and acceptable in the sight of God
  our Saviour; who will have all men to be saved, and to
  come unto the knowledge of the truth." (I Tim. 2:3-4)

———————— ℰ ————————

The Teacher's Outline and Study Bible™
is written for God's people to use
in their study and teaching of God's Holy Word.

9/97

LEADERSHIP MINISTRIES WORLDWIDE

OUR FIVEFOLD MISSION & PURPOSE:

- To share the Word of God with the world.
- To help the believer, both minister and layman alike, in his understanding, preaching, and teaching of God's Word.
- To do everything we possibly can to lead men, women, boys, and girls to give their hearts and lives to Jesus Christ and to secure the eternal life which He offers.
- To do all we can to minister to the needy of the world.
- To give Jesus Christ His proper place, the place which the Word gives Him. Therefore — No work of Leadership Ministries Worldwide will ever be personalized.

This material, like similar works, has come from imperfect man and is thus susceptible to human error. We are nevertheless grateful to God for both calling us and empowering us through His Holy Spirit to undertake this task. Because of His goodness and grace, *The Preacher's Outline & Sermon Bible®* - New Testament is complete in 14 volumes as well as the single volume of **The Minister's Handbook**.

God has given the strength and stamina to bring us this far. Our confidence is that, as we keep our eyes on Him and grounded in the undeniable truths of the Word, we will continue working through the Old Testament Volumes and introduce a new series known as *The Teacher's Outline & Study Bible.* Future materials will include CD-ROM, The Believer's *Outline* Bible, and similar *Outline* and **Handbook** materials.

To everyone, everywhere who preaches and teaches the Word, we offer this material firstly to Him in whose name we labor and serve, and for whose glory it has been produced.

Our daily prayer is that each volume will lead thousands, millions, yes even billions, into a better understanding of the Holy Scriptures and a fuller knowledge of Jesus Christ the incarnate Word, of whom the Scriptures so faithfully testify.

As you have purchased this volume, you will be pleased to know that a portion of the price you paid goes to underwrite providing similar volumes at affordable prices in other languages (Russian, Korean, Spanish and others yet to come) to a preacher, pastor, church leader, or Bible student somewhere around the world, who will present God's message with clarity, authority, and understanding beyond their own.
Amen.

- *Equipping God's Servants Worldwide with OUTLINE Bible Materials* -
— LMW is a 501(c)3 nonprofit, international nondenominational mission agency —   8/97

**LEADERSHIP
MINISTRIES
WORLDWIDE**

P.O. Box 21310, 515 Airport Road, Suite 107
Chattanooga, TN 37424-0310
(423) 855-2181 FAX (423) 855-87616
E-Mail - outlinebible@compuserve.com
www.outlinebible.org [Free download samples]

ACKNOWLEDGMENTS

Every child of God is precious to the Lord and deeply loved. And every child as a servant of the Lord touches the lives of those who come in contact with him or his ministry. The writing ministry of the following servants have touched this work, and we are grateful that God brought their writings our way. We hereby acknowledge their ministry to us, being fully aware that there are so many others down through the years whose writings have touched our lives and who deserve mention, but the weaknesses of our minds have caused them to fade from memory. May our wonderful Lord continue to bless the ministry of these dear servants, and the ministry of us all as we diligently labor to reach the world for Christ and to meet the desperate needs of those who suffer so much.

THE GREEK SOURCES

1   Expositor's Greek Testament, Edited by W. Robertson Nicoll. Grand Rapids, MI: Eerdmans Publishing Co., 1970

2. Robertson, A.T. Word Pictures in the New Testament. Nashville, TN: Broadman Press, 1930.

3. Thayer, Joseph Henry. Greek-English Lexicon of the New Testament. New York: American Book Co.

4. Vincent, Marvin R. Word Studies in the New Testament. Grand Rapids, MI: Eerdmans Publishing Co., 1969.

5. Vine, W.E. Expository Dictionary of New Testament Words. Old Tappan, NJ: Fleming H. Revell Co.

6. Wuest, Kenneth S. Word Studies in the Greek New Testament. Grand Rapids, MI: Eerdmans Publishing Co., 1953.

THE REFERENCE WORKS

7. Cruden's Complete Concordance of the Old & New Testament. Philadelphia, PA: The John C. Winston Co., 1930.

8. Josephus' Complete Works. Grand Rapids, MI: Kregel Publications, 1981.

9. Lockyer, Herbert, Series of Books, including his Books on All the Men, Women, Miracles, and Parables of the Bible. Grand Rapids, MI: Zondervan Publishing House.

10. Nave's Topical Bible. Nashville, TN: The Southewstern Co.

11. The Amplified New Testament. (Scripture Quotations are from the Amplified New Testament, Copyright 1954, 1958, 1987 by the Lockman Foundation. Used by permission.)

12. The Four Translation New Testament (Including King James, New American Standard, Williams - New Testament In the Language of the People, Beck - New Testament In the Language of Today.) Minneapolis, MN: World Wide Publications.

13. The New Compact Bible Dictionary, Edited by T. Alton Bryant. Grand Rapids, MI: Zondervan Publishing House, 1967.

14. The New Thompson Chain Reference Bible. Indianapolis, IN: B.B. Kirkbride Bible Co., 1964,

THE COMMENTARIES

15. Barclay, William. Daily Study Bible Series. Philadelphia, PA: Westminster Press.

16. Bruce, F.F. The Epistle to the Colossians. Westwood, NJ: Fleming H. Revell Co., 1968.

17. Bruce, F.F. Epistle to the Hebrews.Grand Rapids, MI: Eerdmans Publishing Co., 1964.

18. Bruce, F.F. The Epistles of John. Old Tappan, NJ: Fleming H. Revell Co., 1970.

19. Criswell, W.A. Expository Sermons on Revelation. Grand Rapids, MI: Zondervan Publishing House, 1962-66.

20. Greene, Oliver. The Epistles of John. Greenville, SC: The Gospel Hour, Inc., 1966.

21. Greene, Oliver. The Epistles of Paul the Apostle to the Hebrews. Greenville, SC: The Gospel Hour, Inc., 1965.

22. Greene, Oliver. The Epistles of Paul the Apostle to Timothy & Titus. Greenville, SC: The Gospel Hour, Inc., 1964.

23. Greene, Oliver. The Revelation Verse by Verse Study. Greenville, SC: The Gospel Hour, Inc., 1963.

24. Henry, Matthew. Commentary on the Whole Bible. Old Tappan, NJ: Fleming H. Revell Co.

25. Hodge, Charles. Exposition on Romans & on Corinthians. Grand Rapids, MI: Eerdmans Publishing Co., 1972-1973.

26. Ladd, George Eldon. A Commentary On the Revelation of John. Grand Rapids, MI: Eerdmans Publishing Co., 1972-1973.

27. Leupold, H.C. Exposition of Daniel. Grand Rapids, MI: Baker Book House, 1969.

28. Newell, William R. Hebrews, Verse by Verse. Chicago, IL: Moody Press.

29. Strauss, Lehman. Devotional Studies in Philippians. Neptune, NJ: Loizeaux Brothers.

30. Strauss, Lehman. Colossians & 1 Timothy. Neptune, NJ: Loizeaux Brothers.

31. Strauss, Lehman. The Book of the Revelation. Neptune, NJ: Loizeaux Brothers.

32. The New Testament & Wycliffe Bible Commentary, Edited by Charles F. Pfeiffer & Everett F. Harrison. New York: The Iverson Associates, 1971. Produced for Moody Monthly. Chicago Moody Press, 1962.

33. The Pulpit Commentary, Edited by H.D.M. Spence & Joseph S. Exell. Grand Rapids, MI: Eerdmans Publishing Co., 1950.

34. Thomas, W.H. Griffith. Hebrews, A Devotional Commentary. Grand Rapids, MI: Eerdmans Publishing Co., 1970.

35. Thomas, W.H. Griffith. Studies in Colossians & Philemon. Grand Rapids, MI: Baker Book House, 1973.

36. Tyndale New Testament Commentaries. Grand Rapids, MI: Eerdmans Publishing Co., Began in 1958.

37. Walker, Thomas. Acts of the Apostles. Chicago, IL: Moody Press, 1965.

38. Walvoord, John. The Thessalonian Epistles. Grand Rapids, MI: Zondervan Publishing House, 1973.

OTHER SOURCES

39. Bible Illustrator for Windows. Version 2.0b. Copyright © 1990-1997 by Parsons Technology, Inc.

40. Green, Michael P. Illustrations for Biblical Preaching. Grand Rapids, MI: Baker Books, 1996.

41. Hewett, James S. Illustrations Unlimited. Wheaton, IL: Tyndale House Publishers, Inc., 1988.

42. Kennedy Dr. D. James. Is It Nothing to You? Coral Ridge Presbyterian Church, Ft. Lauderdale, Florida.

43. Knight, Walter B. Knight's Master Book of 4,000 Illustrations. Grand Rapids, MI: Eerdmans Publishing Company, 1994.

44. Kyle, Ted & Todd, John. A Treasury of Bible Illustrations. Chattanooga, TN: AMG Publishers, 1995.

45. Larson, Craig B., Editor. Illustrations for Preaching and Teaching. Grand Rapids, MI: Baker Books, 1993

46. Osbeck, Kenneth W. Amazing Grace: 366 Inspiring Hymn Stories for Daily Devotions. Grand Rapids, MI: Kregel Publications, 1990.

47. Rowell, Edward K., Editor. Quotes & Idea Starters for Preaching & Teaching. Grand Rapids, MI: Baker Books, 1996.

48. Zodhiates, Spiros, Th.D. Illustrations of Bible Truths. Chattanooga, TN: AMG Publishers, 1995.

49. Zuck, Roy B. The Speaker's Quote Book. Grand Rapids, MI: Kregel Publications, 1997.

Materials Published & Distributed by LEADERSHIP MINISTRIES WORLDWIDE:

- **THE PREACHER'S OUTLINE & SERMON BIBLE®— DELUXE EDITION**

  Volume 1 . . . . St. Matthew I (chapters 1-15)   3-Ring, looseleaf binder
  Volume 2 . . . . St. Matthew II (chapters 16-28)
  Volume 3 . . . . St. Mark
  Volume 4 . . . . St. Luke
  Volume 5 . . . . St. John
  Volume 6 . . . . Acts
  Volume 7 . . . . Romans
  Volume 8 . . . . 1, 2 Corinthians (1 volume)
  Volume 9 . . . . Galatians, Ephesians, Philippians, Colossians (1 volume)
  Volume 10 . . . . 1,2 Thessalonians, 1,2 Timothy, Titus, Philemon (1 volume)
  Volume 11 . . . . Hebrews -James (1 volume)
  Volume 12 . . . . 1,2 Peter, 1,2,3 John, Jude (1 volume)
  Volume 13 . . . . Revelation
  Volume 14 . . . . Master Outline & Subject Index
  FULL SET — 14 Volumes

- **THE PREACHER'S OUTLINE & SERMON BIBLE® — OLD TESTAMENT**

  Volume 1 . . . . Genesis I (chapters 1-11)
  Volume 2 . . . . Genesis II (chapters 12-50)
  Volume 3 . . . . Exodus I (chapters 1-18)
  Volume 4 . . . . Exodus II (chapters 19-40)   New volumes release periodically

- **THE PREACHER'S OUTLINE & SERMON BIBLE® — SOFTBOUND EDITION**
  Identical content as Deluxe above. Lightweight, compact, and affordable for overseas & traveling.

- **The Minister's Personal Handbook - What the Bible Says...to the Minister**
  12 Chapters — 127 Subjects — 400 Verses *OUTLINED* — Standard, Deluxe, 3-ring
  • More than 400 verses from OT and NT dealing with God's minister and servant; all assembled in
  the unique *Outline* style. Features God's Word for His chosen and called servants who minister the Word.

- **Translations of N.T. Volumes and Minister's Handbook: Limited Quantities**
  Russian — Spanish — Korean • *Future: Portuguese, Hindi, Chinese + others*
  — *Contact us for Specific Language and Prices* —

- **THE TEACHER'S OUTLINE & STUDY BIBLE**™ • **New Testament Books** •
  Average 17 lessons/book & 205 pages • Verse-by-Verse Study •• Also: Student Journal Guides

- **CD-ROM New Testament - (Windows/STEP) - WORD***Search* 4™

**All these great Volumes & Materials are also available at affordable prices in
quantity orders, particularly for overseas ministry, by contacting:**

LEADERSHIP MINISTRIES WORLDWIDE   *Your OUTLINE Bookseller*
PO Box 21310
Chattanooga, TN 37424-0310
(423) 855-2181 (8:30 - 5:00 ET) • **FAX (423) 855-8616 (24 hrs)**
E•Mail - outlinebible@compuserve.com.
↪ **FREE Download Sample Pages — www.outlinebible.org**

• *Equipping God's Servants Worldwide with OUTLINE Bible Materials* •
— LMW is a 501(c)3 nonprofit, international nondenominational mission agency — 8/97

"Go ye therefore, and teach all nations" (Mt. 28:19)

A SPECIAL NOTE FOR THE BIBLE STUDY LEADER, PASTOR, OR MINISTER OF EDUCATION

The teaching material you have before you gives your church the _maximum flexibility_ in scheduling for the church year or for any Bible study program. Below are two options available:

⇒ For those who wish to do a quarterly study on _The Book of Romans {Volume 2}_, the following chart shows you how to combine 18 lessons into 13 sessions.

⇒ For those who wish to follow a self-paced schedule, please note: the outlines marked by an asterisk are outlines of considerable length. You may wish to preview these and break them down into two or more lessons each.

SUGGESTED QUARTERLY SCHEDULE LESSON PLANS FOR ROMANS - VOLUME 2, CHAPTERS 6 - 11,

IV. HOLINESS AND SANCTIFICATION: THE WAY FOR THE BELIEVER TO BE FREE FROM SIN, 6:1-23

WEEK #	LESSON TITLE	SCRIPTURE TEXT	PAGE NUMBER
1	_"The Believer Is Not to Continue in Sin (Part I): He Is to Know His Position in Christ"_	_6:1-10_	
2	_"The Believer Is Not to Continue in Sin:_ ⇒ _(Part II)--He is to Live Out His Position in Christ_ ⇒ _(Part III)--He Does Not Have License to Sin"_	_6:11-13_ _6:14-23_	

V. STRUGGLE AND CONFESSION: THE BELIEVER IS TO BE FREE FROM THE LAW, 7:1-25

WEEK #	LESSON TITLE	SCRIPTURE TEXT	PAGE NUMBER
3	_"The Law:_ ⇒ _The Two Positions of the Law to Man_ ⇒ _The Purpose of the Law"_	_7:1-6_ _7:7-13_	
4	_"The Confessions of a Man's Struggling Soul"_	_7:14-25_	

VI. DELIVERANCE AND REDEMPTION: THE BELIEVER SHALL BE FREED FROM STRUGGLING AND SUFFERING BY THE SPIRIT, 8:1-39

WEEK #	LESSON TITLE	SCRIPTURE TEXT	PAGE NUMBER
5	"The Man in Christ Jesus Is Freed from Condemnation: The Power of the Spirit (Part 1)"	8:1-17	
6	"The Man in Christ Jesus Is Freed from Condemnation: The Power of the Spirit (Part 2)"	8:1-17	
7	"The Whole Creation Shall Be Freed from Struggling and Suffering"	8:18-27	
8	"God Assures Deliverance (Freedom) from Struggling and Suffering"	8:28-39	

VII. ISRAEL AND THE GOSPEL OF RIGHTEOUSNESS, 9:1-11:36

WEEK #	LESSON TITLE	SCRIPTURE TEXT	PAGE NUMBER
9	"The Mystery of Israel: ⇒ The Privileges of Israel and Their Tragic Failure ⇒ The True Israel or Children of God"	9:1-5 9:6-13	
10	"The Rejection of Israel: God's Right to Show Mercy and Justice as He Wills"	9:14-33	
11	"The Tragic Mistake of Israel: ⇒ Missing God's Righteousness ⇒ The Gospel (Righteousness by Faith) Is Not for Israel Alone—It Is Universal"	10:1-11 10:12-21	
12	"The Callous on Israel's Heart: ⇒ The Callous on Israel's Heart is Not Total—There is a Remnant ⇒ The Callous on Israel's Heart is Not Final—There is to be a Restoration ⇒ The Callous on Israel's Heart is a Warning to Other Nations"	11:1-10 11:11-16 11:17-24	
13	"The Restoration of Israel and Its Surety"	11:25-36	

OUTLINE OF ROMANS

Volume 2, Chapters 6 - 11

THE TEACHER'S OUTLINE & SERMON BIBLE™ is *unique*. It differs from all other Study Bibles and Lesson Resource Materials in that every Passage and Subject is outlined right beside the Scripture. When you choose any *Subject* below and turn to the reference, you have not only the Scripture, but you discover the Scripture and Subject *already outlined for you--verse by verse*.

For a quick example, choose one of the subjects below and turn over to the Scripture, and you will find this marvelous help for faster, easier, and more accurate use.

A suggestion: For the quickest overview of Romans, Volume 2, first read *all the major titles* (I, II, III, etc.), then come back and read the subtitles.

OUTLINE OF ROMANS

Volume 2, Chapters 6 - 11

THE EPISTLE OF PAUL THE APOSTLE TO THE

ROMANS

INTRODUCTION

AUTHOR: Paul, the Apostle. Paul clearly states that he is the author (Ro.1:1), and the personal references and facts given in Chapter 15 tell us beyond any doubt that Paul is the author.

DATE: A.D. 55-58.

Paul says, "Now I go unto Jerusalem to minister unto the saints" (Ro.15:25). This journey to Jerusalem was the trip made necessary by the extreme poverty of the believers in the Jerusalem church. Paul had taken a collection from the Gentile churches and felt compelled to deliver the offering himself. This occurred on his third missionary journey.

TO WHOM WRITTEN: "To all that be in Rome, beloved of God, called to be saints."

Several manuscripts have been found with the personal and local touches of chapters 15-16 omitted and the doxology included. This would definitely point to there being several churches. The place of writing seems to be Corinth, for Paul recommended Phoebe to the Romans. Phoebe was a deaconess from Cenchrea, the eastern seaport of Corinth.

PURPOSE: Paul had several reasons for writing.

1.   Paul wished to evangelize Spain (Ro.15:25). To do so he needed a local church from which to launch his ministry--a church that would be much closer to Spain than Antioch. Antioch had been his home base up until now. By writing Romans, he was preparing the Roman church for the day when he would reveal his vision to them. He was making them familiar with his name, his mission, and his love.

2.   Paul had a personal compulsion to visit and witness in Rome itself. His life-long strategy had been to evangelize the great metropolitan cities along the route that stretched from Jerusalem to Rome. He knew that a route so greatly traveled and cities so actively engaged in commerce would assure the spread of the Gospel. Rome was the capital, the center of the world; it provided the greatest strategic opportunity for world evangelism. A Rome conquered for Christ could mean a world conquered for Christ.

3.   Paul was not sure he would ever reach Rome personally. He was going to Jerusalem and knew the danger. There was a chance he might be killed in Jerusalem. He requested the Roman church to pray for him: "I beseech you, brethren...strive together with me in your prayers to God for me, that I may be delivered from them that do not believe in Judea" (15:30-31). Yet despite the danger, Paul was a master strategist: he knew the strategic importance of Rome for the spread of the Gospel worldwide. The church had to be rooted and grounded in the faith; therefore he sat down and wrote this great letter. The message of the letter is what Paul would hammer into the believers' hearts if he ever did get to stand before them.

SPECIAL FEATURES:

1.   The church at Rome. The church was strong. Five factors show its strength.

First, Rome was a *lay church*. A writer of the fourth century said that some Roman citizens "had embraced the faith of Christ...without any sign of mighty works or any of the apostles" (Ambrosiaster, a Latin Father, in his <u>Epistle to the Romans</u>. Quoted by F.F. Bruce. *The Epistle of Paul to the Romans*. "The Tyndale New Testament Commentaries," ed. by RVG Tasker. Grand Rapids, MI: Eerdmans, 1963, p.13). The content of the epistle shows a people of great spiritual depth and maturity. But how did the gospel reach Rome? Who founded the church? The only thing known for sure is that

3

there was a great and flourishing church in the capital. But just when the church was founded is unknown. There are several possibilities.

  a. At Pentecost there were "strangers from Rome, both Jews and proselytes" (Acts 2:10). Were any converted during Pentecost? There is no specific mention of converts among the Romans, but Romans are the only group identified among the European pilgrims.

  b. Many of the members of the Roman church were known by Paul personally. He had met them elsewhere, sometime long ago. The church could have been founded by these. He greets Aquila and Priscilla (16:3; cp. Acts 18:2-3). He also greets some well-known believers whom he says were "in Christ" even before himself: Andronicus and Junia (16:7). Rufus, perhaps the son of Simon of Cyrene who carried the cross of Christ, is also greeted (see note--16:13; cp. Mk.15:21). Paul may have known Rufus and his mother in Antioch.

  c. The lay followers of Christ were probably among the first to carry the gospel to Rome. This was Paul's great strategy as God's chief commander for world evangelization. Paul had penetrated the great cities of the world with the glorious gospel, and he did all he could to establish a strong church in each of the major cities. Each of these cities lay along the world's great roads that led right into the heart of the world's capital, Rome itself. In all the hustle and bustle of business and traveling to and fro, some men, racing throughout the world and carrying on their affairs, were bound to be reached for Christ and to become lay missionaries themselves. It was only inevitable that Rome be penetrated. A church was bound to be founded right in the heart of Rome.

Second, Rome had a *worldwide reputation*. Its faith was strong (1:8). It was spiritually mature, able to digest the *meat* of the Word. Practically every page covers a major doctrine or theological discussion.

Third, Rome was a *Gentile church*. The Gentiles, who comprised a vast majority of the membership, were reminded of the fact that Christianity had come from Jewish roots. Therefore, the Jews were to be deeply respected--even if they were outnumbered (11:18).

Fourth, Rome was a *persecuted church*. The church was severely persecuted seven years after Paul wrote this great letter to the believers. Nero had burned the older section of the great city in a fit of madness, and he blamed the burning of Rome upon the Christians. Believers were also charged with such crimes as cannibalism, immoral practices, and with being enemies of the state. They were actually charged with any other crime that could be connived. However, the blood of the church proved to be its seed (Tertullian, Apology 50. Quoted by F.F. Bruce. *The Epistle of Paul to the Romans*. "The Tyndale New Testament Commentaries," p.17). Believers, fleeing the persecution, spread all over the world; and wherever they went they shared the glorious news of eternal life in Christ Jesus. In addition, the citizens of Rome grew tired of so much savagery and eventually demanded that the savagery against the Christians stop. The church was left alone and the glorious news of salvation was allowed to be freely proclaimed.

Fifth, Rome was a *triumphant church*. The church was unashamed of its life and witness. It was willing to stand up and be counted by the side of those who suffered. When Paul was being escorted into the city as a Roman prisoner, while still some thirty to forty miles away, the Christian church marched forward to meet and give him a triumphant processional over those thirty to forty miles. The sight of these dear believers filled Paul with a sense of glory seldom experienced by men. (See note--Acts 28:13-15.)

  2. Romans is *The Great Epistle of Theology*. It is a statement of what Paul believed, a statement of his theology. Paul was not writing to meet a special problem or danger or error. He was writing primarily to root and ground the Roman believers in the faith as deeply as he could, for they lived in the great strategic center with explosive potential for world evangelization. He was completely free to set forth what he saw to be the essential theology for a living faith.

  3. Romans is *The Epistle Written for Every Man*. It is the Gospel of God (1:1). It is a book for the world (1:4-2:16; etc.); a book for the church (see 1:1-7; etc.); a book

for theologians (see 3:1-5:21; etc.); a book for philosophers (see 1:1-2:16; etc.); a book for legalists (see 7:1f; etc.); a book for immature believers (see 6:1-8:30); a book for mature believers (see 8:12-14; etc.); a book for sufferers (see 7:1-8:39; etc.); a book for unbelievers (see 1:1-2:16; etc.); a book for religionists (see 2:17-5:21; etc.). Romans is the truth desperately needed by every man, whoever or wherever he may be.

4.   Romans is *The Church's Last Testament*. Although one of the driving forces of Paul's heart was to visit the Roman church, he was not sure he would ever get to see them face to face (See Purpose, point 3). Yet, the church's strategic importance necessitated that he do what he could to assure that they use their explosive potential for Christ. Thus, he was forced to write--just in case. And write he did. In the Book of Romans the church has what Paul wished to say to the church--just in case he never got there. In a sense it is *The Church's Last Testament*--just what the church needs to hear. Romans comes closest to being the one written possession a church needs, the most comprehensive statement of Christian truth.

5.   Romans is *The Gospel's Main Truth*. This is evident from Special Features, points 1 and 2.

6.   Romans is *God's WorldWide Plan for Israel and the Gentiles*. More clearly than any other book, Romans shows God's glorious plan for the ages in Israel and the Gentile nations. A panoramic view of history is given from a Christian perspective. This is quickly grasped by a study of the Outline, chapters 9-11.

	CHAPTER 6 **IV. HOLINESS & SANCTIFICATION: THE WAY FOR THE BELIEVER TO BE FREE FROM SIN, 6:1-23**	was raised up from the dead by the glory of the Father, even so we also should walk in newness of life. 5 For if we have been planted together in the likeness of his death, we shall be also in the likeness of his resurrection:	1) Raised by God's glory 2) Purpose: That we should walk in newness of life c. Immersed, identified with the most glorious hope: The believer will be raised just as Jesus was raised
	A. The Believer Is Not to Continue in Sin (Part I): He Is to Know His Position in Christ, 6:1-10	6 Knowing this, that our old man is crucified with him, that the body of sin might be destroyed, that henceforth we should not serve sin.	3. Know 2nd: By position, the believer's old man was crucified with Christ a. To destroy the body of sin b. To enable man to renounce sin
1. The believer & the question of license a. Does grace give a person a free reign to sin? b. God forbid! c. The believer is dead to sin	**W**hat shall we say then? Shall we continue in sin, that grace may abound?	7 For he that is dead is freed from sin.	c. Illustration: A dead man
2. Know 1st: By position, the believer is immersed, placed into Christ a. Immersed, identified with Christ in death b. Immersed, identified with Christ in resurrection	2 God forbid. How shall we, that are dead to sin, live any longer therein? 3 Know ye not, that so many of us as were baptized into Jesus Christ were baptized into his death? 4 Therefore we are buried with him by baptism into death: that like as Christ	8 Now if we be dead with Christ, we believe that we shall also live with him: 9 Knowing that Christ being raised from the dead dieth no more; death hath no more dominion over him. 10 For in that he died, he died unto sin once: but in that he liveth, he liveth unto God.	4. Know 3rd: By position, the believer lives with Christ— now & forever a. Christ has conquered death— once-for-all b. Christ now lives forever for and with God

Section IV
HOLINESS AND SANCTIFICATION: THE WAY FOR THE BELIEVER TO BE FREE FROM SIN
Romans 6:1-23

Study 1: **The Believer Is Not to Continue in Sin (Part I): He Is to Know His Position in Christ**

Text: **Romans 6:1-10**

Aim: To make two strong commitments:
⇒ To break any habitual sins in your life
⇒ To learn all you can about your position in Christ.

Memory Verse:
"Knowing this, that our old man is crucified with him, that the body of sin might be destroyed, that henceforth we should not serve sin" (Romans 6:6).

INTRODUCTION:

Is it possible to live a victorious Christian life, to be free from the power of sin? Look deep inside your own heart and ask yourself this question: *Is there anything—any sin, any bad habit, any vice—that you have found impossible to shake off?* The truth is, many have given in and surrendered to the power of some sin in their lives.

How can anyone live a holy life when the world's pleasures, bright lights, and passions are so attractive and stimulating? Too many believers give up in the struggle against sin when victory is close to becoming a reality.

> *Francis Scott Key found himself to be a prisoner of the British during the War of 1812. His ship captured by attacking British forces, Key was forced to watch as his captors unleashed a fierce bombardment upon Fort McHenry. Smoke filled the sky and darkness flooded the night as the battle raged. From where Key sat that night, the circumstances were not promising: he was a prisoner; his nation was being attacked; and the sight, the sound, and the smell of certain defeat filled the air. But if you know the story, you know that when dawn came, he saw his flag, "Old Glory," still waving. At that moment, Key penned his famous poem that became the National Anthem of the United States: "The Star Spangled Banner."*
>
> *Much like Key, the Christian believer who struggles with sin is also a prisoner. There is every opportunity to lose heart and give up, but for the Christian there is great hope because the dawn has already come! The power of Jesus Christ—His death, resurrection, and work on the Cross—is still our salvation today. His charge to us is simple: "Stand in Me and see the salvation of the Lord." When overcoming sin, the important thing is not what sin surrounds you but where you sit—in Christ.*

The believer who is justified, whose faith is counted as righteousness, is to live a holy life and become a servant of righteousness. A genuinely saved person cannot abuse the mercy of God. He cannot *continually* walk in sin; he cannot make a habit of sinning. To do so is to tread upon the mercy of God and make a mockery of God's grace. It is to say that God's grace gives a person the license to sin, and such is a contradiction of terms—as much a contradiction as to say that a dead man is alive. (See Ro.6:14-15; Gal.5:13.)

Now for the point of the passage. The believer is to know his real position in Christ. Knowledge of his position will help keep him from sin. It will revolutionize his life. Note the word *"know"* is used three times (Ro.6:3, 6, 9).

OUTLINE:

1. The believer and the question of license (v.1-2).
2. Know 1st: by position, the believer is immersed, placed into Christ (v.3-5).
3. Know 2nd: by position, the believer's old man was crucified with Christ (v.6-7).
4. Know 3rd: by position, the believer lives with Christ—now and forever (v.8-10).

1. THE BELIEVER AND THE QUESTION OF LICENSE (v.1-2).

Note three points.

1. Grace means God's undeserved and unmerited favor. It means that God freely accepts and forgives a person's sins; that He freely justifies a person by faith. But does the grace of God give a person free reign to sin? Can a person just go ahead and do what he wants, expecting God to forgive him? Two things bother a lot of people about the teaching of salvation by grace and grace alone.

    a. Grace seems to give free reign to sin, to put no restraint upon sin. These are often the thoughts of the common man, even believers. There is the feeling that if we are forgiven by grace and not by law and doing good, then sin does not matter that much. We do not have to worry too much about the law of God and righteousness, just so we do a fair amount of good. We can pretty much do what we want, for God is going to forgive us anyway. God is gracious and loving and good; therefore, He is going to forgive our sins no matter what we do. Christ died for our sins. All we have to do is ask Him and He will forgive us.

b. Grace seems to encourage sin. Paul had just said that grace is stronger than sin (Ro.5:15-21, esp. 20-21). God's grace is so strong it can forgive any sin, no matter how terrible. In fact, the greater the sin, the more magnified God's grace becomes. When a *great sinner* is forgiven, God's grace is much more magnified than when a morally good person repents and is forgiven. As stated, the greater the sin or sinner, the more God's grace is magnified and glorified.

Now note: some theologians and philosophers, in particular those who stress the law, carry this argument even farther in their position against grace. No doubt Paul was asked this question time and again by the legalists who hounded and fought against him and just did not understand the wonderful grace of God. They argued that if forgiveness is by grace, then is sin not a good thing? Should we not continue in sin so that God will have more opportunity to prove His grace and become more magnified and glorified?

2. Paul's answer is the answer of righteous indignation: "God forbid!" Away with such a thought! Far be it that we ever think such a thing, especially as believers.

3. The *believer's position* in Christ shows the utter impossibility of a true believer's *continuing in sin*. The word "continue" means to practice or to habitually yield to sin. A true believer no longer practices sin and no longer yields to sin. He cannot live *without sin*, not totally, but he no longer lives *in sin*. A true believer is dead to sin, and a dead man cannot do anything: he cannot think, speak, or move. How can a dead man live any longer in sin? It is utterly impossible! It is totally against nature! *Positionally*, the true believer has died to self and has been *placed* into Christ to live for Him. He now possesses the *divine nature*, God's very own nature (2 Pt.1:4). He is *placed* and *positioned* in Christ which means he is dead to self and alive to God. How can he dare think that he can go ahead and sin because God will forgive him anyway?

Note another fact: when a man turns *to* God, he turns *away from* sin. It is a contradiction to say that when a man turns to God he turns to more and more sin. God's grace does not bring a man to God so that he can be *free to sin* more; God's grace brings a man to God so that he can be *free from sin* and its guilt and judgment. Grace does not give license to sin any more than a dead man is able to move about and sin.

ILLUSTRATION:

There are many people who profess to be Christians in order to get their "fire insurance." Wanting to escape the eternal flames of hell, they make a profession of Christ, but they still live for themselves instead of living for God. These people have no trouble justifying...

- telling 'little white lies'
- stealing items from the office for personal use
- focusing on the world and its pleasures instead of God and His treasures

And why not? If grace is free, we can have the best of both worlds...or can we?

There is an old legend about a man who lived his life looking out for "#1"—himself. Having lived for pleasure the majority of his life, he began to take note of some loose ends. "Eternity," he thought to himself. "I need to make sure that when judgment day comes I'll be on the right side." His thinking was that by joining a church and getting his name on the roll, he would secure his 'fire insurance.'

A few months later he died and found himself in a poorly-lit waiting room that reeked of sulfur. "I always thought heaven would be a little bit nicer than this" he mumbled. "This must be a holding room stuck between heaven and hell. It's a good thing I've got my 'fire insurance policy.'"

After a brief wait, the man was summoned inside a large room containing file cabinets, a long table, and a chair. A creature who breathed heavily asked for his insurance policy. "Here it is right here," the man said confidently as he handed over his policy. Glancing at it the creature roared with delight, "Welcome to hell! We've been waiting for you." The man was shocked, "What are you saying? I just gave you my fire insurance policy!" The creature held up the document and pointed to the bottom. "Look, your fire insurance policy was paid for by Jesus Christ but never signed by you! You just failed to follow through! This paper is worthless...and now, so are you."

What are you placing your confidence in—your way or God's way? You cannot have it both ways.

QUESTIONS:
1. How would you respond to those who say that grace allows and encourages others to sin? Have you ever taken license to sin, knowing God will forgive you?
2. What does it mean to be "in Christ"? How does this help keep you from sinful habits?

2. KNOW 1ST: BY POSITION, THE BELIEVER IS IMMERSED, PLACED INTO CHRIST (v.3-5).

First, the believer has been *immersed or placed into Jesus Christ*. This is the first thing the believer should know about his position in Christ. This is one of the most glorious truths in all of Scripture, yet so much controversy has raged over what is meant by baptism that the glorious meaning has often been bypassed. The meaning of baptism is discussed in another note. In the present note, the glorious truth of these verses is being concentrated upon. Christians everywhere agree that baptism is a picture of the death, burial, and resurrection of Jesus Christ. When a true believer is immersed, he is proclaiming to the world that he is being identified with Christ:

⇒ By being placed under the water, he is proclaiming that he has died and been buried with Christ.

⇒ By being raised up from the water, he is proclaiming that he has been raised from the dead with Christ to live a new life.

Now note three glorious points.

1. The believer is immersed, placed into, or identified with Christ *in* death. This is the believer's position in Christ. Very simply, if the believer really died when Christ died, then he has died to sin and is freed from sin, freed from its penalty and punishment. What a glorious gift from God! What a glorious position to receive from God's wonderful grace!

What happens is this: When a person really believes in Christ, then God takes that person's faith and counts the person as having died in Christ. God takes the person's faith (and baptism as stated in this passage) and counts the person as *participating in Christ's death*. God counts and considers the person...

- to have died in Christ's death
- to be identified with Christ's death
- to be in union with Christ's death
- to be placed into Christ's death
- to be a partaker of Christ' death
- to be bound with Christ in death

When a person truly honors God's Son by trusting Him, God honors that person by spiritually placing him into the death of Christ. What is it that causes God to do so much for the believer? Very simply, His love for His Son. God loves His Son so much that He will do anything for anyone who honors His Son by believing in and trusting in Him.

Now note the point: if the believer is *counted* by God as having been immersed into the death of Christ, then the believer...

- has died to sin
- has died to the penalty of sin
- has died to the judgment of sin
- is freed from sin
- is freed from the penalty of sin
- is freed from the judgment of sin

This means that the rule and reign and the habits and desires of sin no longer have control over us. Sin *ceases* to have a place or a position in our lives. We are free from sin, free from...

- sin's habits
- sin's control
- sin's bondage
- sin's enslavement
- sin's rule and reign
- sin's guilt

It means that we no longer live "in" sin, in the *position and place of sin*. We cannot live without sin, not perfectly, but we are *free* from living "in" sin. We no longer practice and desire sin habitually. We desire and practice righteousness, seeking to please God in all that we do. And as glorious as this is, it means that we are freed from the condemnation of sin, the terrible punishment that shall be measured out in the awful day of judgment.

This is the believer's position in Christ. He is immersed, buried, placed into, and identified with Christ in death. And having died, the believer never has to be under the rule and reign of sin and its judgment again. He is a partaker of Christ's death, bound and united to Christ in death; therefore, he is dead to sin and all its effects.

However, note a critical point. A true believer is a person who *really believes*. This simply means he repents, confesses, obeys, and is baptized. It is this person whom God credits as having died in Christ. This is the glorious position of the true believer.

> **"For by one Spirit are we all baptized into one body, whether we be Jews or Gentiles, whether we be bond or free; and have been all made to drink into one Spirit" (1 Cor.12:13).**

2. The believer is immersed, placed into, or identified with Christ in His resurrection. The same picture of baptism is used again to strike home this glorious truth. God counts the true baptized believer as having been raised in Christ. God takes the believer's faith (and baptism as stated in this passage) and counts the person as participating in Christ's resurrection. He counts and considers the person...

- to be raised in Christ's resurrection
- to be placed into Christ's resurrection
- to be identified with Christ's resurrection
- to be a partaker of Christ's resurrection
- to be in union with Christ's resurrection
- to be bound with Christ in His resurrection

Note two significant points.

a. Christ was raised up from the dead by the glory of the Father. This tells how our glorious position in Christ happened. It happened by the glory and the power of God. The "glory" of God means all the excellence of God; all that He is in His might and power, love and grace, compassion and mercy. It means all His attributes: His omnipotence (all power), omniscience (all knowing), omnipresence (being everywhere), and sovereignty. In this particular passage, it refers primarily to His glorious power. It was the glory of His might and power that raised up Jesus from the dead, and it is by the glory of His might and power that he *places and positions* us in Christ.

> **"And God hath both raised up the Lord, and will also raise up us by *his own power*" (1 Cor.6:14).**

b. God's purpose for raising us up with Christ is dynamic and meaningful. It involves walking in a whole new life. The word "walk" means to walk about, to walk step by step, to control and order our behavior, to constantly and habitually walk in "newness of life."

Think about it for a moment. When Christ died, he laid aside His old life, leaving it behind Him. Therefore, when He arose, He took on a totally new life, a changed life, a resurrected life. It is His new life, His changed and resurrected life, that is given to us. In the Bible, the word "new" often carries the idea of purity, righteousness, holiness, godliness. The believer...

- receives a "new birth" (1 Pt.1:23; 2:2)
- receives a "new heart" (Ezk.11:19; 18:31)
- becomes a "new creature" (2 Cor.5:17; Gal.6:15)
- becomes a "new man" (Eph.4:24; Col.3:10)

God's very purpose for *placing* us in the resurrected life of Jesus Christ is that we might walk in Christ, walk soberly, righteously and godly in this present world. The true believer puts off the old man of sin and puts on the new man of righteousness and godliness. He lives a pure, clean, and holy life.

> "Buried with him in baptism, wherein also ye are risen with him through the faith of the operation of God, who hath raised him from the dead" (Col.2:12).

3. The believer is immersed, placed into, or identified with the most glorious hope: that he shall be planted (immersed) in the very likeness of Jesus' resurrection. This simply means that...

- as Jesus was raised to a *new life*, so shall the believer be

> "Even when we were dead in sins, [God] hath quickened us together with Christ, (by grace ye are saved;) and hath raised us up together, and made us sit together in heavenly places in Christ Jesus" (Eph.2:5-6).

- as Jesus was raised to *live with God*, so shall the believer be

> "In my Father's house are many mansions: if it were not so, I would have told you. I go to prepare a place for you. And if I go and prepare a place for you, I will come again, and receive you unto myself; that where I am, there ye may be also" (Jn.14:2-3).

QUESTIONS:
1. What is the first thing a person should know about his position in Christ?
2. What does it mean to die to sin? Does this mean you will never sin again?
3. What is the relationship between baptism and being in Christ? Why is this such a powerful picture of being freed from sin's enslavement?

A CLOSER LOOK:

(6:3-5) **Baptism**: this note is being placed as the last note under verse 10 because of its length and because it is a specialized note dealing with the meaning of "baptism" as used in this passage. Placing the note last allows the reader to study the major points of the outline first and keeps the reader from losing the continuity of thought.

---

3. KNOW 2ND: BY POSITION, THE BELIEVER'S OLD MAN WAS CRUCIFIED WITH CHRIST (v.6-7).

Second, the believer's old man was crucified with Christ. This is the second thing the believer should know about his position in Christ. The Greek definitely uses the past tense: "Our old man <u>was</u> crucified with Christ." It was a *once-for-all act* that Christ

Himself accomplished and completed. He took our "old man" to the cross with Him when He died. The "old man" means...

- our old self
- our old life
- our sinful self
- our sinful life
- our corrupt nature
- our depraved nature
- our unregenerate nature
- our sinful nature

Our "old man" means our old life without God, the old sinful life that is immersed or identified with Christ in death. Now note three points.

1. The old man was crucified so that "the body of sin" might be destroyed. The "body of sin" is not plural (sins) but singular (sin). Sin is seen as a *body*, a *whole package*. The human body is seen as the *seat* of sin and as the *instrument* of sin. The idea is that all sin within a believer is destroyed, conquered, forgiven, and crucified with Christ. The believer is freed from sin. He starts anew, and he *stays* clean and free from sin by walking in constant confession and fellowship before God (1 Jn.1:9).

> **"And he said to them all, If any man will come after me, let him deny himself, and take up his cross daily, and follow me" (Lk.9:23).**

2. The old man was crucified to *enable* and to *empower* the believer to renounce sin. The believer is not to serve sin; he is to renounce it, knowing that it has been crucified and put to death in Christ. By the power of the cross, sin is not to be served; it is...

- to be renounced
- to be refused
- to be repudiated
- to be rejected
- to be denied
- to be conquered

> **"For ye are dead, and your life is hid with Christ in God....Mortify therefore your members which are upon the earth; fornication, uncleanness, inordinate affection, evil concupiscence, and covetousness, which is idolatry" (Col.3:3, 5).**

3. The clearest of all illustrations is given to show the believer's position in Christ. He is not to serve sin because he is dead; he has been crucified with Christ. And a dead man is freed from sin. When we believe that Jesus died for our sins, our belief is counted as righteousness; our belief makes us acceptable to God once-for-all. And it does something else just as wonderful: it gives us constant access into God's presence as we walk about day by day. This means that as we pick up the pollutions of this world and fail here and there, we can constantly come before God and ask forgiveness; and when we ask, He forgives. This is the way we are freed from sin: by constantly walking in *open confession* before God, praying all day long for His forgiveness. And just as He promises, He always forgives us (1 Jn.1:9). Why does He do such a glorious thing as freeing us from sin eternally?

⇒ Because we honor His Son by trusting Christ's death to free us from sin.

⇒ Because He loves His Son and will honor any man who so trusts His Son. He will honor the man by doing exactly what the man believes. If the man honors Christ by *believing* that he is freed from sin by the death of Christ, then God counts the man as being freed from sin.

> **"In whom we have redemption through his blood, the forgiveness of sins, according to the riches of his grace" (Eph.1:7).**

This is the glorious position of the believer in Christ: his old man "was crucified" with Christ in order to free him from sin. Note the most glorious and striking truth: our salvation is *through the death of God's dear Son, Jesus Christ*.

1. Using very simple terms, what does the "old man" or "old self" mean?
2. Why do so many believers struggle with the "old man"? What is the only way to successfully deal with the "old man"?
3. What did Jesus Christ do to the "old man" when He hung on the cross? How enduring is Christ's work in your life?

4. KNOW 3RD: BY POSITION, THE BELIEVER LIVES WITH CHRIST—NOW AND FOREVER (v.8-10).

Third, the believer *shall live with Christ both now and forever*. This is the third thing the believer should know about his position in Christ. We know and possess absolute assurance and confidence that "we shall...live with Christ." The idea is that we shall live eternally with Him. What gives us such belief and absolute assurance?

1. Christ has conquered death—once-for-all. Think about it. Christ has already died. Now we are to *know*...

- "that Christ being raised from the dead dieth no more"
- "that death hath no more dominion over Him"
- that He is freed from death

> **"But [God's purpose and grace] is now made manifest by the appearing of our Saviour Jesus Christ, who hath abolished death, and hath brought life and immortality to light through the gospel" (2 Tim.1:10).**

2. Christ now lives forever with and for God. We are to know...

- that Christ died unto sin once
- that Christ now lives in the presence of God forever
- that Christ lives unto God; that is, He lives in an unbroken devotion and service to God

The believer is to live with and for God through all eternity, beginning right now, from the moment of his conversion. Death has no more dominion over him. He is immersed or placed into the resurrected life of Christ. He is an eternal person *now*; therefore, he is to live with and for God beginning right now, even as he will live with and for God through all eternity.

> **"I came forth from the Father, and am come into the world: again, I leave the world, and go to the Father" (Jn.16:28).**

APPLICATION:

This, of course, means that we too shall be living on and on in an unbroken devotion and service to God—forever.

> **"For God so loved the world, that he gave his only begotten Son, that whosoever believeth in him should not perish, but have everlasting life" (Jn.3:16).**
> **"Verily, verily, I say unto you, He that heareth my word, and believeth on him that sent me, hath everlasting life, and shall not come into condemnation; but is passed from death unto life" (Jn.5:24).**

1. What causes some people to put off living for God until the last minute? Why is this such a wrong thing to do? Does anyone even know when the *last minute of his or her life* will be?
2. How can you be sure that you will live with Christ forever?

ILLUSTRATION:

The pressures of society invite us to forsake a life of commitment to God. But the Christian believer has no excuse to turn back, to fall away from the Lord. Are you willing to be fully committed to His cause?

> *"Many men of the world have understood the necessity for commitment if they are to accomplish great things. For example, when Spanish explorer Cortez landed at Vera Cruz in 1519 to begin his conquest of Mexico with a small force of seven hundred men, legend has it that he purposely set fire to his fleet of eleven ships. Presumably, his men on the shore watched their only means of retreat sink to the bottom of the Gulf of Mexico. There was now only one direction to move—forward into the Mexican interior to meet whatever might come their way.*
>
> *"As part of our commitment as Christian disciples, we must purposefully destroy all avenues of retreat. We must resolve that whatever price is required for being his follower, we will pay it."*[1]

As this simple spiritual song reminds us,
> *I have decided to follow Jesus*
> *I have decided to follow Jesus*
> *I have decided to follow Jesus*
> *No turning back, no turning back.*

A CLOSER LOOK

(6:3-5) **Baptism**: remember, this note is being placed as the last note of this outline because of its length and its dealing with a specialized subject. Men have dissected and argued over how a person is "saved" so much that the preciousness and, in too many cases, the truth of the experience have been lost. The result is a confused public. Many people think if they have been baptized and do half-way right, then they are saved and God will never reject them. Others who are highly disciplined and have reformed their lives think they are as acceptable to God as anyone else because they do live moral and decent lives. A confused public, including both those within and without the church, is basing their eternal fate upon one or more of the following. They think they are saved...

- by baptism
- by doing good deeds
- by being as good as they can
- by church membership
- by faith alone
- by repentance

Much of the confusion has been caused by men *over-stressing or misunderstanding* one of the truths of Scripture. Too often too many of us have been guilty of abusing Scripture; and once we have taken a strong position, we have been unwilling to back off or to give balance to the whole truth, even when we realized we had gone too far. It is time for us to totally commit our lives to the Lord, to lay aside our *bandwagons* and exhaustively labor to proclaim the whole truth both to the church and to the world. Again, it is time for the truth to be proclaimed, the whole balance of Scripture—time for us to help straighten out the confusion of the public, for many within the church are deceived and are without Christ; and the world cannot come to Christ with a genuine experience until they come as *Scripture dictates*.

---

[1] Michael P. Green. *Illustrations for Biblical Preaching.* (Grand Rapids, MI: Baker Books, 1996), p.71-72.

In the passage before us, an argument rages over the word baptism (v.3-4). Does "baptism" mean the actual baptism experience of a person, or is it being used in a symbolic or spiritual sense? Those who hold to baptism's being essential for salvation say it means the actual baptism experience; whereas those who hold to salvation by faith tend to say it is speaking symbolically and spiritually. And the battle rages on. The great tragedy is...

- many within and without the church have become confused
- many have never had a true experience of salvation because they have never heard the truth of Scripture
- many have never heard nor understood the truth of Scripture
- many have mocked the divisiveness and irrelevance of church positions

And all with whom we have failed to share the truth are doomed, and we are responsible. Now, note several points.

1. Scripture speaks strongly in unmistakable terms on the subject of salvation—on just how we are saved—and to an *honest and thoughtful mind* it speaks clearly.

a. We are saved by *faith*.

> **"For by grace are ye saved through <u>faith</u>; and that not of yourselves: it is the gift of God: not of works, lest any man should boast" (Eph.2:8-9; cp. Jn.1:12; 3:16; Ro.10:9-10).**

b. We are saved by *obedience*.

> **"And being made perfect, he became the author of eternal salvation unto all them that <u>obey</u> him" (Heb.5:9; cp. Mt.7:21; Jn.15:10; Rev.22:14).**

c. We are saved by *repentance*.

> **"I came not to call the righteous, but sinners to <u>repentance</u>" (Lk.5:32; cp. Acts 11:18).**

d. We are saved by *confession*.

> **"Whosoever therefore shall <u>confess</u> me before men, him will I confess also before my Father which is in heaven. But whosoever shall deny me before men, him will I also deny before my Father which is in heaven" (Mt.10:32-33; cp. Ro.10:9-10; 1 Jn.4:15).**

e. We are saved by *baptism*.

> **"Then Peter said unto them, Repent, and be <u>baptized</u> every one of you in the name of Jesus Christ for the remission of sins, and ye shall receive the gift of the Holy Ghost" (Acts 2:38).**

Now, in all honesty, what does this show? Is it not that the true experience of salvation is a *whole* experience, a *comprehensive* experience, an experience that involves the *whole life* of a believer? Is salvation not a past and a present and a future experience?

What Scripture declares is that salvation is looked upon as the *whole* experience of a truly *born again* person. When Scripture speaks...

- of believing in Christ, it means a person who repents, confesses, obeys, and is baptized
- of obedience to Christ, it means a person who believes, repents, confesses, and is baptized
- of repentance toward Christ, it means a person who believes, confesses, obeys, and is baptized
- of baptism in Christ, it means a person who believes, repents, confesses, and obeys
- of confession to Christ, it means a person who believes, repents, obeys, and is baptized

Now note a most critical point: just because a person professes and does some of these things does not mean the person is saved. Just because a person...

- professes faith
- lives a moral and good life
- is baptized
- claims to live as Jesus taught

...does not mean he is saved. The power of salvation is not in these things, not in profession and moral goodness and baptism and the teachings of Jesus. The power to save is *in Jesus Christ Himself*, in believing that He is the crucified Savior, the Son of God Himself who has the power to save.

The point is this: Scripture speaks of the true believer in different ways at different times, anyone of which means that he is saved. Scripture says that a *true believer* is a person...

- who believes
- who obeys
- who repents
- who is baptized
- who confesses

Each of these terms is *inclusive*; that is, sometimes Scripture uses each term to include the others. The present passage says that believers who "were baptized into Jesus Christ were baptized into his death." Paul is using the *symbolic meaning* of our baptism experience to picture our "death" and "resurrection" with Christ. He is not saying that baptism is the "substance" that has the power to "place" us into Christ. Only God has that power. Paul is saying that the baptized person (as a person who believes, repents, obeys, and confesses) is the person who is *placed* into the death of Christ. Our baptism experience is being used as an inclusive term, not as an exclusive term or in an exclusive sense.

2. Among the believers in the New Testament, faith and baptism were not so much two experiences as two parts of one experience.[2] A person who genuinely believed *was baptized*, and a person who was baptized *was to be a genuine believer*. To be "baptized into Jesus Christ" did not mean "to be baptized *without faith*" and to "believe in Jesus Christ" did not mean to believe *without being baptized*. Scripture definitely indicates this. Therefore, *when Scripture speaks of baptism*, it means that baptism is for a genuine believer: a genuine believer is baptized, and a baptized person is to be a genuine believer. There just was no such thing as a *genuine believer* who was not baptized unless he was providentially prohibited, and there was no such thing as a *genuinely baptized* person who was not to be a true believer.

3. Scripture definitely teaches that the power to make a person acceptable to God, to place a person into Christ, is not in the water of baptism but *in Christ*. For example, this is the whole point of Romans up to this point, the whole teaching of justification. If the power to save is in water, then what do we do with the thousands who have been baptized and live like the devil himself, the thousands who show no changed life at all?

The power is definitely in Christ; Christ is the One who saves. And He saves the person who believes, not the person who is merely physically baptized. This is clearly evident from the *unholy lives lived by so many who have been baptized*.

However, as mentioned in point one, the person who truly believes does repent; and he does turn from his old life to follow Christ. He does what Christ says, and the first commandment is to follow Him in baptism. Baptism is the very first act, the very first proof that a person believes and repents.

2 F.F. Bruce. *The Epistle of Paul to the Romans*. "The Tyndale New Testament Commentaries." (Grand Rapids, MI: Eerdmans Publishing Co., Began in 1958), p.136.

There is another way to see the connection between faith and baptism or between our union with Christ and baptism. The power to save—to make a person acceptable to God—is not in the waters of baptism, but in Christ; therefore...

- not everyone who is baptized is saved. Their unbelieving and unholy lives prove the fact.
- everyone who is saved will be baptized immediately as an *act of belief and obedience* in Christ. The person will be baptized unless he is physically unable.

4. The physical symbol is never the truth itself; it is a picture of the truth. No physical substance has the power to bring about anything spiritual. The whole physical world and everything in it passes away, including water. Physical substances can symbolize spiritual truth, but they cannot be the cause or the power to bring about the spiritual reality. If a physical substance such as water baptism had such power, it would mean that the spiritual reality had its basis in the physical and material which pass away. And if the basis passes away (water baptism), then the substance (spiritual salvation) itself would also pass away.

Another way to say the same thing is this: the physical can never penetrate nor create the spiritual; it is the spiritual that must penetrate and create the physical. Philosophically, we must always remember this or else we doom ourselves and cause thinking men in the world to mock us. Why? Because the philosophical and thinking men of the world know that if we are saved by water (the physical and material), then we are doomed; for no physical substance can impart something it does not have, an eternal quality (eternal life, salvation, forgiveness of sins). Only the spiritual—only God and His power—can impart the spiritual quality of eternal life and salvation and forgiveness of sins. God can impart spiritual salvation and then say, "Immersion in water is a picture of what I do for you. And if you really believe in Me, then the very first evidence of your faith is for you to be baptized."

5. Practical experience tells us that belief and baptism are *separate acts* involved in salvation, yet they are both involved. They are both involved in the sense that baptism is an immediate act of obedience and repentance. A true believer should be baptized, and no true believer will fail to be baptized unless he is providentially stopped.

⇒ Example: a believer, flying across country, leads another person to truly trust Christ to save him. The plane crashes, and the new believer is killed before he can be baptized. He is not doomed to hell. Scripture teaches no such thing. To say he is doomed is to say that the power of salvation is in the waters of baptism and not in God's Son. In fact, to say such is to dishonor God's Son, to take the love and power and grace that belong to Him and to ascribe it to a physical substance. If the new believer truly believes within his heart, truly honors God's Son by trusting Jesus to save him, God accepts that man and will do anything for him. The man is thereby accepted by God, accepted because he honors God's Son by believing and committing his life to Him.

However, the man who reaches the ground and is not baptized as soon as he can make arrangements is not genuine. His faith is suspect, for he is not putting God first in his life. He has not turned to Christ *ready* to obey and live for Him. The man who truly believes is the man who is not only *ready* to obey Christ, he *does* obey and live for Christ.

⇒ Note another example. There are masses of people who live in arid and desert countries where thousands are starving and dying of thirst. What about them and baptism? What if a missionary leads some to Christ. *Are they to be immersed or sprinkled when there is so little water and multitudes are dying of thirst?* The point is clear, not only in the teaching of Scripture, but in the love of God and in practical terms. A person is justified *by faith*, but he is to be baptized immediately, as soon as he possibly can. Why? Because he is genuine, he does believe in the Lord Jesus, loving Him and wishing to obey Him in all things and thereby fulfilling all righteousness. However, his salvation does not depend upon baptism; it depends upon God's dear Son, our Lord and Savior, Jesus Christ.

QUESTIONS:
1. Why is the physical act of baptism powerless to save you? What is the only way a sinner can be saved?
2. What role does baptism play in your relationship with Jesus Christ?

SUMMARY:

We are not under the power of sin, not any longer. There is no reason for sin to dominate and control us any longer. We can break loose from sin, be freed from sin. Sin can be conquered through the power of Jesus Christ. Jesus Christ has won the battle over sin and will set us free. How do we know this is true? Remember...

1. The believer does not have license to sin.
2. Know 1st: by position, the believer is immersed, placed into Christ.
3. Know 2nd: by position, the believer's old man was crucified with Christ.
4. Know 3rd: by position, the believer lives with Christ—now and forever.

PERSONAL JOURNAL NOTES:
(Reflection & Response)

1. The most important thing that I learned from this lesson was:

2. The thing that I need to work on the most is:

3. I can apply this lesson to my life by:

4. Closing Prayer of Commitment: (put your commitment down on paper).

	B. The Believer Is Not to Continue in Sin (Part II): He Is to Live Out His Position in Christ, 6:11-13	fore reign in your mortal body, that ye should obey it in the lusts thereof.	a. Does not let it reign b. Does not obey its lusts
		13 Neither yield ye your members as instruments of unrighteousness unto sin:	3. He does not yield the members of his body to sin a. He yields himself to God
1. He counts himself dead to sin but alive to God a. Dead to sin b. Alive to God c. Source: Thru Christ	11 Likewise reckon ye also yourselves to be dead indeed unto sin, but alive unto God through Jesus Christ our Lord.	but yield yourselves unto God, as those that are alive from the dead, and your members as instruments of righteousness unto God.	b. He yields the members of his body to be instruments of righteousness or to do right
2. He resists sin	12 Let not sin there-	ness unto God.	

Section IV
HOLINESS AND SANCTIFICATION: THE WAY
FOR THE BELIEVER TO BE FREE FROM SIN
Romans 6:1-23

Study 2: **The Believer Is Not to Continue in Sin (Part II): He Is to Live Out His Position in Christ**

Text: **Romans 6:11-13**

Aim: To learn a much needed lesson: we must do right; we must not continue in sin.

Memory Verse:
> **"Likewise reckon ye also yourselves to be dead indeed unto sin, but alive unto God through Jesus Christ our Lord" (Romans 6:11).**

INTRODUCTION:
How much willpower do you need in order to resist the things that tempt you the most? It might be easy to muster up a little willpower on the first occasion, but if the same temptation continues to batter you, the will to fight weakens. Unless you resolve to live in the power of the Holy Spirit, you will quickly find ways to dull your conscience to sin.

> *"A man consulted a doctor. 'I've been misbehaving, Doc, and my conscience is troubling me,' he complained.*
> *"'And you want something that will strengthen your will power? asked the doctor.*
> *"''Well, no,' the man said. 'I was thinking of something that would weaken my conscience.'"*[1]

We do not need any help in gaining a weakened conscience. On the contrary, we need to possess a strong conscience that will resist temptation. Jesus Christ has guaranteed every believer eternal life. And yet, Christians still struggle with sin that acts like a ball and chain. God's best for you is not to *put up with* the problem of habitual sin. God's best for you is VICTORY over sin. He wants us to be victors not victims. Which one are you?

---

[1] Roy B. Zuck. *The Speaker's Quote Book*. (Grand Rapids, MI: Kregel Publications, 1997), p.354.

The true believer does not continue in sin; he does not live in sin. He conquers and triumphs over sin. In very clear terms, this passage tells exactly what the believer must do to live in victory over sin.

OUTLINE:
1. He counts himself dead to sin but alive to God (v.11).
2. He resists sin (v.12).
3. He does not yield the members of his body to sin (v.13).

1. HE COUNTS HIMSELF DEAD TO SIN BUT ALIVE TO GOD (v.11).

How does the believer keep from walking in sin?

1. The believer must count himself *dead to sin*. If a person is a true believer, then God takes his belief, his faith, and counts him as having died in Christ; and a dead man can do nothing. He cannot sin. God frees him from sin and its power as well as from its consequences and penalty. Therefore, the believer is to...

- count himself
- treat himself

- consider himself
- regard himself

- reckon himself
- credit himself

...as being *dead in Christ*, as being free from sin and its power. He is to *receive* this truth into his heart and life, become totally *convicted and convinced* of it.

(Note a crucial point: the true believer is not left only to the power of his own mind or thoughts to convince himself of this glorious truth. It is not only a matter of *human thought and reasoning* or of mental control. God has given the Holy Spirit to stir and build confidence of the glorious truth within the believer. The Holy Spirit is our "seal," our guarantee, of salvation. But this is the subject of another discussion, of chapter eight. The present chapter concerns *our part* in overcoming sin. God does help us to overcome sin through the Holy Spirit, but we also have a part. And it is our part that is presently being considered.)

> **"I am crucified with Christ: nevertheless I live; yet not I, but Christ liveth in me: and the life which I now live in the flesh I live by the faith of the Son of God, who loved me, and gave himself for me" (Gal.2:20).**

2. The believer must count himself *alive to God*. The true believer is not only identified with Christ in death, he is identified with Christ in resurrection. God not only counts the believer's faith as *death in Christ*, He counts his faith as *life in Christ*. The resurrection of the Lord Jesus counts as the resurrection of the believer. As Jesus Christ was raised to a new life, so the believer is raised to a new life. As Jesus Christ was raised to live in the presence of God and to serve Him forever, so the believer is raised to live in the presence of God and to serve Him forever.

The point is this: the believer is to receive into his heart and life the truth of *his resurrected life*. The believer is now to *live for and with God*. The believer is now to *serve God and not sin*. The believer is to *walk before God* in his new, resurrected life; to walk soberly, righteously, and godly in this present world. He is to walk...

- counting himself
- treating himself

- considering himself
- regarding himself

...as alive to God, now and forever serving God.

> **"For he is not a God of the dead, but of the living: for all live unto him" (Lk.20:38).**

3. Note the most glorious truth: the believer's life is due to Christ and Christ alone. All that the believer knows—his glorious deliverance from sin and the wonderful victory of eternal life—is due to Christ's death and resurrection. And note: it is the be-

liever who really *keeps his mind* upon the death and resurrection of Christ who *walks above sin*. It is he who walks free from sin who conquers it every step of the way and glorifies God by the victory of his righteous life.

In conclusion, the believer's first step in conquering sin is to count himself dead to sin but alive unto God. The believer must *know and live out* his position, the glorious life God has given him in the death and resurrection of Jesus Christ our Lord. The believer who keeps his mind and thoughts upon *his position* in Christ's death and resurrection will conquer sin—every time.

ILLUSTRATION:

The way to protect yourself from the power of sin is to hide in Christ. This point is illustrated perfectly by this story.

> *"In the second century, a Christian was brought before a pagan ruler and told to renounce his faith. 'If you don't do it, I will banish you,' threatened the king. The man smiled and answered, 'You can't banish me from Christ, for He says, 'I will never leave you nor forsake you.'"*
>
> *"To this the king angrily retorted, 'Then I will confiscate your property and take all your possessions.' Again the man smiled and said, 'My treasures are laid up on high; you cannot get them.' The king became furious and shouted, 'I will kill you!' 'Why,' the man answered, 'I have been dead forty years; I have been dead with Christ, dead to the world, and my life is hid with Christ in God, and you cannot touch it.'*
>
> *"In desperation the king turned to his advisers and asked, 'What can you do with a fanatic like that?'"*[2]

In order to defeat the power of sin in your life, you must treat it in a fanatical way. You must become dead to sin and alive to God. Is your life marked by a fanatical hatred for sin, or is it marked by failure and overcome by sin?

QUESTIONS:

1. How do you keep from walking in sin if sin is alive in your life? Why is it so hard to overcome sin? What must you do today in order to be freed from habitual sin?
2. What habits can you begin to cultivate in your life that will make you alive to God?
3. Your life is due to Christ and to Christ alone. What, therefore, must you do when you are tempted to sin?

A CLOSER LOOK # 1

(6:11) **Reckon—Impute**: to credit; to set to one's account; to lay to one's charge; to impute; to judge; to consider; to treat; to count; to compute; to ascribe. It is an accounting word; it implies something put to a man's credit. It is used many times throughout Romans, about eleven times in chapter four of Romans alone. It is an extremely important idea in Scripture.

1. Scripture says that righteousness is credited to the genuine believer by God.

> **"And therefore it was imputed to him for righteousness. Now it was not written for his sake alone, that it was imputed to him; but for us also, to whom it shall be imputed, if we believe on him that raised up Jesus our Lord from the dead; who was delivered for our offences, and was raised again for our justification"** (Ro.4:22-25).

---

[2] Spiros Zodhiates, Th.D. *Illustrations of Bible Truths*. (Chattanooga, TN: AMG Publishers, 1995), p.267.

2. Scripture says that the genuine believer is immersed, imputed, reckoned, or counted as dead in Christ's death; that is, his "old man" is imputed or reckoned as crucified in Christ's death.

> **"Know ye not, that so many of us as were baptized into Jesus Christ were baptized into his death? Therefore we are buried with him by baptism into death: that like as Christ was raised up from the dead by the glory of the Father, even so we also should walk in newness of life" (Ro.6:3-4).**

3. Scripture says that a new life, a resurrected life, is imputed, reckoned, or put to the account of the believer through Christ's resurrection.

> **"For if we have been planted together in the likeness of his death, we shall be also in the likeness of his resurrection" (Ro.6:5).**

Very simply stated, God counts the believer righteous because of what Christ has done. Christ is seen to be "the Lord our righteousness," and His righteousness is said to be put to a man's account through faith (cp. Phile.18).

QUESTIONS:
1. What did Christ do to make you righteous? What did *you* do?
2. Righteousness has been described as something that has been deposited to your spiritual account. Before Christ deposited His righteousness to your account, what types of things were filling your life?

2. HE RESISTS SIN (v.12).

This is an imperative—a forceful command. It is up to the believer to resist sin; he is responsible for resisting it.

1. He must not let sin *reign*: have authority, rule, control, occupy, hold sway, prevail over him. The present tense is used, so the idea is a continuous attitude and behavior. The believer is always to keep his mind off sin. He is to keep his mind under control by keeping his mind off...

- wealth and material things
- position and power
- recognition and fame
- the lust of the eyes
- the lust of the flesh
- the pride of life
- parties and sex
- appearance and clothes

The believer is not to let sin dominate, control, or reign in his mortal body. Sin is not to dominate his thoughts and life. He is to resist sin by standing against it, by rebuking and fighting against it. He is to oppose sin with all his might.

> **"Behold, thou art made whole: sin no more, lest a worse thing come unto thee" (Jn.5:14).**
> **"My little children, these things write I unto you, that ye sin not. And if any man sin, we have an advocate with the Father, Jesus Christ the righteous" (1 Jn.2:1).**

2. He must not obey sin in its *lusts*. The word means strong desire or craving or passion. The pull of sin is sometimes strong, very strong. All men know what it is to lust after things, after more and more, whether it be money, property, security, position, pleasure, fun, or fleshly stimulation. The true believer must not *yield* to these pulls. He must not let the lusts of his eyes and flesh rule and regulate his mind and behavior. He must not let lust *order* his life. He must resist the lusts of his mortal body.

"But put ye on the Lord Jesus Christ, and make not provision for the flesh, to fulfil the lusts thereof" (Ro.13:14).

"Dearly beloved, I beseech you as strangers and pilgrims, abstain from fleshly lusts, which war against the souls" (1 Pt.2:11).

QUESTIONS:
1. Why is it *your* responsibility to resist sin?
2. What are some practical examples of things people lust after?
3. What can you do to conquer lustful cravings and desires?

3. HE DOES NOT YIELD THE MEMBERS OF HIS BODY TO SIN (v.13).

Three things need to be said about sin at this point in Romans. (1) Sin is an offense and a disease in chapters 1-4. In chapter 6 it is a master or a ruling power. (2) Sin is not "destroyed" in the believer. It is still active and can still injure. The believer is to fight against its pull. (3) The body is not the source of sin, but the Bible says and man's experience proves that the body is the *instrument* of sin, the *organ* which sin uses to manifest and satisfy itself. The body is under the *heavy influence* and *severe power* of sin and corruption—so much so that the sensual appetites of the body tend to enslave the soul and lead men to sin, even against his better judgment. Therefore, the believer is strongly exhorted to resist: "Let not sin therefore reign in your mortal bodies" (Ro.6:12).

ILLUSTRATION:
Soldiers in every nation have been awarded medals for courageous acts of bravery. At great personal risk, these brave soldiers performed in such a way that others marveled at what they had done. Throughout the history of the Christian church, there have also been brave soldiers. Here is the story of one such soldier.

> Ronald was an energetic young man and a popular worker at the sales office where he worked. Ronald was friendly to all, sometimes to a fault. He was a fairly new Christian and had recently been married. Ronald loved his new bride Cindy. She was the girl of his dreams. He would never do anything to hurt her—not ever...not intentionally...not on purpose...not in his wildest imaginations.
>
> Karen was on the rebound. Hurt by a failed marriage, she was longing for someone to treat her with respect. Working with Ronald on the same project was something she looked forward to every day. It did not take long for Karen to see Ronald as more than just a fellow employee. She saw him as the answer to all her problems. Karen's body language began to betray her hidden agenda.
>
> Ronald saw it coming...in a way. He really liked working with Karen. She was interesting and attractive. One day this neutral relationship finally came to a head and disaster struck. Karen put her hand on his shoulder in a very inappropriate way and stared into his eyes. Frozen in his tracks, the first thing that ran through Ronald's mind was, "This is no big deal. I can handle this." The longer he thought about it, the more he realized there was nothing heroic about trying to stare down the woman who was tempting him. He had to get out immediately.
>
> "Karen, this is not right. I love my wife too much to allow this to go on for a moment longer." Ronald pulled back, promptly left the room, and requested an immediate transfer to another division within the company.

As we can learn from this story, there is nothing heroic about trying to stare down the things that tempt us. The courageous Christian soldier will immediately run to Christ and find refuge in Him.

QUESTIONS:
1. What is your definition of sin? Is God's definition the same? What changes in your life do you need to make to make sure—absolutely sure—that you do not slip into sin?
2. Sin is not dead in your life. It is a dormant but deadly foe. What should be your attitude with this in mind?

A CLOSER LOOK # 2

(6:13) Sin—Life, Victorious: the believer must not yield the members of his body to sin. The word "yield" means to offer; to put at the disposal of; to give; to grant; to turn over to. The believer *is not* to yield the members of his body to be instruments or tools of unrighteousness. If he takes a member of his body to use as an instrument or tool of unrighteousness, he sins. The members of a person's body refer to all the parts of the body: the eyes, ears, mouth, tongue, hands, feet, mind, or any of the covered and dressed parts. No believer is to offer or give any part of his body over to unrighteousness. To do so is to sin. The tense is present action, so the believer is constantly to be on guard against allowing any member of his body to be yielded to sin. Note: the word "yield" has the idea of struggling. It is a struggle to fight against sin and to control and protect the members of our body.

1. The believer is to yield himself to God. Note a significant fact: in the Greek this is not written in the present tense but in the aorist tense. This simply means the believer is to make a *one-time* decision for God, a *once-for-all* dedication of his life to God. The presentation of his life to God is to be sincere and genuine. He is to yield himself—his body, his life, all that he is—to God; and his decision is to be a permanent one.

2. The believer is to yield the members of his body as instruments of righteousness *unto* God. The believer is to *turn* the members of his body over to God: his eyes, ears, mouth, tongue, hands, feet, mind—all his members. Every part of his body is to be given over to God as an instrument or tool for the purpose of working righteousness.

> **"And if thy right eye offend thee, pluck it out, and cast it from thee: for it is profitable for thee that one of thy members should perish, and not that thy whole body should be cast into hell. And if thy right hand offend thee, cut it off, and cast it from thee: for it is profitable for thee that one of thy members should perish, and not that thy whole body should be cast into hell" (Mt.5:29-30; cp. Mt.18:8-9).**
>
> **"I beseech you therefore, brethren, by the mercies of God, that ye present your bodies a living sacrifice, holy, acceptable unto God, which is your reasonable service. And be not conformed to this world: but be ye transformed by the renewing of your mind, that ye may prove what is that good, and acceptable, and perfect, will of God" (Ro.12:1-2).**

QUESTIONS:
1. When are you most likely to yield the members of your body to sin? Why?
2. Have you given God every member of your body, your...
   * eyes—do they tend to lose their focus upon Him?
   * ears—do they keenly listen to His voice?
   * mouth—does it allow hurtful words to escape or does it participate in things it should not?
   * mind—does it meditate on things that would bring shame if exposed?
   * hands—do they long for service or for selfishness?
   * feet—do they bring peace wherever they go?

SUMMARY:

We live in a world where sin is excused, condoned, explained away, diminished, and denied. Sin has become the acceptable, unchangeable trait of the world. In a world gripped by sin and death, the believer must live free from the power of sin. How can the Christian believer conquer sin?

1. He must count himself dead to sin but alive to God.
2. He must resist sin.
3. He must not yield the members of his body to sin.

PERSONAL JOURNAL NOTES:
(Reflection & Response)

1. The most important thing that I learned from this lesson was:

2. The thing that I need to work on the most is:

3. I can apply this lesson to my life by:

4. Closing Prayer of Commitment: (put your commitment down on paper).

C. The Believer Is Not to Continue in Sin (Part III): He Does Not Have License to Sin, 6:14-23

1. Learn something: Sin shall not dominate the true believer
   a. Because he is not under law, but under grace
   b. Shall he continue to sin? Take license to sin?
2. Know something: You can serve only one master, sin or God
   a. Do you serve or yield to sin? You shall die
   b. Do you serve or yield to God? You shall live
3. Remember something: Remember your decision—you chose righteousness
   a. Fact: You were a servant of sin but now you have obeyed
   b. Result: Freed from sin, the op-pressive master
4. Do something: Serve God with the same fervor that you served sin
   a. Your sin prompted more sin—resulted in more & more sin
   b. Now let your righteousness work holiness
   c. You never had such opportunity before
5. Question something: What fruit is there in sin?
6. Consider something: The wages of sin vs. the gift of God—eternal life

14 For sin shall not have dominion over you: for ye are not under the law, but under grace. 15 What then? shall we sin, because we are not under the law, but under grace? God forbid. 16 Know ye not, that to whom ye yield yourselves servants to obey, his servants ye are to whom ye obey; whether of sin unto death, or of obedience unto righteousness? 17 But God be thanked, that ye were the servants of sin, but ye have obeyed from the heart that form of doctrine which was delivered you. 18 Being then made free from sin, ye became the servants of righteousness. 19 I speak after the manner of men because of the infirmity of your flesh: for as ye have yielded your members servants to uncleanness and to iniquity unto iniquity; even so now yield your members servants to righteousness unto holiness. 20 For when ye were the servants of sin, ye were free from righteousness. 21 What fruit had ye then in those things whereof ye are now ashamed? for the end of those things is death. 22 But now being made free from sin, and become servants to God, ye have your fruit unto holiness, and the end everlasting life. 23 For the wages of sin is death; but the gift of God is eternal life through Jesus Christ our Lord.

Section IV
HOLINESS AND SANCTIFICATION: THE WAY FOR THE BELIEVER TO BE FREE FROM SIN
Romans 6:1-23

Study 3: The Believer Is Not to Continue in Sin (Part III): He Does Not Have License to Sin

Text: Romans 6:14-23

Aim: To renounce your right to sin: to recommit yourself to righteousness.

Memory Verse:
"For the wages of sin is death; but the gift of God is eternal life through Jesus Christ our Lord" (Romans 6:23).

INTRODUCTION:

Sin is running rampant throughout society. Group after group and person after person is promoting...

- homosexuality
- promiscuity, immorality
- physician-assisted suicide
- indulgence
- greed

- radical rights
- abortion
- humanism
- license
- secularism

On and on the list could be compiled. There is a certain attitude that expresses itself with a rebellious fist shaken in the face of God. Every Christian would agree that this is not a good thing to do. However, the believer is sometimes guilty of the same attitude. Thinking that the grace of God excuses his sin, the believer goes about doing his own thing. He shakes a rebellious fist in the face of God and does exactly what he wants to do instead of doing what God commands. He sins; he rebels against God. He forgets this crucial fact: just because we have been forgiven our sin does not permit us to continue in sin. God's grace is given to keep us from sin, not to be a reason to sin. This is the very point of this study: *The believer is not to continue in sin; he does not have license to sin.*

OUTLINE:

1. Learn something: sin shall not dominate the true believer (v.14-15).
2. Know something: you can serve only one master, sin or God (v.16).
3. Remember something: remember your decision—you chose righteousness (v.17-18).
4. Do something: serve God with the same fervor that you served sin (v.19-20).
5. Question something: what fruit is there in sin (v.21-22)?
6. Consider something: the wages of sin vs. the gift of God—eternal life (v.23).

1. LEARN SOMETHING: SIN SHALL NOT DOMINATE THE TRUE BELIEVER (v.14-15).

There is a strong reason for this: the believer is under grace and not under the law.

1. A person under the law is always struggling to keep the law, yet he is constantly aware that he fails, coming short of the law. The law is ever before his face. He struggles and strives, wrestles and grapples, works and labors to obey; but his experience is full of tension and pressure, disappointment and discouragement. The person under law never lives a victorious life, for he is constantly coming short of God's glory and perfection. When he fails, he goes through periods of self-accusation, of reproaching and censoring himself for having failed. He accuses and downs himself, feeling unworthy and undeserving, wretched and vile before God. He is constantly feeling unacceptable to God, as though he no longer has the right to approach God; and he often does not approach God for long periods of time, living a defeated life, always bearing the burden of his sin and failure.

"Tribulation and anguish, upon every soul of man that doeth evil, of the Jew first, and also of the Gentile" (Ro.2:9).

2. The true believer is under grace not under the law. God is not a legal judge hovering over the believer to punish him every time he sins by breaking a particular law. The believer is not under such frightening dominion: he is not under the law but under grace. What does this mean?

a. It means that the believer accepts the grace of God demonstrated in Jesus Christ. That is, the believer accepts the righteousness, the sinless perfection, of Christ as his own righteousness. The believer identifies his life with the life of Christ, and God takes the believer's acceptance of Christ and counts his acceptance as righteousness. Such is the *great love of God*. But note, this is the *position of grace*; that is, the believer is counted righteous and placed in the *posi-*

tion of righteousness when he believes in Christ. He is *placed into Christ* and *positioned in Christ* once-for-all when he truly believes. Such is the *righteous position* of the believer.

However, what about the *righteous life* of the believer? Very practically, how does the believer keep from serving sin, from living under sin, from displeasing God? How can he honestly live *under* grace day by day? How can he live under God's favor all the time? How can he go about pleasing God and receiving His approval and acceptance?

b. The genuine believer *must constantly* keep before his face this glorious truth: he is *under* God's grace. God is the believer's Father, and the believer has become a true child of God. Therefore, the true believer is favored and accepted by his Father. What the child has to do is stay in that favor. He must keep his Father's favor and approval. When he sins, he needs to go to His Father in all sincerity to ask forgiveness, repenting of his sin. If he keeps an open relationship with his Father—always approaching Him, asking His forgiveness, and repenting—he is forgiven. The slate is wiped clean—sin does not have dominion over him. All has been discussed and forgiven. The offense is gone, resolved, put away forever. Therefore, sin does not dominate and rule over the child.

Now, note the point: God is a gracious and loving Father. He cares and suffers long with growing children. When His child falls into sin, God is long-suffering, ever willing to forgive His erring child—if the child will only come to ask forgiveness, turning from his sin (Lk.17:3-4; 1 Jn.1:9). Just how long-suffering is God? "His mercy endureth forever"; His mercy covers every sin and all sin (Ps.106:1; 107:1; 118:1-4).

> "It were better for him that a millstone were hanged about his neck, and he cast into the sea, than that he should offend one of these little ones. Take heed to yourselves: If thy brother trespass against thee, rebuke him; and if he repent, forgive him" (Lk.17:2-3).
>
> "In whom we have redemption through his blood, the forgiveness of sins, according to the riches of his grace" (Eph.1:7).

3. In light of so wondrous a relationship, a question needs to be asked. Is the child of God allowed to continue in sin? Can he sin and sin, expecting God to forgive and forgive him? Scripture shouts: God forbid! Then Scripture argues that a true child of God must not continue in sin. He does not set God aside for a night or two so he can sin. He does not rationalize that he can sin because God is going to forgive him anyway. Why does the true child of God not do this? Why does he keep away from sin?

⇒ Because his Father (God) loves him, and he loves his Father. A true child of God does not want to hurt and displease his Father, and his Father is displeased with sin. Consequently, the true child of God strives not to sin (Ro.2:23-24; Heb.6:6). He fights against it, for sin is contrary to the nature of his Father and cuts the heart of his Father beyond all else. Therefore, he does all he can to keep away from sin.

> "If they shall fall away, to renew them again unto repentance; seeing they crucify to themselves the Son of God afresh, and put him to an open shame" (Heb.6:6).

⇒ Because he turned to God in order to get away from sin, its shame and destruction. He did not turn to God in order to have the freedom to sin, but to be set free from the enslavement and habits of sin, to break the bondage and consequences of sin.

> "For the wages of sin is death; but the gift of God is eternal life through Jesus Christ our Lord" (Ro.6:23).

To summarize what is said above, the believer must learn something: sin will not dominate the true believer. There are three reasons.

1. God is not a legal judge hovering over the child to punish him every time he sins by breaking a particular law. The child is not under such a frightening rule and reign.

2. God is a gracious and loving Father. He cares and suffers long with growing children. When His child falls into sin, God is long-suffering, ever willing to forgive His erring child—if the child will only come to ask forgiveness and turn from his sin (Lk.17:3-4; 1 Jn.1:9).

3. God is a teaching Father who disciplines. He exhorts His child not to fall into the dominating trap of sin (cp. Heb.12:5-11; 1 Jn.2:1-2).

The emphasis of this chapter, however, is of supreme importance. A believer who is genuine—who really belongs to Christ—shows his genuineness by obeying Christ as Master. He does not consistently practice sin.

QUESTIONS:
1. What frustrations does a person face who lives under the law?
2. Is there any sin that dominates (controls) you? What is the key to being set free from sin's dominance?
3. How would you describe what it is like to live under grace?
4. What is the role that grace plays in keeping you from sin?

2. KNOW SOMETHING: YOU SERVE ONLY ONE MASTER, SIN OR GOD (v.16).

The word "servant" means slave. A person is either the slave of sin or of God, and there is a very simple test to tell which master a person serves.

⇒ Do you yield to sin, that is, serve sin?
⇒ Do you yield to God, that is, serve God?

If you yield to sin, you shall die. If you yield to God and obey Him, you shall be counted righteous and live.

Now note a crucial point. Either sin is your master or God is your Master. You either yield to sin or you yield to God. This does not mean that you become sinless and perfect, but that...

- you do not plan to sin
- you hate sin and fight against it
- you struggle to please God by not sinning
- you diligently seek to make God the Master of your life by obeying Him
- you study God's Word so that you will know His commandments and can obey Him
- you immediately seek God's forgiveness when you do sin and you repent— you turn away from the sin (1 Jn1:9; 2:1-2)
- you walk in open confession before God, talking to Him all day long, ever gaining an unbroken fellowship with Him as the Master of your life

Again, note the results, for *whom* you serve determines your destiny. If you yield to sin, you shall die; but if you yield to God, you shall be counted righteous and live eternally.

> **"No man can serve two masters: for either he will hate the one, and love the other; or else he will hold to the one, and despise the other. Ye cannot serve God and mammon" (Mt.6:24).**

ILLUSTRATION:

You have probably heard the riddle, "What do you get when an elephant sits on a fence?" Answer: "A broken fence!" There is more truth to this silly riddle than most would think. It is impossible to sit on the fence between serving God and serving sin. Here is the story of one man whose attempt to sit in both worlds found him crashing to the ground.

> *Wally's life is like many others who started well but did not finish the race of maturity and responsibility. Raised in a Bible-believing home, Wally still sowed a lot of wild oats during his youth. His rationale to choose a life-style of sin was "I'll get things right with God when I get older." After getting through college with his degree in hand (some would say Wally majored in partying), Wally was still acting like a kid in a man's body. What had started out as a spontaneous experiment with the drug culture had turned into a serious habit that craved more and more—never to be satisfied.*
>
> *Wally did not let his drug dependency slow him down from having fun. He just spread his destructive habit to others who were willing to join him on his trip. Supplying his friends with drugs boosted his feelings of importance and gave him the boldness to explore even more deeply into forbidden territory.*
>
> *Wally entered into that new territory and never found his way out. He never had time to get things right with God. He never had time to make up for all of the wasted years. Wally died from a drug overdose.*

How are you spending your time: serving God or serving sin?

QUESTIONS:

1. If others were to observe you, would they say you serve God or serve sin? God sees your every move, knows your every motive. Whom would He say you serve?
2. What does it mean to yield to God? Does this mean you will never sin again? Why?
3. What is the end result of the man who yields to sin? What is your duty as a believer toward a person who continually chooses to serve sin?

3. REMEMBER SOMETHING: REMEMBER YOUR DECISION—YOU CHOSE RIGHTEOUSNESS (v.17-18).

1. Note the stated fact: believers "were the servants of sin." They used to yield to sin, all kinds of sin ranging from...

- simple off-colored jokes to using God's name in vain
- immoral thoughts to adultery
- simple thoughts of pride to drunkenness
- simple acts of selfishness to stealing
- simply wanting more to actually indulging
- seeking position and power to hurting and crushing people

But *now* believers have obeyed the doctrine of God, the gospel of God, doing exactly what God commanded. They obeyed God's commandment. They "believed" on the name of God's Son, Jesus Christ; therefore, God counted their faith as righteousness. They chose God and righteousness, and because they did, God accepted them as righteous.

> **"And this is his commandment, That we should <u>believe</u> on the name of his Son Jesus Christ, and love one another, as he gave us commandment" (1 Jn.3:23).**

2. Note the stated result: believers are freed from sin. They are counted righteous, *not sinful*, by God. Therefore, believers are freed from sin and its consequences. God does not charge believers with sin; He does not lay sin against them. Believers are freed from the accusation of sin, and they shall never be charged with sin. God has freed them from sin through His Son, the Lord Jesus Christ (cp. Ro.8:33-34).

Now this means something significant, very significant. The believer becomes the servant of righteousness. There is no way he could ever serve sin again, not if he has really been justified, not if he has really come to know God's love revealed in the Lord Jesus Christ. Once he truly knows God's glorious love, he is driven to serve God in appreciation for what God has done for him in Christ Jesus. He is driven to be the servant of God by living righteously and godly in this present world.

APPLICATION:

The degree to which a believer grasps the love of God is the degree to which he is driven to serve God and to live righteously.

> **"Who shall lay any thing to the charge of God's elect? It is God that justifieth. Who is he that condemneth? It is Christ that died, yea rather, that is risen again, who is even at the right hand of God, who also maketh intercession for us" (Ro.8:33-34).**

> **"For the love of Christ constraineth us; because we thus judge, that if one died for all, then were all dead: and that he died for all, that they which live should not henceforth live unto themselves, but unto him which died for them, and rose again" (2 Cor.5:14-15).**

QUESTIONS:

1. Believers used to be servants of sin. What things have you served in the past that you no longer serve? What took place that changed you from a servant of sin to a servant of righteousness?
2. What does it mean to be freed from sin? How does this great truth help you live a life that is pleasing to God?

4. DO SOMETHING: SERVE GOD WITH THE SAME FERVOR THAT YOU SERVED SIN (v.19-20).

1. Your sin prompted more sin; it resulted in more and more sin. The word "members" means the parts of a person's body: the eyes, ears, mouth, tongue, hands, feet, mind, or any of the covered and dressed parts. Before a person obeyed the gospel, truly believed in Jesus Christ, he yielded parts of his body to serve uncleanness and to work sin upon sin. He sinned and found that *sin prompted and induced more sin;* sin increased and grew. He found that sin enslaved him, became a bondage, a habit that he could not easily break. Sin simply led to more sin, no matter what the sin was...

- smoking
- drinking
- immorality
- overeating
- greed
- lust
- gossip
- criticism
- grumbling
- cursing
- selfishness
- popularity
- recognition
- power
- fame

The point is this. The believer had found that his sin worked more sin and that he could not break the power of sin, not the power of *all* sin. Therefore, he had turned to the only hope he had, God Himself.

> **"For when we were in the flesh, the motions of sins, which were by the law, did work in our members to bring forth fruit unto death" (Ro.7:5).**

2. Now the believer is to let righteousness work *holiness*. The word means sanctification or separation. The believer is to yield the parts of his body to serve righteousness, and he is to let righteousness sanctify him more and more, to become more and more holy like God.

3. The believer never had the opportunity to work righteousness before he was justified. Before believing in Christ, the believer was not counted righteous, not by God. God never credits a person with righteousness unless the person honors His Son by believing in His Son's glorious name. Only those who believe are counted righteous. Therefore, the message is loud and clear: when you served sin, you were free from righteousness: you were not credited with righteousness. You did not have the opportunity to live righteously before God. *But now* you have obeyed God; you have believed. Now you have the opportunity to live righteously; so begin to serve God with the same fervor and energy with which you were serving sin. Let righteousness enslave you and become the bondage and habit of your life.

> **"This I say then, Walk in the Spirit, and ye shall not fulfil the lust of the flesh" (Gal.5:16).**

QUESTIONS:
1. If you spent the same amount of energy serving God as you have spent (and still spend) in serving sin, what would your life be like? (Keep in mind that anything that is not pleasing to God is sin.)
2. Why is it so difficult to escape the power of sin? What is the only hope given that will free you from sin's power?
3. Before you became a believer, why were you powerless to live a righteous life? Have you taken advantage of the power available to you to live a righteous life?

5. QUESTION SOMETHING: WHAT FRUIT IS THERE IN SIN (v.21-22)?

Note several clear facts.
1. The true believer is ashamed of his past sin.

> **"And he said, I heard thy voice in the garden, and I was afraid, because I was naked; and I hid myself" (Gen.3:10).**

2. The fruit of sin is death (see A Closer Look # 1, Death—Ro.6:23). The fruit of sin is not good; there is nothing good about it. Sin corrupts, destroys, and dooms all who seek its fruits. This should always be remembered by men.

3. Believers are "made free" from sin by justification, through the glorious love of God. Therefore, they have become slaves to God...
- bearing the fruit of holiness

> **"And ye shall know the truth, and the truth shall make you free" (Jn.8:32).**
> **"That he would grant unto us, that we being delivered out of the hand of our enemies, might serve him without fear. In holiness and righteousness before him, all the days of our life" (Lk.1:74-75).**
> **"Because it is written, Be ye holy; for I am holy" (1 Pt.1:16).**

- bearing the glorious hope and end of eternal life

> **"He that believeth on the Son hath everlasting life: and he that believeth not the Son shall not see life; but the wrath of God abideth on him" (Jn.3:36).**

QUESTIONS:
1. If a person is not ashamed of his sin, what does that tell you about his relationship with God? How can you witness to a person who has no shame?
2. God's Word clearly says that the fruit of sin is death. Why do men continue to sin, disregarding the inevitable results?
3. What are some fruits a believer produces when he becomes a slave to God?

6. CONSIDER SOMETHING: THE WAGES OF SIN VS. THE GIFT OF GOD— ETERNAL LIFE (v.23).

1. The wages of sin is death. Sin deserves death for two very clear reasons.
   a. Sin is acting against God, acting against His very nature. Sin strikes out against God, attempts to tear down God's nature...
      - of purity and morality
      - of holiness and glory
      - of justice and righteousness
      - of love and grace

   b. Sin is rebellion against God. It is rejecting God, ignoring God, disobeying God, denying God, and refusing to live for God.
      The point is this. True justice demands that sin receive its payment or its wages. Since sin is so opposed to God's nature and is actually rebellion against God, it deserves to die...
      - to be cast far, far away from God
      - to have no part of God
      - to be banished from God's sight
      - to be separated from God's presence forever
      - to be condemned and punished for having dishonored and cursed God so much

   As a laborer receives his wages, so sin shall receive its wages. Just as it would be unjust not to pay the laborer, it would be unjust not to pay sin for its work. In fact, if sin did not receive its just punishment, it would be the most gross injustice of eternity. Why? Because sin is against the Sovereign Majesty of the universe, against God Himself. Sin must receive its just wages. Sin must die; it must be banished forever from the presence of God.

   > **"Wherefore, as by one man sin entered into the world, and death by sin; and so death passed upon all men, for that all have sinned" (Ro.5:12).**
   > **"Then when lust hath conceived, it bringeth forth sin: and sin, when it is finished, bringeth forth death" (Jas.1:15).**

2. The gift of God is eternal life. Note that eternal life *is not* the payment of wages. A man cannot work to earn eternal life. It is the gift of God, and it is only through Jesus Christ our Lord.

   > **"For God so loved the world, that he gave his only begotten Son, that whosoever believeth in him should not perish, but have everlasting life" (Jn.3:16).**

ILLUSTRATION:
How can we get rid of sin? Not by giving in to the sin and 'getting it over with' or 'out of our systems.' Thinking this is deception, terrible deception. Lust does not decrease in a heart that is not yielded to God. Lust pours gas on a flame that explodes, resulting in death.

"In one movie some shipwrecked men are left drifting aimlessly on the ocean in a lifeboat. As the days pass under the scorching sun, their rations of food and fresh water give out. The men grow deliriously thirsty. One night while the others are asleep, one man ignores all previous warnings and gulps down some salt water. He quickly dies.

"Ocean water contains seven times more salt than the human body can safely ingest. Drinking it, a person dehydrates because the kidneys demand extra water to flush the overload of salt. The more salt water someone drinks, the thirstier he gets. He actually dies of thirst.

"When we lust, we become like this man. We thirst desperately for something that looks like what we want. We don't realize, however, that it is precisely the opposite of what we really need. In fact, it can kill us."[1]

What we need is not another dose of deadly salt water. What we need is an eternal dose of Living Water, water that will give eternal life.

"Jesus answered and said unto her, If thou knewest the gift of God, and who it is that saith to thee, Give me to drink; thou wouldest have asked of him, and he would have given thee living water. The woman saith unto him, Sir, thou hast nothing to draw with, and the well is deep: from whence then hast thou that living water?" (Jn.4:10-11).

"He that believeth on me, as the scripture hath said, out of his belly shall flow rivers of living water" (Jn.7:38).

<u>QUESTIONS:</u>
1. Unbelievers sin and believers sin. Why is the sin of unbelievers deadly? Why is the sin of believers not deadly? Why does sin deserve death?
2. When you sin, do you stop to think how it affects God? Others? Yourself?
3. The gift of God is eternal life. What have *you* done to deserve such a gift? What *must* you do to receive it?

<u>SUMMARY:</u>

As a Christian believer, you have no right to live as you please. But always remember this: what you are to receive is far, far greater—eternal life. Every right that you had before you became a believer was left at the foot of the cross. Now, it is Jesus Christ who has the right to tell you how to live. This is what He requires from you:

1. Learn something: sin shall not dominate you, the true believer.
2. Know something: you can serve only one master, sin or God.
3. Remember something: remember your decision—you chose righteousness.
4. Do something: serve God with the same fervor that you served sin.
5. Question something: what fruit is there in sin?
6. Consider something: the wages of sin vs. the gift of God—eternal life.

---

[1] Craig B. Larson. *Illustrations for Preaching and Teaching.* (Grand Rapids, MI: Baker Book House, 1994), p.147.

ROMANS 6:14-23

<u>**PERSONAL JOURNAL NOTES:**</u>
(Reflection & Response)

1. The most important thing that I learned from this lesson was:

2. The thing that I need to work on the most is:

3. I can apply this lesson to my life by:

4. Closing Prayer of Commitment: (put your commitment down on paper).

CHAPTER 7

V. STRUGGLE AND CONFESSION: THE BELIEVER IS TO BE FREE FROM THE LAW, 7:1-25

A. The Two Positions of the Law to Man, 7:1-6

1. The law dominates man only as long as he lives

a. The two positions are illustrated by marriage
   1) The law is alive & active for the living
   2) The law is dead & inactive through death
b. The conclusion
   1) The law condemns the living

Know ye not, brethren, (for I speak to them that know the law,) how that the law hath dominion over a man as long as he liveth?
2 For the woman which hath an husband is bound by the law to her husband so long as he liveth; but if the husband be dead, she is loosed from the law of her husband.
3 So then if, while her husband liveth, she be married to another man, she shall be called an adulteress: but if her husband be dead, she is free from that law; so that she is no adulteress, though she be married to another man.
4 Wherefore, my brethren, ye also are become dead to the law by the body of Christ; that ye should be married to another, even to him who is raised from the dead, that we should bring forth fruit unto God.
5 For when we were in the flesh, the motions of sins, which were by the law, did work in our members to bring forth fruit unto death.
6 But now we are delivered from the law, that being dead wherein we were held; that we should serve in newness of spirit, and not in the oldness of the letter.

who violate its demands
   2) Death frees a person from the law

2. Position 1: The law is dead to believers
a. How: By Christ's death
b. The purpose for the believer's death
   1) To unite him to Christ
   2) To bear fruit

3. Position 2: The law is alive to those "in the flesh"
a. How: By arousing sin
b. Result: Death

4. The law is inactivated by conversion
a. How: By death "in" Christ
b. Purpose: To serve in newness of Spirit

Section V
STRUGGLE AND CONFESSION: THE BELIEVER IS TO BE FREE FROM THE LAW
Romans 7:1-25

Study 1: **The Two Positions of the Law to Man**

Text: Romans 7:1-6

Aim: To come out from under the pressure of the law; to live free "in Christ."

Memory Verse:
> "But now we are delivered from the law, that being dead wherein we were held; that we should serve in newness of spirit, and not in the oldness of the letter" (Romans 7:6).

INTRODUCTION:

One of the most popular children's stories is that of "Cinderella." As you recall, Cinderella was scorned by her step-mother and two evil step-sisters. While Cinderella lived under their roof, life was impossible. She worked as hard as she could, but it was never enough to please her family. One day Cinderella was locked in her room as the evil step-sisters made their way to the palace for a big ball. But good fortune finally shone down upon Cinderella. Her fairy godmother suddenly appeared; and in a flash, Cinderella, equipped with the finest clothes and coach, was sent off to join the others at the palace. You probably know how the rest of the story goes.

Cinderella's beauty caught everyone's attention. Furthermore, she captured not only the eye of the prince, but his heart as well. He treated her as a prized gem, like royalty. But as the clock struck twelve, she remembered her godmother's warning: at midnight her clothes would begin to change back into rags and her coach would become a pumpkin. In Cinderella's rush to escape, her glass slipper was left behind and was claimed by the prince. His mission was clear: to find the foot that fit this slipper.

The prince went from house to house in his kingdom in search of his missing princess. Finally, his journey brought him to Cinderella's house. The evil step-sisters tried to force their large feet into the slipper. Obviously, they failed. Their effort to hide Cinderella from his presence also failed. She gently slipped her foot into the slipper, and the rest is history: they lived happily ever-after.

The point is clear. The law, like the evil step-sisters, dominates those who live under its roof. The only way to escape is to do what Cinderella did: leave behind the place of bondage and live with the Prince of Peace. The fairy godmother is not real, but God is. He can free you from the bondage of the law. He will treat you as a prized gem. He has already paid the ultimate sacrifice to seek you out and free you from the penalty of the law. But the law stands in two positions that must be understood if you wish to secure peace in this life.

OUTLINE:
1. The law dominates man *only* as long as he lives (v.1-3).
2. Position 1: the law is dead to believers (v.4).
3. Position 2: the law is alive to those "in the flesh" (v.5).
4. The law is inactivated by conversion (v.6).

1. THE LAW DOMINATES MAN ONLY AS LONG HE LIVES (v.1-3).

The law applies only to the living; it has no bearing whatsoever upon the dead. A dead man is freed from the law; it has no jurisdiction or power over a dead man.
1. Note the two positions of the law illustrated by the law of marriage (v.2).
   a. The law is alive or active to the living. (Cp. the husband and wife who are living and the law of marriage and divorce.)
   b. The law is dead or inactive when death enters the picture. (Cp. the wife who is loosed or freed from the law when her husband dies.)
2. Note the conclusion of the illustration (v.3).
   a. The law condemns the living who violate its demands. (Cp. the woman who marries another man while her husband lives.)
   b. Death frees a person from the law. (Cp. the wife who is free from the law when her husband dies.)

The point is clear. When death enters the picture, a person is *no longer under* the law, and he can *no longer be condemned* by the law. Death forever frees a person from the law, from its demands, guilt, and condemnation.

QUESTIONS:
1. Death voids the law. Understanding this and being able to explain it is vitally important as you witness to unbelievers. How can you simply convey this picture?
2. When you die, are all your problems over? Why or why not?

2. POSITION 1: THE LAW IS DEAD TO BELIEVERS (v.4).

The first position of the law is a glorious truth—the law is dead to "brothers" (believers). Note: Scripture says that believers are "dead to the law," whereas the outline states that the law is dead to believers. Both are true and are saying the same thing.
   ⇒ Believers are "dead to the law"; therefore, the law is bound to be dead and inactive to believers.

The law has no jurisdiction, power, rule, authority, or dominion over the true believer. This is a shock to most people, but it is exactly what Scripture is declaring. The believer is no longer under the law and its accusing finger, no longer under its...

*   guilt and shame
*   condemnation and punishment
*   discouragement and frustration
*   tension and pressure
*   sense of failure and unworthiness
*   sense of disappointment

1. Note how the glorious truth becomes a reality in the life of a person. The believer is dead to the law by the [crucified] body of Christ. The believer is slain or put to death *in Christ*. The believer's death in Christ is a *vicarious death*; that is, he does not literally die himself, but he participates in the death of Christ *spiritually*. When a man believes in Christ's death, God takes that man's belief and counts him as having died in Christ. Why does God do this? Because Christ died on man's behalf, in man's stead, taking the penalty and punishment of the law upon Himself. Therefore, the believer—being dead in Christ—is freed from the law, from its demands and guilt and punishment.

The believer is freed "by the body of Christ," that is, by His slain body or by His death. Christ redeemed the believer from the law...

*   by being a curse

    "For as many as are of the works of the law are under the curse: for it is written, Cursed is every one that continueth not in all things which are written in the book of the law to do them. Christ hath redeemed us from the curse of the law, being made a curse for us: for it is written, Cursed is every one that hangeth on a tree" (Gal.3:10, 13).

*   by His blood

    "In whom we have redemption through his blood, the forgiveness of sins, according to the riches of his grace" (Eph.1:7).

*   by His flesh

    "Having abolished in his flesh the enmity, even the law of commandments contained in ordinances; for to make in himself of twain one new man, so making peace" (Eph.2:15).

*   by the cross

    "And that he might reconcile both unto God in one body by the cross, having slain the enmity thereby" (Eph.2:16).

*   by the body of His flesh

    "In the body of his flesh through death, to present you holy and unblameable and unreproveable in his sight" (Col.1:22).

These are equivalent expressions. They teach the same truth: Christ bore our sins in His own body upon the tree (1 Pt.2:24). His sufferings satisfied justice. His death makes us acceptable to God, delivering us from the penalty of the law; therefore, the believer is free from the law.

    "Who his own self bare our sins in his own body on the tree, that we, being dead to sins, should live unto righteousness: by whose stripes ye were healed" (1 Pt.2:24).

ILLUSTRATION:

Jesus Christ has set you free from the law. This He did when He died upon the cross. How tragic it is when men become ignorant of what He has done for them upon the cross. Men in sin are starving for a freedom that is simply theirs for the asking.

> *"A few days after the [American] Civil War had been officially ended, a man was riding along a road in West Virginia. Sudden[ly] a soldier, clad in a dirty and tattered Confederate uniform, sprang out of a thicket, seized the horse's bridle, and with twitching face demanded, 'Give me bread! Give me bread! I don't want to hurt you, but give me bread—I'm starving.' The man on horseback replied, 'Then why don't you go to the village and get food?' 'I don't dare—they will shoot me,' was the soldier's answer.*
>
> *"'What for?' inquired the man; 'tell me your trouble.'....the confederate soldier related that he had deserted his company several weeks before. Upon approaching the Union pickets, however, he had been informed that no fugitives from Lee's army were to be taken in. What was he to do? If he returned to his company, he would be shot as a deserter. In desperation, he had taken to the woods and lived there on roots and berries until starvation had driven him to the point of madness.*
>
> *"The man on horseback listened, and then exclaimed: 'Don't you know the war is over? Lincoln has pardoned the whole Confederate army. You can have all the food that you want.'"*[1]

The price that Jesus Christ paid for you is much too expensive for you to be starving for freedom from the law. The question is, "Will you continue to scavenge for what the world has to offer or will you feed on the Bread of Life?"

2. Note the glorious purpose for the believer's death to the law.
   a. The believer dies to the law so that he can be united to Christ, the risen and living Lord. Note the picture of marriage is used again. Before coming to Christ, the believer was married and united to the law; he was under its rule and authority. But now, since coming to Christ, he is married and united to Christ; he is under His rule and authority. The believer no longer lives as the law says, but as Christ lived and commanded. (Note: Christ came to fulfill the law; therefore, He and His commandments include not only the law, but much more. See Mt.5:17-18.) Note that believers are married to Christ, the risen and living Lord. The marriage is not a dead or an inactive marriage, but a living, active marriage.

   > **"Know ye not that your bodies are the members of Christ? shall I then take the members of Christ, and make them the members of a harlot? God forbid" (1 Cor.6:15).**

   b. The believer dies to the law so that he can bring forth fruit to God. Bearing fruit would mean...
   - to bear righteousness (Ro.6:21-23; Ph.1:11)
   - to bear converts (Ro.1:13; Jn.15:16)
   - to bear Christian character, the fruit of the Spirit (Gal.5:22-23; Col.1:10)

---

[1] *Dr. Vernon C. Grounds, in 'Our Hope.'* Walter B. Knight. *Knight's Master Book of 4,000 Illustrations.* (Grand Rapids, MI: Eerdmans Publishing Co., 1994), p.594-595.

1. How can you be physically alive but dead to the law? What one thing frees a person from being under the obligations of the law? Can you adequately explain this to a lost soul?
2. Why did Christ free you from the law? What was His eternal purpose? What should be your response to Him? Have you accepted His gift?

3. POSITION 2: THE LAW IS ALIVE TO THOSE "IN THE FLESH" (v.5).

The second position of the law is a warning—the law is alive to those "in the flesh." A man "in the flesh" is the natural man: the man without Christ, the unsaved, the unjustified, the unregenerate man. To be "in the flesh" means that a man is still "under the law," that he must keep its demands, suffer its guilt, and bear its punishment. Note two significant points.

1. The law is alive and active to the man without Christ.
   a. It is alive and active in that it points out sin and arouses guilt within a man when he violates the law.

> **"By the law is the knowledge of sin" (Ro.3:20).**
> **"Wherefore the law was our schoolmaster to bring us unto Christ, that we might be justified by faith" (Gal.3:24).**

   b. It is alive and active in that it arouses sinful passions or "the passions of sins." The law not only points out sin; it actually arouses feelings and stirs the emotions to do the forbidden. Sinful feelings are actually brought about by the law in our members. When the law prohibits and forbids something, it actually creates within us...

   - an interest
   - an attraction
   - an excitement
   - an appeal
   - a tug or pull
   - a fascination
   - a seduction
   - an arousal

There is within man something that makes him want to do that which he is forbidden to do. When he is restricted or fenced in, he wants to break through the restriction or fence. He wants to go beyond where he is allowed, to take control of his own life as he wishes and wills.

> **"But every man is tempted, when he is drawn away of his own lust, and enticed. Then when lust hath conceived, it bringeth forth sin: and sin, when it is finished, bringeth forth death" (Jas.1:14-15).**

2. The result of combating the law—of refusing to obey the law—is that one bears the fruit of sin. When a man violates the law, he bears transgression and sin, and sin leads to death. In fact, sin deserves death.

> **"Wherefore, as by one man sin entered into the world, and death by sin; and so death passed upon all men, for that all have sinned" (Ro.5:12).**

1. What risks does a man face who is under the law?
2. Are the consequences of living under the law severe enough to make you seek Christ personally? Enough to make you share Christ with others? Or do you feel it is not worth the trouble and effort?

4. THE LAW IS INACTIVATED BY CONVERSION (v.6).

Believers are "delivered," that is, have been *discharged,* from the law. How? By their death "in" Christ (see note 2—Ro.7:4 for discussion).

The believer is freed from the law so that he might serve in "newness of spirit," not in the "oldness of the letter."

⇒ The "oldness of the letter" refers to the law. It is the *written* law which a man tries to keep in order to please God. But note: the law was the *old way* for man to live; it is no longer the way for a man to approach God.

⇒ The "newness of spirit" can refer either to the Holy Spirit or to the believer's new spirit. The Holy Spirit is the One who brings new life to the believer and bears fruit within the believer. (Cp. Ro.8:13-17; Gal.5:22-23.)

The believer's new spirit is also focused upon God and upon his relationship with God. The believer is now a child of God, a true member of God's family who has open access into God's presence anytime and under any condition. The believer seeks to serve God knowing that if he fails, God will forgive him and allow him to continue on as if nothing had ever happened. The believer no longer serves God in a legal and slavish spirit that dooms him to discouragement and defeat; but he serves God in "the new spirit" of love, joy, peace, forgiveness, and acceptance.

> **"For if ye live after the flesh, ye shall die: but if ye through the Spirit do mortify the deeds of the body, ye shall live. For as many as are led by the Spirit of God, they are the sons of God. For ye have not received the spirit of bondage again to fear; but ye have received the Spirit of adoption, whereby we cry, Abba, Father. The Spirit itself beareth witness with our spirit, that we are the children of God: and if children, then heirs; heirs of God, and joint-heirs with Christ; if so be that we suffer with him, that we may be also glorified together" (Ro.8:13-17).**

ILLUSTRATION:

God has offered every person a wonderful opportunity: the gift of life in exchange for the certain destiny that sin brings—death. God could have kept His love all to Himself. He could have refused to sacrifice His only Son. He could have just ignored us and given us what we really deserved, but instead He gave us the greatest gift of all—salvation through Jesus Christ.

> *"One Mercedes Benz TV commercial shows their car colliding with a cement wall during a safety test. Someone then asks the company spokesman why they do not enforce their patent on the Mercedes Benz energy-absorbing car body, a design evidently copied by other companies because of its success.*
>
> *"He replies matter-of-factly, 'Because some things in life are too important not to share.' How true. In that category also falls the gospel of salvation, which saves people from far more than auto collisions."*[2]

God has given every believer a brand new start at the point of salvation. Who would ever want to go back to the old way of doing things, the way of bondage to the law?

QUESTIONS:

1. Since your conversion, do you ever fall into the habit of trying to satisfy the law? Do you allow the law to condemn and judge you? What is the only antidote to being freed from the law's bondage?

2. How can you keep your focus on God, His power, His Spirit, His love? Can you ever really be totally free of the law and its tug?

---

[2] Craig B. Larson. *Illustrations for Preaching and Teaching,* p.71.

SUMMARY:

Have you secured true peace in your life? True freedom from the bondage of sin? There is no reason for you to be at the mercy of an unforgiving and domineering law that always destroys and brings you down. Jesus Christ has made a way of escape, a way whose only path goes through the cross. If you want to be free, remember...

1. The law dominates man *only* as long as he lives.
2. Position 1: the law is dead to believers.
3. Position 2: the law is alive to those "in the flesh."
4. The law is inactivated by conversion.

PERSONAL JOURNAL NOTES:
(Reflection & Response)

1. The most important thing that I learned from this lesson was:

2. The thing that I need to work on the most is:

3. I can apply this lesson to my life by:

4. Closing Prayer of Commitment: (put your commitment down on paper).

	B. The Purpose of the Law, 7:7-13	10 And the commandment, which was ordained to life, I found to be unto death.	
1. Is the law sin; that is, is it evil?	7 What shall we say then? Is the law sin? God forbid. Nay, I had not known sin, but by the law: for I had not known lust, except the law had said, Thou shalt not covet.	11 For sin, taking occasion by the commandment, deceived me, and by it slew me.	5. The law reveals the deceitfulness of sin
2. The law reveals the fact of sin			
3. The law gives sin the opportunity to be a-roused & to work every kind of evil	8 But sin, taking occasion by the commandment, wrought in me all manner of concupiscence. For without the law sin was dead.	12 Wherefore the law is holy, and the commandment holy, and just, and good.	6. The law reveals the way of God: Holiness, righteousness, & goodness
4. The law reveals the fact of condemnation & death	9 For I was alive without the law once: but when the commandment came, sin revived, and I died.	13 Was then that which is good made death unto me? God forbid. But sin, that it might appear sin, working death in me by that which is good; that sin by the commandment might become exceeding sinful.	7. The law shows that sin is exceedingly sinful & that it is the cause of death

Section V
STRUGGLE AND CONFESSION: THE BELIEVER IS TO BE FREE FROM THE LAW
Romans 7:1-25

Study 2: **The Purpose of the Law**

Text: Romans 7:7-13

Aim: To examine and understand God's purpose for the law.

Memory Verse:
> **"Wherefore the law is holy, and the commandment holy, and just, and good" (Romans 7:12).**

INTRODUCTION:
When you are driving your car down the road, the laws of the highway have a significant effect upon you. The law tells you such things as...
⇒ which side of the road to drive on
⇒ how fast you can go legally
⇒ that you must have a license
⇒ that you must come to a complete stop at a stop sign

Chances are if a policeman sees you breaking a traffic law, he will pull you over. What will your excuse be? Do you think any of your excuses will impress the policeman?
⇒ "I was daydreaming."
⇒ "I was in a real hurry."
⇒ "I forgot and left my license at home."
⇒ "I did not see anyone else coming."

The purpose for highway laws is not up for discussion or negotiation. Their purpose is simple: to keep the roads safe from lawbreakers. In the same sense, God's law is not up for discussion or negotiation. God's law is to keep people from becoming lawbreakers and to protect society from lawbreakers, from those who would make up laws as they see fit. God's law is firm, unchanging, and established. When His law is applied to our lives, we quickly see what poor spiritual drivers we really are. We are spiritual wrecks who are in desperate need of a Savior who can put us on the right road.

The purpose of the law is clearly pointed out in this passage. It is a passage that needs to be carefully studied by both the world and believers. It is a passage that needs to be proclaimed from the housetops, for the law was given by God to show man his desperate need for a Savior.

OUTLINE:

1. Is the law sin, that is, evil (v.7)?
2. The law reveals the fact of sin (v.7).
3. The law gives sin the opportunity to be aroused and to work every kind of evil (v.8).
4. The law reveals the fact of condemnation and death (v.9-10).
5. The law reveals the deceitfulness of sin (v.11).
6. The law reveals the way of God: holiness, righteousness, and goodness (v.12).
7. The law shows that sin is exceedingly sinful and that it is the cause of death (v.13).

1. IS THE LAW SIN, THAT IS, EVIL (v.7)?

This is a legitimate question because of what Romans has declared about the law.

1. *The law judges and condemns men*: "As many as have sinned in the law shall be judged by the law" (Ro.2:12).
2. *The law and ritual do not make a person a Christian*: "He is a Jew [Christian], which is one inwardly; and circumcision [a ritual] is that of the heart, in the spirit, and not in the letter [law], whose praise is not of men, but of God" (Ro.2:29).
3. *The law cannot make a man righteous and acceptable to God*: "Therefore by the deeds of the law there shall no flesh be justified in his sight: for by the law is the knowledge of sin" (Ro.3:20; cp. Ro.3:27).
4. *The purpose of the law is not to save man but to bear witness that man desperately needs the righteousness of God*: "But now the righteousness of God without law is manifested, being witnessed by the law and the prophets; even the righteousness of God which is by faith of Jesus Christ unto all and upon all them that believe: for there is no difference" (Ro.3:21-22).
5. *The law leads man to boast in himself—in his own works and self-righteousness—not in God*: "Where is boasting then? It is excluded. By what law? Of works? Nay: but by the law of faith" (Ro.3:27; cp. Ro.4:2, 4; 2:29).
6. *The law does not justify a person*: "If Abraham were justified by works [the law], he hath whereof to glory; but not before God. For what saith the scripture? Abraham believed God, and it was counted unto him for righteousness. Now to him that worketh is the reward not reckoned of grace, but of debt. But to him that worketh not, but believeth on him that justifieth the ungodly, his faith is counted for righteousness" (Ro.4:2-5).
7. *The law is not the way a person receives the promise of God*: "For the promise, that he should be the heir of the world, was not to Abraham, or to his seed, through the law, but through the righteousness of faith" (Ro.4:13).
8. *The law works wrath in that it accuses man of sin and condemns him*: "Because the law worketh wrath: for where no law is, there is no transgression" (Ro.4:15).
9. *The law causes sin to increase and multiply*: "Moreover the law entered, that the offence might abound. But where sin abounded, grace did much more abound" (Ro.5:20).
10. *The law enslaves and brings men into bondage*: "For sin shall not have dominion over you: for ye are not under the law, but under grace" (Ro.6:14; cp. Ro.7:1).

11.   *The law arouses men to sin*: "For when we were in the flesh, the motions of sins, which were by the law, did work in our members to bring forth fruit unto death" (Ro.7:5).

Such facts as these can naturally cause a person to question the value of God's law. If the law lays such a burden of sin upon man, what good is it? Is it not evil? Scripture declares loud and clear: "God forbid! Let it never be! Such a thought is far from the truth!"

QUESTIONS:

1. What would society be like without laws? Do any lawless societies exist now? If so, do these societies have advantages of which you would like to be a part ?
2. In what ways has the law affected your life? Do you consider these ways to be to your benefit or to your detriment? Depending on your answer, does that dictate that the law is good or evil?

2. THE LAW REVEALS THE FACT OF SIN (v.7).

Apart from the law, man would be aware that some acts are wrong, such as stealing and killing. However, there would be much that man could not know if he did not have the law, much that he would desperately need to know in order to live a full and peaceful life.

The law reveals the fact of sin, the fact...
- that men are not in a right relationship with God
- that men are not in a right relationship with other men
- that men are living selfishly, thereby dooming themselves
- that men are coveting and lusting, thereby destroying their world and their future
- that men are displeasing God and have become unacceptable to Him

The point is this: when a man sees the fact of sin, the fact that he is a sinner, he can *correct it* and *do something* about it. The knowledge of sin is a great and glorious thing, for we can take our knowledge and use it to *correct the wrong*. Without the law, we would roam in ignorance, not knowing what was wrong and what was right, what was dooming us and what was freeing us. If there were no restraint, that is, no law, every man would be doing what he wanted when he wanted; he would be doing his own thing—fulfilling his own desires—regardless of the fallout and the hurt inflicted upon others.

Now note: the law reveals sin; it awakens man to three facts about sin.

1.   *The law reveals the fact of sin*, that sin actually exists. The law awakens man to the reality and truth of sin. Man knows that coveting is wrong because the law says, "Thou shalt not covet." He knows that some things are good and other things are bad because the law tells him. He knows that certain things please and other things displease God because the law says so. In simple and clear language, the law tells a man...
- what the nature and will of God is
- what he must do to be acceptable to God

2.   *The law reveals the fact of man's own sin*, that man is unquestionably a sinner. The law awakens man to the reality that he himself is a sinner. The law shows man...
- that he does not always do the will of God
- that he cannot keep the law of God, not perfectly
- that he is guilty of acting contrary to the nature of God
- that he is imperfect, guilty of violating God's law
- that being imperfect, he comes short of God's glory
- that being short of God's glory, he is unacceptable to God

3.   *The law reveals the fact of man's sinful nature*, that man is actually aroused to do some of the things that are forbidden. The law shows man that he has a sinful, de-

praved, polluted, and corrupted nature. The law shows man that he covets and lusts, enjoys and is aroused...

- to take more than his share and more than he needs—whether it be food, clothing, shelter, or other material possessions
- to take those things which are not his
- to keep up with the status of his neighbor
- to go after the excitement and stimulation of the forbidden
- to fulfill the lust of the flesh
- to feed the lust of the eyes
- to satisfy the pride of life

The purpose of the law is to reveal sin so that man can correct his behavior and save himself and his world. Apart from God's law, he would not know that he needed to be saved.

> **"Therefore by the deeds of the law there shall no flesh be justified in his sight: for by the law is the <u>knowledge of sin</u>" (Ro.3:20).**
> **"Wherefore the law was our schoolmaster to bring us unto Christ, that we might be justified by faith" (Gal.3:24).**

<u>QUESTIONS:</u>
1. How can the knowledge of your sin be a blessing to you? Under what circumstances would this knowledge not be a blessing?
2. Since man has a sinful nature, can he be responsible for his sin? How? Are you as responsible as you can be?

3. THE LAW GIVES SIN THE OPPORTUNITY TO BE AROUSED AND TO WORK EVERY KIND OF EVIL (v.8).

Note the exact words of the Scripture: "Sin, taking occasion [opportunity] by the commandment, works in men all manner of evil"; that is, sin *uses* the commandment. Sin is *not within* the commandment; it is *separate* from it. The commandment or law itself is not sinful. Sin is within man, not within the law. Man's aging, deteriorating, and corrupt nature has within it...

- the principle of sin
- the tendency to sin
- the fondness for sin
- the urge to sin

- a diseased flesh
- a selfish appetite
- a self-centered mind
- a dead spirit

Note three points.
1. It is the law that gives sin the opportunity to be aroused. The law actually stirs, awakens, and arouses sin to work all manner of evil. When a man is told not to do something, there is something within him that is stirred, causing him to want to do it. Sometimes the desire to do the forbidden is so strong it becomes a rage, inflamed to such a point that the person just has to do it.
2. It is man who takes and misuses the law; it is not the law that takes and misuses man. The law does not violate man; man violates the law. It is not the law that *takes* man and forces him to sin. It is man who *takes* the law and breaks it, who deliberately goes against what it says. It is sin within man that takes and misuses the law to work all manner of sin. Therefore, it is not the law that is evil; it is man who is evil.
3. Without the law, *sin was dead*; that is, the law was not alive and active. It was not guiding and directing man; it was not able to fulfill its function which was so desperately needed: showing man his critical need for deliverance from sin and its condemnation of death.

Without the law, *sin is dead*; but with the law, sin becomes alive. Man is able to look at the law and his true condition, that he is a sinner who must be saved if he is to become acceptable to God and live eternally. The law is not evil but good, gloriously good, for it shows us our desperate need for salvation.

> **"For when we were in the flesh, the motions of sins, which were by the law, did work in our members to bring forth fruit unto death" (Ro.7:5).**
> **"For the flesh lusteth against the Spirit, and the Spirit against the flesh: and these are contrary the one to the other: so that ye cannot do the things that ye would" (Gal.5:17).**

ILLUSTRATION:

The law is a constant companion to sinful man who thinks he can take care of his own sin. One thing is true. No fallen man has ever kept himself from falling and being condemned. Only Jesus Christ can keep a person from falling and from condemnation.

> *"The story is told of a carpenter who was nailing shingles on the roof of a house. He lost his footing and started to slide off. As he was sliding he began praying, 'Lord, oh, Lord, help me!' Still he kept sliding. Again the man prayed, 'Lord, oh, Lord, help me!' He kept sliding until he got to the edge and a nail sticking up caught hold of his pants. After he came to a stop he said, 'Never mind, Lord. The nail's got a hold of me now.'"[1]*

The law is God's haunting reminder, a haunting reminder that without the nails that Christ allowed to pierce His hands and feet, life would be absolutely hopeless and full of despair. Remember this: the next time you are tempted to take credit for keeping yourself from falling, thank God for the law and for the nails!

QUESTIONS:

1. Have you ever been given a rule, a law, an instruction—only to turn right around and break it? What is it about boundaries or guidelines that tempt us to step outside and disobey? Would you be better off without the boundaries? Why or why not?
2. Man can take any good thing and make it bad by misusing it. Why is the law such a temptation for man to abuse?
3. Have you ever thanked God for His law? That it points the way to Him and His glorious salvation? Why not thank Him right now?

4. THE LAW REVEALS THE FACT OF CONDEMNATION AND DEATH (v.9-10).

This is a major purpose of the law. Note three points.

1.   A man who does not know or pay attention to the law feels alive. He is just not aware of the law; therefore, he does not pay attention to sin. He is not aware that he is a sinner and short of God's glory, violating God's will and going contrary to God's nature. He is ignorant of God's law; he pays little attention to right and wrong. When he does wrong and fails to do right, he is not aware of it. Therefore he feels...

- no consciousness of sin
- no guilt
- no sense of judgment
- no dread of punishment

He feels alive, safe, secure, confident, and assured that he is pleasing to God, that he will be approved and accepted by God—if he is even aware of God's existence! He feels alive despite the reality of his sinful state and condition. Without the law he does not know the truth, that he is a sinner, condemned and unclean, ever so short of God's glory and acceptance.

---

[1] Michael P. Green. *Illustrations for Biblical Preaching*, p.327.

2.   A man who does know God's law and pays attention to it sees sin come alive. By knowing the law, the man becomes *acutely aware* of sin when he breaks the law. It is the law that gives him...

- a painful awareness of sin
- a sense of guilt
- a sense of judgment to come
- a dread of punishment and of death

It is the law that causes his spirit to die, that destroys his confidence and assurance, comfort and security. It is the law that shows him the true state and condition of man: that he is a sinner who is to face condemnation and death; that he desperately needs to be delivered from sin and death; that he desperately needs a Savior who can make him acceptable to God.

3.   The point is this: the law is ordained to bring life, but not in the way men think. Men think that the law was given to be kept and that by keeping the commandment, they can earn the acceptance of God, working their way into heaven. However, this is not the way the law brings life to man. The law brings life to man...

- by destroying his self-centeredness and self-righteousness
- by revealing the truth to him, his true state and condition
- by showing him that he is a corrupt, sinful being
- by demonstrating that he desperately needs to be delivered from sin and death
- by proving that he desperately needs a Savior, One who can make him acceptable to God

When a man really looks at the law of God, he learns his true condition: he is corrupt and destined to face condemnation and death. In learning this fact, he is driven to seek the salvation of God. Therefore, the law is not evil; it is good.

> "For I delight in the law of God after the inward man: but I see another law in my members, warring against the law of my mind, and bringing me into captivity to the law of sin which is in my members. O wretched man that I am! who shall deliver me from the body of this death?" (Ro.7:22-24).

QUESTIONS:
1. How does ignorance of the law cause a man to misjudge the true condition of his soul? Is ignorance an acceptable excuse for not knowing the truth? Why or why not?
2. Has the law caused you to come to God for deliverance from your sinful self? How can you make a difference to the lost souls who are ignorant of the law?

5. THE LAW REVEALS THE DECEITFULNESS OF SIN (v.11).

Note again: it is sin that takes the law and misuses it; it takes the law and deceives us. How? There are at least two ways.

1.   Sin misuses the law and deceives a person by making him feel safe and secure. Sin, that is, self-righteousness, says obey the law and you shall live. But this is deception, for no man can keep the law perfectly. Down deep, the thinking and honest man knows he can never achieve perfection by keeping God's law; but his sin, his self-righteousness, drives him onward to try and try; thus he is forever deceived and doomed. The point is this: the law reveals the deceitfulness of sin or of self-righteousness. The law proves that man is not perfect, that he cannot live without sinning, that he sins continually and cannot keep from sinning. When a man honestly looks at the law, the law destroys the deceitfulness of sin.

2.   Sin misuses the law and deceives a person by discouraging him, making him feel helpless and hopeless. Sin deceives men into thinking that the law has been given to bring life to man. Therefore, when a man continues to break the law, he is keenly aware that he is condemned and unable to achieve the righteousness of the law. He knows that he has displeased God, senses that he is unacceptable to God. Feelings of helplessness and hopelessness swarm over him; he becomes defeated, down and out.

Sin simply takes the law and uses man's failure to discourage him. Sin uses the law, so to speak, to whip man; to make him feel unworthy, helpless, and hopeless; to drive him deeper and deeper into despair.

> **"For sin, taking occasion by the commandment, deceived me, and by it slew me" (Ro.7:11).**
> **"For we ourselves also were sometimes foolish, disobedient, deceived, serving divers lusts and pleasures, living in malice and envy, hateful, and hating one another" (Tit.3:3).**

Now note: such an attitude toward the law is the attitude of sin. The law was never given to drive men to despair, and in truth, it cannot. It is sin *within* men that drives them to despair. Twisted minds and ungodly thoughts drive men into a state of hopelessness. The law was given to reveal sin to men, to take the sin that already exists and to reveal its shame and consequences to men. When the law was first given, man was already in a state of sin and death: he was sinning and he was dying. God gave the law to man because He loved man, because He knew that men needed to be pointed toward Christ, needed to be shown their terrible condition and desperate need for a Savior. Such is the glorious purpose of the law, a purpose which is far from being evil.

QUESTIONS:
1. Do you ever take pride in your obedience to the law? Why is this attitude sinful, and why is it dangerous? How can you keep from being prideful?
2. Have you ever been so deep in sin or so addicted to a sin that you felt hopeless and helpless? That you were too unworthy to be forgiven or accepted by God? The law was not meant to discourage but to point toward a glorious hope. How can you turn despair into hope?

6. THE LAW REVEALS THE WAY OF GOD: HOLINESS, RIGHTEOUSNESS, AND GOODNESS (v.12).

1. The law is holy: set apart and full of purity, majesty, and glory—set apart in that it reveals God's nature and will—set apart in that it exposes sin, all that is contrary to God's nature and will. The law is holy in that it is different and set apart from everything else on earth. The law is God's way of holiness, the way to live a life of holiness, the way that is so different and so set apart that no man can reach its purity.

2. The law is just: righteous, fair, impartial, equitable, straight. The law treats a man exactly as he should be treated; it shows no partiality to anyone. It also reveals how a man should treat others. The law is just in that it reveals exactly how a man should live. It shows him how to live in relation to God and his fellow man; it judges him fairly and impartially.

3. The law is good: it shows man how to live and tells him when he fails to live that way. It exposes his sin and demonstrates his desperate need for a Savior. The law tells man the truth about the nature of man in a most explicit way, and it points him toward the need for *outside* help in order to be saved.

> **"The law of the LORD is perfect, converting the soul: the testimony of the LORD is sure, making wise the simple" (Ps.19:7).**
> **"But we know that the law is good, if a man use it lawfully" (1 Tim.1:8).**

1. God's law is holy, just, and good. If the law were of man, how would it be different?
2. What are some practical examples of the differences between God's law and man's laws?
3. Would you rather live under God's law or man's law? Why?

7. THE LAW SHOWS THAT SIN IS EXCEEDINGLY SINFUL AND THAT IT IS THE CAUSE OF DEATH (v.13).

Note three points.

1. The law is good; it is not the cause of death. "God forbid! Such is impossible!"

2. The law was given to expose sin and to make men deeply aware of its presence and consequences. Men needed to know just how appalling sin is. Men needed to know that sin...
- is the worst possible affront to God
- is the worst imaginable rebellion against God
- is against all that God represents

The law proves that sin is against God: against all that He is, against all of His nature and will. Sin is selfish, destructive, dirty, ugly, and impure. The law is the very opposite. The law was given to show how exceedingly sinful sin is, to show just how terrible it is. Take any sin and stand it up against the law that prohibits it, and the great contrast is seen. For example, take murder and stand it beside the commandment "Thou shalt not kill." Look at the great contrast.
⇒ The commandment protected man's life, but sin took his life away.
⇒ The commandment protected man's presence with loved ones, but sin took his presence away.
⇒ The commandment protected man's existence upon earth, but sin took his existence away.
⇒ The commandment protected man's contribution to society, but sin took his contribution away.
⇒ The commandment said that man could live, but sin said "no," and killed him.

So it is with every sin, whether adultery, stealing, or taking God's name in vain. The law was given to make men think of their sinful state and condition, of their desperate need for deliverance and salvation.

3. The law was given to make men think about death, to make men aware that they die because they violate the will and nature of God. Men died *before* the law was ever given. They died because they did not live holy and righteous lives, did not live according to the nature and will of God. God gave the law so that sin and its condemnation of death would be *exposed* more than ever before. Men had to be shown that they were great sinners and that they died because they sinned. The law shows men clearer than ever before and in no uncertain terms...
- that they do sin
- that they are not perfect
- that they are condemned to die

Therefore, they need a Savior who will deliver them from sin and its terrible consequence of death. The law shows man his desperate need to be saved from sin, death, and judgment.

"For all have sinned, and come short of the glory of God"
(Ro.6:23).

ILLUSTRATION:

When does a man get desperate enough to seek a savior greater than himself? People who are willing to look into the mirror and admit their need for Jesus Christ will escape eternal judgment.

> *Herbert was living the American dream: married to his high-school sweet-heart, two beautiful children, a large home in a good neighborhood, two new cars, involved in the civic life of his community, and a member of the largest church in town.*
>
> *Like many men who live close to the edge, Herbert thought he could get away with anything. A wandering eye became his Achilles' heel, his weakness that betrayed him. Spotting an attractive co-worker, he did not take long to develop an affair. Herbert's dream life became a tragic nightmare. His adultery severely damaged his relationship with his faithful wife and his two children. After his sin was exposed, his employer no longer had use for a man who could not be trusted.*
>
> *Herbert was a crushed and broken man. Self-reliant for all his adult life, he quickly came to the end of his rope. Broken-hearted, he repented of his sin and asked God to forgive him. Fortunately for Herbert, God had given him a wife far more spiritual and loving than himself. Through the ministry of his church, they were able to get the needed counseling that put their marriage back on a solid foundation.*
>
> *After several difficult months, Herbert asked God this question: "Lord, why did you take such a risk on someone like me?" In that small, still voice in his heart, he heard this reply: "Herbert, I did not take a risk on you. There is no risk in My love. And you should know that you are not taking a risk when you trust Me to change you."*

As Herbert fell asleep that night, he meditated on this great truth: when he had come to the end of his rope, he found God right there, waiting for him with open arms. He was thankful for the law, God's short leash, that saved his life.

QUESTIONS:

1. It is sin that causes death, not the law. What things has sin killed in your life? What has the law helped preserve?
2. If the punishment for sin were not death, do you think you would try as hard to obey the law? Is death too severe a penalty for breaking the law? Why or why not?

SUMMARY:

A day should not go by when you do not thank God for the law. Through the law, God shows you your desperate need for help. After Jesus Christ, the law is the best thing God has ever done for you. The law has a critical purpose in your life:

1. The law is not sin, that is, evil.
2. The law reveals the fact of sin.
3. The law gives sin the opportunity to be aroused and to work every kind of evil.
4. The law reveals the fact of condemnation and death.
5. The law reveals the deceitfulness of sin.
6. The law reveals the way of God: holiness, righteousness, and goodness.
7. The law shows that sin is exceedingly sinful and that it is the cause of death.

ROMANS 7:7-13

PERSONAL JOURNAL NOTES:
(Reflection & Response)

1. The most important thing that I learned from this lesson was:

2. The thing that I need to work on the most is:

3. I can apply this lesson to my life by:

4. Closing Prayer of Commitment: (put your commitment down on paper).

C. The Confessions of a Man's Struggling Soul, 7:14-25

1. The law is spiritual

2. Confession 1: Man is carnal, given over & enslaved to sin

　a. A carnal life is a helpless, unceasing struggle

　b. A carnal life demonstrates that human nature & knowledge are inadequate

　c. The conclusion: man has a sinful, depraved, & corrupt nature

3. Confession 2: Man is void of any good thing

　a. He wills & resolves, but it is all inadequate

14 For we know that the law is spiritual: but I am carnal, sold under sin.
15 For that which I do I allow not: for what I would, that do I not; but what I hate, that do I.
16 If then I do that which I would not, I consent unto the law that it is good.
17 Now then it is no more I that do it, but sin that dwelleth in me.
18 For I know that in me (that is, in my flesh,) dwelleth no good thing: for to will is present with me; but how to perform that which is good I find not.
19 For the good that I would I do not: but

the evil which I would not, that I do.
20 Now if I do that I would not, it is no more I that do it, but sin that dwelleth in me.
21 I find then a law, that, when I would do good, evil is present with me.
22 For I delight in the law of God after the inward man:
23 But I see another law in my members, warring against the law of my mind, and bringing me into captivity to the law of sin which is in my members.
24 O wretched man that I am! who shall deliver me from the body of this death?
25 I thank God through Jesus Christ our Lord. So then with the mind I myself serve the law of God; but with the flesh the law of sin.

　b. The conclusion: he has a sinful, depraved, & corrupt nature

4. Confession 3: Man finds two laws or forces within

　a. The law of God works inwardly

　b. The law of sin wars against the law of his mind

5. Confession 4: Man is a desperate, wretched man who needs a Deliverer

6. Confession 5: The Deliverer is Jesus Christ

**Section V
STRUGGLE AND CONFESSION: THE BELIEVER
IS TO BE FREE FROM THE LAW
Romans 7:1-25**

Study 3:　The Confessions of a Man's Struggling Soul

Text:　Romans 7:14-25

Aim:　To acknowledge the great need of your soul: Jesus Christ.

Memory Verse:
　　"O wretched man that I am! who shall deliver me from the body of this death? I thank God through Jesus Christ our Lord. So then with the mind I myself serve the law of God; but with the flesh the law of sin" (Romans 7:24-25).

INTRODUCTION:
　Think for a moment. When are you most honest with yourself and with others? Are you more prone to be honest...
- when no one is around to see or hear you?
- when you are among trusted friends?
- when the truth is the only believable explanation?
- when you have been caught in a lie?

No one is perfect, although there are many who live under the pressure of trying to be perfect. Living under such a false pretense is unscriptural as well as a recipe for disaster. A lot of people hide behind an air of bravado, trying to fool everyone. In reality, they fool no one, not even themselves. Everyone has problems. Everyone has struggles. Everyone wants to do good in some area of life while evil pulls at him in another area. As we will soon see, there is only one answer to this dilemma.

This is a great passage of Scripture in that it portrays the struggling soul of the believer as he plows through life. It is a rare picture of the life of Paul, of what he sensed, learned, and experienced as he struggled to please God and to become conformed to the glorious image of the Lord Jesus. It is the confession of a man's soul as the man struggles through life.

OUTLINE:
1. The law is spiritual (v.14).
2. Confession 1: he is carnal, given over and enslaved to sin (v.14-17).
3. Confession 2: he is void of any good thing (v.18-20).
4. Confession 3: he finds two laws or forces within (v.21-23).
5. Confession 4: he is a desperate, wretched man who needs a Deliverer (v.24).
6. Confession 5: the Deliverer is Jesus Christ (v.25).

1. THE LAW IS SPIRITUAL (v.14).

It is spiritual in at least three senses.
1. The law was given to man by the Spirit of God. The Greek word used is the very name of the Holy Spirit. The Holy Spirit is the source of the law.
2. The law is the expression of the will and nature of God. The law is spiritual because it describes the will of God and tells man just what God is like. The rules of the law reveal both the mind and nature of God.
3. The law is spiritual because of its purposes. Remember:
   ⇒ The law reveals the fact of sin (v.7).
   ⇒ The law gives sin the opportunity to be aroused and to work every kind of evil (v.8).
   ⇒ The law reveals the fact of condemnation and death (v.9-10).
   ⇒ The law reveals the deceitfulness of sin (v.11).
   ⇒ The law reveals the way of God: holiness, righteousness, and goodness (v.12).
   ⇒ The law shows that sin is exceedingly sinful, that it is the cause of death (v.13).

ILLUSTRATION:
Bear in mind one clear fact: the law points out what is wrong but has no power to fix your problems. Have you ever thought, "How could the law be spiritual when all it does is make my flesh miserable?" What purpose does the law serve?

David had just hired a new work crew to build a house in a very affluent neighborhood. No expense was to be spared. After the foundation was laid, the walls went up quickly. The new crew worked fast. "This is going to be a great job," David thought to himself. The more quickly they finished the job, the sooner he got paid. Before moving on to the next phase, David placed his plumbline on a wall and to his surprise, the wall was crooked. He checked another wall and found that it was crooked as well. In fact, every wall in the house was crooked.

To the natural eye, the walls looked perfectly straight. But the plumbline testified to the truth: the walls were crooked. David's anger boiled over. He flung the plumbline across the lot. He glared at and fired each of his workers because of their sloppy, costly, and inexcusable work. Then, he got mad at himself for having hired them.

The fault was not in the plumbline. It only showed David the problem. Just like the law: the law was not given to fix our lives, bent by the crookedness of sin; the law was given to reveal God's will for us, to reveal His nature, to reveal how He wants us to behave. The law is God's gift to the believer. It is a gift that shows us the problem so that we will be desperate enough to ask for help from the Carpenter from Nazareth.

QUESTIONS:
1. Since the Holy Spirit is the source of the law, can it be anything but good? Why is this important to know when you struggle with the law?
2. Is there a difference between the law and the nature of God? Between the law and the will of God? Which are you to revere and respect: the law or God? Or both?

2. CONFESSION 1: HE IS CARNAL, GIVEN OVER AND ENSLAVED TO SIN (v.14-17).

The word "carnal" or "fleshly" means to be made of flesh; to consist of flesh; to have a body of flesh and blood. It means the flesh with which a man is born, the fleshly nature one inherits from his parents when he is born.

The word carnal also means to be given up to the flesh, that is, to live a fleshly, sensual life; to be given over to animal appetites; to be controlled by one's sinful nature.

Paul says that he is "sold under sin." He simply means that as a creature of flesh, that is, as a man, he is...

- enslaved to sin
- given over to sin
- under sin's influence
- subject to sin
- capable of sinning
- guilty of sinning

- cannot free himself from being short of God's glory
- cannot keep from sinning—not perfectly
- cannot erase sin's presence—not completely
- cannot cast sin out of his life—not totally
- cannot get rid of sin—not permanently

> "His own iniquities shall take the wicked himself, and he shall be holden with the cords of his sins" (Pr.5:22).
> "Jesus answered them, Verily, verily, I say unto you, Whosoever committeth sin is the servant of sin" (Jn.8:34).

Paul makes three points about his being carnal and sold under sin.
1. He says that a carnal life is a helpless, unceasing struggle.
   a. "That which I do I allow not": the word "allow" means to recognize, to know, to perceive. A carnal man finds himself doing things, and he cannot understand why he is doing them. He fights and struggles against them, but before he knows it, he has sinned and come short. The sin was upon him before he even recognized and saw it. If he had known that the behavior was sin, he never would have done it, but he did not recognize it as coming short of God's glory and God's will for his life.
   b. "What I would, that do I not." Paul says that he wanted to do right and to please God as he walked throughout life day by day. He wanted to be conformed to the image of Christ, becoming all that God wanted him to be. But despite his desire and expectation, before he knew it, he found himself coming short of God's glory and will.
   c. "What I hate, that do I." Paul hated sin and hated coming short of God's glory. He struggled against failing and displeasing God; he hated everything that hurt and cut the heart of God, and he fought to erase it completely from his life. But no matter how much he hated and struggled against coming short, he still found himself failing.

> **"For the flesh lusteth against the Spirit, and the Spirit against the flesh: and these are contrary the one to the other: so that ye cannot do the things that ye would" (Gal.5:17).**

2. A carnal life demonstrates that human nature and knowledge are inadequate. A carnal man fails to live for God as he should. No matter how much he tries to please God and to be conformed to the image of Christ, he comes short.

Now note: it is the law that tells man that he comes short. The law tells him that despite all his efforts to please God, he is short and unacceptable to God. He may know the law and he may try to keep the law, but his desire to know and to seek God will not save him. His nature and knowledge are not enough; they fail. What he needs is a Savior, One outside his own flesh who can forgive his sins and impart eternal life to him.

Note another fact: a carnal life proves the law is good. The word "consent" means to agree; to say the same thing; to speak right along with the law; to prove, demonstrate, and show that the law is right. The law proves and demonstrates that a man cannot live a perfectly righteous life. A carnal man proves the very same thing. He sins, finding himself doing exactly what the law says not to do and what he himself prefers not to do.

The point is this: when a carnal man sins, the law points out his sin. The law tells the carnal man the truth: he is a sinner doomed to die. Knowing this, the carnal man is able to seek the Lord and His forgiveness. Therefore, the carnal man agrees with the law; the law is very good, for it tells him that he must seek the Savior and His forgiveness. He may not actually follow through and seek the Lord, but the law has at least fulfilled its function in showing the carnal man what he needs to do.

> **"The way of peace they know not; and there is no judgment in their goings: they have made them crooked paths; whosoever goeth therein shall not know peace" (Is.59:8).**
>
> **"Having the understanding darkened, being alienated from the life of God through the ignorance that is in them, because of the blindness of their heart" (Eph.4:18).**

3. Paul's conclusion is that man has a sinful, depraved, and corrupt nature. What causes him to conclude this? As a man who was a genuine believer, he did not want to sin; he actually willed not to sin. However, he found that he could not keep from sinning. He continually came short of the glory of God, failing to be consistently conformed to the image of Christ. Why?

⇒ Not because he failed to exercise his will
⇒ Not because his mind was not focused upon Christ
⇒ Not because he did not know God's will
⇒ Not because he did not seek to do God's will
⇒ Not because he did not call upon every faculty and power of his being

Paul came short and failed because of *sin that dwelled in him*, because of *sin within* his flesh. The carnal man finds a principle, a law of sin *within* his flesh that tugs and pulls him to sin. He finds that no matter what he does, he sins...

- by living for himself before he lives for God and for others
- by putting himself before the laws concerning God and the laws concerning man

(This refers to the Ten Commandments where the first four laws govern our relationship to God and the last six laws govern our relationship to man.)

No matter what resources and faculties man uses and no matter how diligently he tries, he is unable to control sin and to keep from sinning. Sin is *within* his flesh; it *dwells in* him. In fact, man is corrupt and dies for this very reason. He was never made to be corruptible nor to die; he was not created with the *seed of corruption* that causes him to age and deteriorate and decay (Ro.5:12). The *seed of corruption* was planted in his flesh, in his body and life, when he sinned. The carnal life proves that man cannot keep from sinning, that man is diseased with the *seed of corruption*, the seed of a sinful and a depraved nature.

> "Jesus answered them and said, Verily, verily, I say unto you,
> Ye seek me, not because ye saw the miracles, but because ye did
> eat of the loaves, and were filled" (Jn.6:26).
> "Unto the pure all things are pure: but unto them that are
> defiled and unbelieving is nothing pure; but even their mind and
> conscience is defiled" (Tit.1:15).

QUESTIONS:
1. Paul said he was a carnal man. What thoughts run through your mind when you think about a man who was such a spiritual giant but was still carnal? How does this effect how you feel about yourself? Why?
2. In practical terms, what does it mean to be "sold under sin"?
3. Why is it impossible for a carnal man to give his best for God? What do you need to do in order to give your best for God?
4. Why is it impossible for you to keep a perfect record of not sinning? What makes your situation different from that of an unbeliever?

3. CONFESSION 2: HE IS VOID OF ANY GOOD THING (v.18-20).

By "flesh" Paul means the human, sinful, depraved, and corrupt nature of man. Paul declares: there is no "good thing" in his flesh. This does not mean that he never did any good thing or work. It means that his flesh...
- is unable to please the goodness of God
- is unable to be as good as it should be
- is unable to be perfectly good
- is unable to conquer the tendency and push toward sin
- is unable to be conformed to the image of Christ
- is corrupted and short of God's glory
- is contaminated and diseased by sin
- is incapable of reaching God on its own and by itself
- is aging and deteriorating, dying and decaying
- is condemned to face the judgment of God

1. Note why Paul says his flesh is void of any good thing: he wills and resolves not to sin, but it is all to no avail, he still fails and comes short. Note that being *willing to do good is ever present* with him. The word "present" means that it is constantly before his face. He is __always__ willing to do good and to please God. There is no lack of will in him. It is not the weakness of will nor of his resolve that causes him to come short of God's glory and will. How does he know this?
⇒ Because what he wills to do, he fails to do
⇒ Because the evil he tries not to do, he does

2. Paul's conclusion is the same as that of point one. He is void of any good thing because he has a sinful, depraved, and corrupt nature. He is held in spiritual bondage to sin.

QUESTIONS:
1. Do you really believe there is no good thing in you? How can this be true? What is the distinction between *being* good and *doing* good?
2. If you accept that there is no good thing in you, does that mean you should quit trying?
3. How can you use this point (v.18-20) to help identify with an unbeliever and witness to him?

4. CONFESSION 3: HE FINDS TWO LAWS OR FORCES WITHIN (v.21-23).

Very simply, as soon as Paul wills to do good, he is immediately confronted...
- by a law of evil (v.21)
- by the law of sin (v.23)

The law of sin and evil battles *the law of the inward man* (v.22), *the law of his mind* (v.23).

1. The *law of evil* or the *law of sin* means that sin is a law, a rule, a force, a principle, a disposition, an urge, a tendency, a pull, a tug, a corruption, a depravity within man's nature or inner being. It is called a law...
- because of its regularity; it rises up and rules all the time
- because of its permanent and controlling power
- because it is impossible to break its rule and to keep from sinning
- because it has captivated and enslaved the nature of man (Ro.7:14f)
- because it is not passive but active, constantly struggling to gain the ascendancy over the law of the mind

Any man who allows the law of sin to rule in his life is a miserable and helpless victim of sin.

2. The *law of the inward man* or *the law of the mind* means...
- the divine nature of God implanted within the believer

> **"Whereby are given unto us exceeding great and precious promises: that by these ye might be partakers of the <u>divine nature</u>, having escaped the corruption that is in the world through lust" (2 Pt.1:4).**

- the "new man" created when a believer is born again

> **"And be renewed in the spirit of your mind; and that ye put on the new man, which after God is created in righteousness and true holiness" (Eph.4:23-24).**

- the abiding presence of Christ in the believer's life

> **"I will not leave you comfortless: I will come to you....At that day ye shall know that I am in my Father, and ye in me, and I in you" (Jn.14:18, 20).**

- the indwelling presence of the Holy Spirit

> **"And I will pray the Father, and he shall give you another Comforter, that he may abide with you for ever; even the Spirit of truth; whom the world cannot receive, because it seeth him not, neither knoweth him: but ye know him; for he dwelleth with you, and shall be in you....But the Comforter, which is the Holy Ghost, whom the Father will send in my name, he shall teach you all things, and bring all things to your remembrance, whatsoever I have said unto you" (Jn.14:16-17, 26).**

- the "hidden man of the heart"

> **"But let it [one's appearance] be the hidden man of the heart, in that which is not corruptible, even the ornament of a meek and quiet spirit, which is in the sight of God of great price" (1 Pt.3:4).**

Very simply stated, the *law of the inward man* is the law, rule, disposition, urge, tendency, pull, and tug of the Holy Spirit to please God and to delight in doing His will.

The confession of Paul is striking. He declares that the law of sin wars against the law of his mind and that it gains the ascendancy. The law of sin captivates and enslaves him.

<u>QUESTIONS:</u>

1. Have you ever resolved to do something 'just right' or to behave in a certain way, only to turn around and do just the opposite? Why did this happen? Was it because you didn't try? Didn't care? What should this shortcoming cause you to do?
2. How *should* you respond when you get that "pulled-apart" feeling? How *do* you respond when you get that "pulled-apart" feeling?

5. CONFESSION 4: HE IS A DESPERATE, WRETCHED MAN WHO NEEDS A DELIVERER (v.24).

There is a sense in which man is a walking civil war. He has the ability to see what is good, but he is unable to do it. He can see what is wrong, but he cannot keep from doing it. Paul says he was pulled in two directions, pulled so much that he was almost like two men in the same body. He knew *the right*, yet he did *the wrong*. He knew what was wrong, yet he was unable to stay away from it.

There is no believer, no matter how advanced in holiness, who cannot use the same language used by the Apostle. There is a bondage, a power of sin, within the believer's nature that he cannot totally resist. True, he may and does struggle against the power, and he desires to be free from it; but despite all his efforts, he still finds himself under its influence. This is precisely the bondage of sin, of coming short of the glory of God. Too often he finds himself distrusting God, being hard of heart, loving the world and self, being too prideful, too cold, too slothful—disapproving what he knows to be right and approving what he hates. He groans under the weight of sin, of being short of God's glory and of failing to be conformed to the image of Christ. He aches to walk in humility and meekness and to be filled with the fruit of love, joy, and peace. But day by day, he finds the force of sin reasserting its power over him. He struggles and struggles against it, but he finds that he cannot find the power to free himself. The believer senses an utter helplessness, longing and desiring for God to free him. He is a slave looking and longing for liberty. As has been said, this conflict between the flesh and spirit "continues in us so long as we live, in some more, and in others less, according as the one or the other principle is the stronger."[1]

It is this consciousness that drives the believer to the awareness that deliverance is found only through Jesus Christ our Lord.

> **"If they shall fall away, to renew them again unto repentance; seeing they crucify to themselves the Son of God afresh, and put him to an open shame" (Heb.6:6).**

<u>QUESTIONS:</u>

1. Note Paul's personal view of himself: "a desperate, wretched man who needs a Deliverer." This is the Apostle Paul, the man who wrote a large portion of the New Testament. What lessons can you draw from his gut-level honesty?
2. How serious is your need for Jesus Christ? Have you really acknowledged and confessed it? Why do some believers take Him for granted? How do you take Christ for granted?

---

[1] Martin Luther as quoted by Charles Hodge. *Commentary on the Epistle to the Romans*. (Grand Rapids, MI: Eerdmans Publishing Co., 1950), p.236.

6. CONFESSION 5: THE DELIVERER IS JESUS CHRIST (v.25).

This is an exclamation! Paul bursts forth with praise to God, for there is a glorious deliverance from sin! But note: the deliverance *does not come* through...
- some man-made law
- some man-possessed power
- some man-possessed ability
- some superior physical quality or faculty
- some great spiritual force

1. The deliverance comes through the great Deliverer Himself, Jesus Christ our Lord. He alone can deliver from sin. He is perfectly clear about this.

**"Jesus saith unto him, I am the way, the truth, and the life:
no man cometh unto the Father, but by me" (Jn.14:6).**

Jesus Christ delivers the believer from sin in two ways.
a. Jesus Christ justifies the believer.
b. Jesus Christ places the believer under God's grace.
2. Paul's conclusion is that he serves the law of God with his mind, that is, with his *renewed mind*. The believer who truly *knows* that his deliverance is through Jesus Christ our Lord learns something. He learns that his *mind* is *transformed* and *renewed* by Jesus Christ; he learns that his mind is born again and experiences a new birth just as his "old man" does. He learns that his *old mind* becomes the *new mind* and that his "old man" becomes the "new man."

**"And be not conformed to this world: but be ye transformed
by <u>the renewing of your mind</u>, that ye may prove what is that
good, and acceptable, and perfect, will of God" (Ro.12:2).**

Because of Jesus Christ, the believer takes his *new mind* and does all he can to serve the law of God. When he fails—when his flesh caves in to sin—he knows that it is the law or force of sin that has caused it, not the law of his *new mind*. He knows that he is still flesh as well as spirit, that he is still indwelt by two laws, two forces that struggle for allegiance; therefore, he does all he can to focus his mind upon the law of God. He simply serves God—His will and His nature (that is, His law)—trying to please God in all that he does. He dedicates himself not to come short of God's glory but to be conformed to the image of Christ. He knows that he is delivered from the law (force) of sin through Jesus Christ; therefore, the believer keeps justification and God's grace ever before his face. The believer knows that when his flesh serves the law of sin by failing, he has open access into God's presence to ask forgiveness. Therefore, he "girds up the loins of his mind" and comes before God for forgiveness. And after receiving a fresh surge of God's forgiveness and grace, he starts all over again. The believer begins to sense the law of God with renewed fervor, the fervor of his renewed mind.

ILLUSTRATION:

Every person who has ever lived has tried at some point to overcome some sin using his own strength. But every person has also failed. Success comes only when we see our mortal limits and call upon the One who can make a difference.

One day at a local restaurant, four friends met around a table in the corner. Over the years they had developed a good friendship and met to share what was going on in their lives. On this occasion, Jim confessed to his friends that he was having a struggle with his thought-life. "You guys need to pray for me. You would not believe some of the things that are going through my mind." Bill was the next one to confess a weakness. "I've put on 25 pounds in the last 3 months. I eat everything in sight. I just can't walk away from food. I need help." Fred was next. *"I've been tempted to go back to drinking. The pull to have a drink has at times been almost irresistible. I don't know how much longer I can go before I give in. You guys are going to have to watch out for me."*

At this point, every man had confessed a weakness and great need for help. Everyone, that is, except Andy. Jim, Bill, and Fred recognized their needs and their shortcomings and were asking God for help. They were at His mercy. Then all eyes fell upon Andy who was squirming in his seat. But Andy, although he had some problems, did not want to be freed from them. In fact, he took pleasure in his vices. Andy is typical of those who would rather surrender to sin than fight its power.

There are many who know right from wrong but do not accept the consequences of continuing to live in sin. Jim, Bill, and Fred are going to make it. They have gone to the only One who can set them free from sin's power, Jesus Christ. On the other hand, there will always be men like Andy who will search for their own way out of the maze of sin. They will look and fail, look and fail, finally surrendering and subjecting themselves to a life of sin.

QUESTIONS:

1. Have you confessed that Jesus Christ is the Deliverer, the only Deliverer, from your sin? Are you living like you believe it?
2. In what ways does a carnal man try to deliver himself from trouble? When are you most tempted to ignore God's help and go your own way?
3. What role does your mind play in being delivered from sin? What is the best way to keep your mind spiritually sharp?

SUMMARY:

The inward struggle you face between right and wrong and good and bad is not a problem unique to you. Everyone struggles with the problem. Will you always be trapped in a hopeless cycle of bondage and misery? No! Jesus Christ has come to set you free from the power of habitual sin. The challenge for you is to acknowledge your sinfulness and your need for deliverance, and then to set your mind on the resurrected Christ, the One who has the power to set you free. Remember:

1. The law is spiritual.
2. Confession 1: you are carnal, sold under sin.
3. Confession 2: you are void of any good thing.
4. Confession 3: you find two laws or forces within.
5. Confession 4: you are a desperate, wretched man who needs a Deliverer.
6. Confession 5: the Deliverer is Jesus Christ.

PERSONAL JOURNAL NOTES:
(Reflection & Response)

1. The most important thing that I learned from this lesson was:

2. The thing that I need to work on the most is:

3. I can apply this lesson to my life by:

4. Closing Prayer of Commitment: (put your commitment down on paper).

CHAPTER 8

VI. DELIVERANCE & REDEMPTION: THE BELIEVER SHALL BE FREED FROM STRUGGLING & SUFFERING BY THE SPIRIT, 8:1-39

A. The Man in Christ Jesus Is Freed from Condemnation: The Power of the Spirit, 8:1-17

1. **Now, since Christ has come** (3:21-22)
   a. The believer is not condemned
   b. Why: He is "in" Christ

2. **The Spirit gives life**
   a. By freeing the believer from sin & death

   b. By doing what the law could not do

   c. By Christ's condemning sin in the flesh
   d. By Christ's providing righteousness: For those who do not walk after the flesh, but after the Spirit

3. **The Spirit pulls the mind to spiritual things**
   a. The carnal mind vs. the spiritual mind

   b. The fate of both minds: Death vs. life & peace

   c. The reason the carnal mind dwells in death
   1) It is bitterly set

There is therefore now no condemnation to them which are in Christ Jesus, who walk not after the flesh, but after the Spirit. 2 For the law of the Spirit of life in Christ Jesus hath made me free from the law of sin and death. 3 For what the law could not do, in that it was weak through the flesh, God sending his own Son in the likeness of sinful flesh, and for sin, condemned sin in the flesh: 4 That the righteousness of the law might be fulfilled in us, who walk not after the flesh, but after the Spirit. 5 For they that are after the flesh do mind the things of the flesh; but they that are after the Spirit the things of the Spirit. 6 For to be carnally minded is death; but to be spiritually minded is life and peace. 7 Because the carnal mind is enmity against God: for it is not subject to the law of God, neither indeed can be. 8 So then they that are in the flesh cannot please God. 9 But ye are not in the flesh, but in the Spirit, if so be that the Spirit of God dwell in you. Now if any man have not the Spirit of Christ, he is none of his. 10 And if Christ be in you, the body is dead because of sin; but the Spirit is life because of righteousness. 11 But if the Spirit of him that raised up Jesus from the dead dwell in you, he that raised up Christ from the dead shall also quicken your mortal bodies by his Spirit that dwelleth in you. 12 Therefore, brethren, we are debtors, not to the flesh, to live after the flesh. 13 For if ye live after the flesh, ye shall die: but if ye through the Spirit do mortify the deeds of the body, ye shall live. 14 For as many as are led by the Spirit of God, they are the sons of God. 15 For ye have not received the spirit of bondage again to fear; but ye have received the Spirit of adoption, whereby we cry, Abba, Father. 16 The Spirit itself beareth witness with our spirit, that we are the children of God: 17 And if children, then heirs; heirs of God, and joint-heirs with Christ; if so be that we suffer with him, that we may be also glorified together.

against God

   2) It cannot please God

4. **The Spirit dwells within the believer**
   a. He removes him from being "in" the flesh
   b. He identifies him as being "in" Christ

5. **The Spirit gives life to the spirit of the believer**
   a. He gives life <u>now</u>

   b. He gives life, quickens the mortal body <u>later</u>

6. **The Spirit gives the power to mortify— to put to death— evil deeds**
   a. Believers are debtors to the Spirit
   b. Believers determine their own fate: Death or life

7. **The Spirit leads the believer, identifying him as a son of God**

8. **The Spirit adopts**
   a. He delivers from the bondage of fear
   b. He gives access to God

9. **The Spirit bears witness with our spirit**
   a. We are God's children
   b. We are heirs of God
   c. We are equal heirs with Christ
   d. We are conquerors over suffering

ROMANS 8:1-17

(Note: Because of the length of this outline and commentary, you may wish to split this passage into two or more studies.)

Section VI
DELIVERANCE AND REDEMPTION: THE
BELIEVER SHALL BE FREED FROM STRUGGLING
AND SUFFERING BY THE SPIRIT
Romans 8:1-39

Study 1: The Man in Christ Jesus Is Freed from Condemnation: The Power of the Spirit

Text: **Romans 8:1-17**

Aim: To learn the function of the Holy Spirit and to experience His power: to become forever free from guilt and condemnation.

Memory Verse:
> "There is therefore now no condemnation to them which are in Christ Jesus, who walk not after the flesh, but after the Spirit" (Romans 8:1).

INTRODUCTION:
What has been the greatest display of power on earth? You might remember when:
⇒ atomic bombs were used and how they annihilated both life and property
⇒ killer earthquakes, hurricanes, typhoons, floods, blizzards, or fires hit various continents, leveling buildings and bridges, burying people under deadly debris, destroying the land and devastating hundreds of thousands of people
⇒ giant rockets lifted men into space, projecting them to land on the moon and walk in space
⇒ bombs made out of crude or sophisticated materials were used to blow up buildings, subways, and buses, killing thousands of innocent victims

It seems that every generation exposes man to more and more technological power. As weighty as these examples are, their power combined is no match for what occurred on earth over 2,000 years ago. In a far-a-way land, the greatest display of power on earth occurred in a time when it seemed that such power was non-existent. Jesus Christ was born, and He lived and died in a land called Palestine. His death came at the hands of a government whose power was the greatest on earth. But as history records, Jesus Christ became the first man to defy death and win over its power. The power of death and sin was defeated when the Holy Spirit raised the Son of God from the tomb. Now, note this very important fact: the same Holy Spirit who raised Christ from the grave lives in you—if you are a believer. Just imagine: the same power that resurrected Jesus Christ is at your disposal—if you just believe.

This is one of the most important passages in all of Scripture. Its subject cannot be overemphasized: the power of God's Spirit in the life of the believer. If the believer needs anything, he needs the power of God's Spirit. Forcefully, Scripture spells out point by point what the power of the Holy Spirit is.

OUTLINE:
1. Now, since Christ has come (v.1).
2. The Spirit gives life (v.2-4).
3. The Spirit pulls the mind to spiritual things (v.5-8).
4. The Spirit dwells within the believer (v.9).
5. The Spirit gives life to the spirit of the believer (v.10-11).

6. The Spirit gives the power to mortify—to put to death—evil deeds (v.12-13).
7. The Spirit leads the believer, identifying him as a son of God (v.14).
8. The Spirit adopts (v.15).
9. The Spirit bears witness with our spirit (v.16-17).

1. NOW, SINCE CHRIST HAS COME (v.1).

Since Christ has come, a most wonderful thing has happened. The people who believe *in* Christ are not condemned.

1. "No condemnation" means that the believer is not doomed and damned, but is freed from the penalty and condemnation of sin; he is not judged as a sinner, but is delivered from the condemnation of death and hell; he is not judged to be unrighteous, but is counted to be righteous.

Very simply stated, the person who is *in* Christ is safe and secure from condemnation now and forever. He will not be judged as a sinner; he shall never be separated from the love of God which is *in* Christ Jesus our Lord (cp. Jn.3:16; Ro.8:33-39). (But remember: the believer is to be judged for his faithfulness to Christ. He will be judged for how responsible he is—for how well he uses his spiritual gifts for Christ—for how diligently he serves Christ in the work of God. The judgment of the believer will take place at the great *judgment seat of Christ*.)

2. Now note the most crucial point: only the believer who is *in* Christ Jesus will not be condemned. All non-believers will face condemnation for sin. A genuine believer is a person who does not "walk after the flesh, but after the Spirit." Note what it means to be *in* Christ Jesus (see A Closer Look # 1, Believer—Ro.8:1 for discussion).

QUESTIONS:
1. Christ has freed us from condemnation. As a believer, how secure do you feel? When are you most likely to feel condemned? Why?
2. What is the only way to avoid condemnation? Have you ever done this? If not, what are you waiting for?

A CLOSER LOOK # 1
(8:1) **Believer, Position In Christ**: What does it mean for a person to be *in* Christ?

1. In the simplest terms, being *in Christ* means placing your faith in Christ, in all that Christ is. Christ lived and died and arose; so being *in* Christ means living, dying, and arising *in* Christ. Christ is the person's Representative, his Agent, his Substitute, his Mediator in life, death, and resurrection. The person who believes *in* Jesus Christ is *identified* with Christ: counted and considered to be "in" Christ.

The believer's faith actually causes God to identify the believer *with Christ*, to count the believer...

- as having lived *in* Christ when Christ lived upon earth; therefore, the believer is counted sinless and righteous because Christ was sinless and righteous
- as having died *in* Christ; therefore, the believer never has to die (Jn.3:16). The penalty and condemnation of his sins are already paid for in the death of Christ
- as having been raised in Christ; therefore, the believer has received the "new life" of Christ. Just as Christ had a new life after His resurrection, even so the believer receives the "new life" of Christ when he believes in Christ.

2. To be *in* Christ means that a believer walks and lives *in* Christ day by day. He is in union with Christ. To truly believe is to walk, and to truly walk is to believe. A true believer...

- lays his life—his past sins, his present behavior, all that he is—upon Christ
- entrusts his present welfare and destiny—all that he is or ever will be—into the hands of Christ

To live and walk *in* Christ means that we do not "walk after the flesh, but after the Spirit" (Ro.8:1, 4). It means that "denying ungodliness and worldly lusts, we should live soberly, righteously, and godly, in this present world" (Tit.2:12). It means that we bear the fruit of the Spirit (Gal.5:22-23). It means that we abide *in* Christ, that we become as connected and attached to Christ...

- as the members of the body are connected and attached to each other (1 Cor.12:12-27)
- as the branch is connected and attached to the vine (Jn.15:4-7)

This is what it means for a person to be "in" Christ. A person simply *believes* in Christ, putting all he is and has into the hands and keeping of Christ. The person honestly believes that Christ will take care of his past sins, present welfare, and future destiny. Therefore, the believer simply places and positions himself—his faith and welfare—*in* Christ; and God in turn identifies the person with Christ, with all that Christ is. God counts and considers the person to be *in* Christ.

QUESTIONS:
1. Using your own words, what does it mean to be *in Christ?*
2. Can a person be a true believer and not live *in Christ?* Why or why not?
3. In what ways does being *in Christ* make a difference in your life...
   - as a friend?
   - as an employee?
   - as a witness to the lost?
   - as a member of your church?

2. THE SPIRIT GIVES LIFE (v.2-4).

The term "the law of the *Spirit* of life" means two things. It means...
- the *law* of the Holy Spirit
- the *Spirit of life* which is in Christ Jesus

Within the universe there is a law so important that it has become the law of the Holy Spirit. It is called *"the law of the Spirit of life."* What is meant by this law? Very simply, life is in Jesus Christ and in Him alone. Whatever life is—energy, being, spirit, love, joy, peace—it is all in Jesus Christ and nowhere else. Within Christ, within His very being, is the *Spirit of life*, the very energy and being of life. This fact is important, so important that God has written it into the laws of the universe. The Spirit of life for which we long and ache is available *in* Christ Jesus.

"In him was <u>life</u>; and the <u>life</u> was the light of men" (Jn.1:4).
"I am come that they might have <u>life</u>, and that they might have it more abundantly" (Jn.10:10).

Now for the critical question. How does the Spirit give life? How does a person go about securing "the Spirit of life" so that he may not die but live forever?

1. The Spirit gives life by freeing the believer from sin and death, that is, from the "law of sin and death." This simply means that the believer lives in a consciousness of being free. He breathes and senses a depth of life, a richness, a fulness of life that is indescribable. He lives with power—power over the pressure and strain, impediments and bondages of life—even the bondages of sin and death. He lives now and shall live forever. He senses this and knows this. Life to him is a *spirit, a breath, a consciousness* of being set free through Christ. Even when he sins and guilt sets in, there is a tug, a power (the Holy Spirit) that draws him back to God. He asks for forgiveness and removal of the guilt (1 Jn.1:9), and immediately upon asking, the same power (the Holy Spirit) instills an instantaneous assurance of cleansing. The spirit of life instantaneously takes up its abode within him again. He feels free again.

"Now the Lord is that Spirit: and where the Spirit of the Lord is, there is liberty" (2 Cor.3:17).

2. The Spirit gives life by doing what the law could not do. The law could not make man righteous because man's flesh is too weak to keep the law. No man has ever been able to keep the law of God, not to perfection or even close to perfection. All flesh has miserably failed—come far short of God's glory and law. Consequently, all flesh dies physically and spiritually. Therefore, righteousness and life just cannot come by the law. *But,* what the law could not do, the Spirit is able to do. He can provide righteousness and life.

3. The Spirit gives life by Christ's condemning sin in the flesh (see <u>A Closer Look # 2</u>, <u>Christ, Fulfills Law</u>—Ro.8:3 for discussion).

4. The Spirit gives life by Christ's providing righteousness for us. He provides righteousness for those who do not walk after the flesh but after the Spirit. This is a most marvelous statement, a glorious truth.

    a. The Spirit "fulfills righteousness <u>in</u> us." He credits righteousness as being *in* us. When?

        ⇒ When we believe that Jesus Christ is our righteousness, the sinless and perfect Son of God.

        ⇒ When we believe that Jesus Christ is our Savior, the One who died *for* us.

When we believe in Jesus Christ, the Spirit of God takes the righteousness of Jesus Christ (which is the righteousness of the law) and credits it to us. He actually places within us the perfect righteousness of Jesus Christ. He places the Divine nature (righteousness) of God *in* us (2 Pt.1:4).

It is critical to see this fact, for the Spirit fulfills righteousness *in us, not by us.* We do not and cannot even come close to keeping the law perfectly, but Christ did. If His righteousness cannot be credited and fulfilled *in* us, then we are hopeless and doomed.

"For he hath made him to be sin for us, who knew no sin; that we might be made the righteousness of God in him" (2 Cor.5:21).

    b. Now note: righteousness is not fulfilled or credited *in* everyone. It is only fulfilled in those...

    • who <u>do not</u> walk after the flesh
    • who <u>do</u> walk after the Spirit

The point is this: the Spirit gives life to men, but He gives life only to those who forsake the flesh and walk after the Spirit. The spiritual man, the man who walks after the Spirit, loves Christ and wants to honor Christ *in all that he does.* Therefore, he strives to follow Christ and His example. Such love and honor of Christ pleases God to no end, for God loves His Son with a perfect love. He loves His Son so much that He will take whatever honor a man gives His Son and match it for the man. Whatever recognition and honor a man heaps upon Christ, God matches it for the man.

    ⇒ If a man trusts Christ for righteousness, then God gives that man righteousness.

    ⇒ If a man trusts Christ for meaning, purpose, and significance, then God gives the man meaning, purpose, and significance.

    ⇒ If a man trusts Christ to lead him through some trial or need, then God leads him through the trial or need.

Whatever the man sows in Christ, he reaps: God matches it. Whatever a man measures out to Christ, the same is measured back to the man: God matches it. In fact,

Scripture says that God will even go beyond and do much more than we ask or think (cp. Eph.3:20).

Therefore, the man who *walks after* the "Spirit of life" which is in Christ Jesus is given the Spirit of life. The Holy Spirit fulfills and credits him with the righteousness of the law, with the right to live eternally.

> **"Therefore we are buried with him by baptism into death: that like as Christ was raised up from the dead by the glory of the Father, even so we also should <u>walk in newness of life</u>" (Ro.6:4).**

<u>QUESTIONS:</u>
1. Do you really believe it is possible for the Spirit of God to give life to a physical being? How?
2. In what ways have you experienced the life given by the Spirit? Are you conscious of the freedom you have been given by the Spirit of life? Do you thank God for that freedom?
3. How is the law of the Spirit different from the letter of the law? Which law is more likely to control you?
4. What would keep a person from walking after the Spirit of life?

A CLOSER LOOK # 2

(8:3) <u>Christ, Fulfills Law—Sin</u>: Christ condemned sin in the flesh by three acts.

1. Christ pointed to sin and condemned it as being evil. The very fact that He never sinned points out that sin is contrary to God and to God's nature. Christ rejected sin, and by rejecting it He showed that it was evil, that it was not to be touched. He condemned it as evil and unworthy of God and man.

2. Christ secured righteousness for all men. When He came into the world, He came with the same flesh that all men are born with—the same flesh with all its desires, passions, and potential for evil. However He never sinned, not once. Therefore, He secured a perfect righteousness, and because His righteousness is perfect and ideal, it becomes the model and pattern for all men. It stands for and covers the unrighteousness of all men; it overcomes sin and its penalty. It is to be noted that He condemned sin "through the flesh"; therefore, all flesh finds its power to condemn sin "in Christ," in His ideal righteousness.

> **"Which of you convinceth me of sin? And if I say the truth, why do ye not believe me?" (Jn.8:46).**
> **"For we have not a high priest which cannot be touched with the feeling of our infirmities; but was in all points tempted like as we are, yet without sin" (Heb.4:15).**

3. Christ allowed the law of sin and death to be enacted upon Him instead of upon the sinner. Man has sinned, so the natural consequence is corruption and death. However, Christ allowed God to accept His *Ideal righteousness* for the unrighteousness of man. He allowed God to lay man's sin and death upon Himself. He allowed God to let Him bear the law of sin and death for man and to experience hell for man. He allowed God to let Him condemn sin and death "in His own body upon the tree" (1 Pt.2:24). He was the perfect, ideal Man. Therefore, He could bear all the violations of the law and all the experiences of death for *all* men. This was God's design and purpose, and God bore the awful price of having to condemn sin and death in His very own Son. Sin and its power have been made powerless—to those who will turn to Christ and believe in Him. Death has been conquered (1 Cor.15:1-58, esp. v.54-57), and he who had the power of death has been destroyed, that is, Satan.

> **"For when we were yet without strength, in due time Christ died for the ungodly" (Ro.5:6).**
> **"But God commendeth his love toward us, in that, while we were yet sinners, Christ died for us" (Ro.5:8).**

3. THE SPIRIT PULLS THE MIND TO SPIRITUAL THINGS (v.5-8).

This is one of the most important passages in all of Scripture, for it discusses the human mind: **"As [a man] <u>thinketh</u> in his heart, so is he" (Pr.23:7).** Where a man keeps his mind and what he thinks about determine who he is and what he does. If a man keeps his mind and thoughts in the gutter, he becomes part of the filth in the gutter. If he keeps his mind upon the *good*, he becomes good. If he focuses upon achievement and success, he achieves and succeeds. If his mind is filled with religious thoughts, he becomes religious. If his thoughts are focused upon God and righteousness, he becomes godly and righteous. A man becomes and does what he thinks. It is the law of the mind. Scripture says three things about the power of the Spirit and of the human mind.

1. There is the carnal mind vs. the spiritual mind. The carnal mind is the mind of man's flesh or body. The phrase "to be carnally minded" means the *mind of the flesh*. It is the mind with which man is born, the fleshly mind which he inherits from his parents.

The carnal mind also means something else, something that must be heeded. It means the mind that is *given over to the flesh*; that focuses upon the flesh and its worldly urges and desires; that gives its attention and pursuits over to the flesh; that savors tasting and partaking of the flesh; that is controlled by one's sinful nature.

There are three directions of thought the carnal mind may take:

    a. The carnal mind may focus upon the base, the immoral, the violent, the material, or the physical. This is usually the life style most people think about when a carnal or fleshly person is mentioned. The minds of some are consumed with the lust for sex, power, money, houses, lands, furnishings, recognition, position—concerned and filled with the earthly and the worldly.

    b. The carnal mind may focus upon the moral, upright, and cultured life. Some minds are centered upon the welfare and comfort of themselves and of their society. They want themselves and their society to be as refined and educated, as moral and upright, as possible, so they focus their minds upon such *commendable* ends. And they are commendable purposes, but a person can be refined and well educated and live as independently and as separate from God as the base and immoral person. Most cultured people depend upon their *good works* and service to make them acceptable to God. Most just think that God will accept them because their lives and efforts have been focused upon building a good life and better society for all. What they fail to see is that God is interested in building a God-centered society and not a world-centered society. God wants the needs of every man to be met, but He wants it to be done from a spiritual basis, not from a human basis. He wants men led to Christ—their minds and lives focused upon God—so that they may have life, life that is both *abundant* and *eternal*. Just taking care of the physical needs of man does not meet the spiritual needs of man. It leaves a gaping hole in man's life; for the *spirit* of man determines how a man lives, either defeated or victorious, either with or apart from God.

    c. The carnal mind may also focus upon religion: upon living a religious life of benevolence and good works, of ceremony and ritual. However, note again: a person can be a strict religionist and still live separate from God. He can have his mind *set on religion* and its welfare instead of God. He can be living for religion instead of for God, carrying out the function of *institutional religion* instead of the mission of God. He can be depending upon his commitment to religion to make him acceptable to God instead of believing and trusting God's Son, Jesus Christ our Lord. In all of this, note where the religionist's mind is—note where his thoughts are. There is little if any stress upon a *personal relationship* with God; little stress upon knowing God—really knowing, believing, and understanding Him—little stress upon walking and living in Him. The stress of the carnal religionist is his religion and its rituals and ceremonies, its welfare and projects. Such a focus is fleshly and carnal. It is of the earth, attached to the physical and material *institution* which passes away and dies.

The point is this: a carnal mind does not necessarily mean that a man's thoughts are upon the base, immoral, and vicious. A carnal mind means any mind that does not find its basis in God, any mind that is not focused upon God first. A carnal mind may focus upon a moral, upright, and cultured life but still ignore, neglect, and exempt God. A carnal mind may also focus upon religion and still exempt God. A carnal mind is a mind that finds its basis in this world, that focuses its thoughts upon the physical and material instead of upon God.

> **"And even as they did not like to retain God in their knowledge, God gave them over to a reprobate mind, to do those things which are not convenient" (Ro.1:28).**

2. There is the spiritual mind. It is the natural mind of man that has been *renewed by the Spirit of God*.

> **"And be not conformed to this world: but be ye transformed by the renewing of your mind, that ye may prove what is that good, and acceptable, and perfect, will of God" (Ro.12:2).**

The words "spiritually minded" mean to be possessed by the Spirit or to be controlled and dominated by the Spirit. It means that the man who walks after the Spirit *minds* "the things of the Spirit" day by day. And note: it is the Spirit of God who draws the believer's mind to focus upon spiritual things. The Spirit of God lives within the believer. He is there to work within the believer, both to will and to do God's pleasure; He is there to keep the mind and thoughts of the believer focused upon spiritual things.

   a. The believer *keeps* his mind upon developing spiritual character and fruit.

> **"But the fruit of the Spirit is love, joy, peace, longsuffering, gentleness, goodness, faith, meekness and temperance" (Gal.5:22-23).**

   b. The believer *keeps* his mind upon carrying out the ministry and mission of Christ.

> **"Even as the Son of man came not to be ministered unto, but to minister, and to give his life a ransom for many" (Mt.20:28).**
> **"For the Son of man is come to seek and to save that which was lost" (Lk.19:10).**

c. The believer *keeps* his mind upon knowing, believing, and understanding God.

> **"Ye are my witnesses, saith the LORD, and my servant whom I have chosen: that ye may know and believe me, and understand that I am he: before me there was no God formed, neither shall there be after me" (Is.43:10).**

d. The believer *keeps* his mind upon being conformed more and more to the image of Christ.

> **"For whom he did foreknow, he also did predestinate to be conformed to the <u>image</u> of his Son, that he might be the firstborn among many brethren" (Ro.8:29).**

e. The believer *keeps* his mind upon casting down imaginations and making *every thought* obedient to Christ.

> **"Casting down imaginations, and every high thing that exalteth itself against the knowledge of God, and bringing into captivity every thought to the obedience of Christ" (2 Cor.10:5.)**

ILLUSTRATION:

Do you ever feel that you just cannot conquer the flesh, that you just cannot keep from being carnal? You know the feeling: you want to think pure thoughts, but the more you try, the more tempting things are sent your way. Here is an example of one man's struggle.

> *James was an avid reader, consuming every book that made the best sellers' list—regardless what kind of material it was. On the rare occasion when he tried to read the Bible, his mind would immediately wander to his most recent thriller.*
>
> *One day he prayed, asking God how he could discipline his mind. As he prayed and thought, this impression came to his mind, an impression that he knew was the tug of the Holy Spirit. "The reason you have such a hard time concentrating on Me is because you are not concentrating on Me." How simple, and yet so profound! What you fill your mind with is what you will think about. Right then and there, James made a new commitment. He would spend more time thinking about the Lord and His Word, whom he would spend eternity with, and less time consuming books that had no eternal value, that drew him further and further into the world.*

God has given you a choice: fill your mind with the world or fill your mind with Him. What are you thinking about the most?

QUESTIONS:

1. What kinds of things does the carnal mind focus upon? Are these things always immoral? If not, does it matter whether you think about them? Are there dangers involved?
2. Think about your average day. If you had to give an account of what your mind stayed on the most, would it be the 'things of the flesh' or the 'things of the Spirit'? Are you satisfied with your answer? What can you do about it?

3. There is the fate of both minds. The carnal mind is strongly warned, whereas the spiritual mind is assured and comforted.
   a. The fate of the carnal mind is death. By death is meant spiritual death, being separated and cut off from God eternally. It means the soul is dead *now*, while the man lives on this earth, and it means that the soul remains dead (separated

and cut off from God) even when the man enters the next world. The carnal mind...

- cannot ignore God now and expect to have thoughts of God in the next world.
- cannot focus upon the flesh now and expect to focus upon God in the next world.
- cannot think as it wills now and expect to think as God wills in the next world.
- cannot have a worldly mind now and expect to have a spiritual mind in the next world.
- cannot choose the flesh now and expect to be saved from the flesh in the next world.
- cannot reject God now and expect to be accepted by God in the next world.

Very simply stated, whatever the mind chooses will continue on and on. If the mind chooses the flesh instead of God, then the choice is made. The mind will continue on without God from now on, forever and ever. The mind is allowed to do as it chooses. If it chooses to be separated and cut off from God so that it can dwell upon the flesh, then the soul *shall* have the flesh; it shall be separated and cut off from God. God loves man; God will not violate man's mind to force man to choose Him. The choice is man's: he may choose God, or he may choose flesh and death (to be separated and cut off from God).

"The man that wandereth out of the way of understanding shall remain in the congregation of the dead [spiritually dead]" (Pr.21:16).
"Then Jesus said unto them, Verily, verily, I say unto you, Except ye eat the flesh of the Son of man, and drink his blood, ye have no life in you" (Jn.6:53).

b. The fate of the spiritual mind is life and peace. It is the very opposite of death. The spiritual mind lives all that life was intended to be and lives it eternally. The spiritual mind is full of...
- meaning, purpose, and significance
- assurance and confidence
- joy and rejoicing
- knowing, believing, and understanding God
- spiritual fruit, the fruit of love, joy, and peace (Gal.5:22-23)

The spiritual mind is also full of peace. The man who is spiritually minded is at *peace with God*: he has peace with God because he knows beyond question that his sins are forgiven, that he is now acceptable to God. He also dwells in the *peace of God*: he has the *peace of God* because he experiences the day-by-day care and guidance of God in his life. He actually walks through life in the peace of God, knowing that God is looking after him and working all things out for his good. He knows his eternity is taken care of, that he shall be given the glorious privilege of living eternally and serving God in some glorious responsibility. Note something else as well: the man who is spiritually minded is at peace with all other men. He loves and cares for all men, no matter who they are, just as Jesus loves and cares for them.

The spiritual mind, the mind that focuses upon the things of the spirit, knows and experiences life and peace. Life and peace are its destiny forever and ever. Such is the promise of God and the testimony of His saints who have gone on before.

"Verily, verily, I say unto you, He that heareth my word, and believeth on him that sent me, hath everlasting life, and

shall not come into condemnation; but is passed from death unto life" (Jn.5:24).

4. There is the reason the carnal mind dwells in death. The carnal mind dwells in death because it is at enmity with God. This is simply seen.

⇒ God is holy, righteous, and pure; whereas the carnal mind is impure, immoral, polluted, or self-righteous. The carnal or fleshly mind is opposed to God by its very nature.
⇒ God acts only in morality and justice and goodness; whereas the carnal mind behaves immorally, unjustly, and selfishly. The carnal or fleshly mind is opposed to God by its very behavior.
⇒ God is eternal, from everlasting to everlasting; whereas the carnal mind ages, deteriorates, dies, and decays. The carnal or fleshly mind is opposed to God by its very destiny—death.

Now note: all this is saying one simple thing: the carnal mind "is not subject to the law of God, nor indeed can be." The carnal mind cannot be subject to God's law because it is not "like" God: not by nature, not by behavior, not by destiny. A carnal mind has no interest in the law of God nor in trying to live as God wishes. The carnal mind wants to live as it wishes and do its own thing. The carnal man wants to indulge his flesh, whether by food, sex, pride, power, position, money, recognition, fame, or self-righteousness.

The fate of the carnal mind is clearly stated, a fate that must be strongly heeded.

> "So then they that are in the flesh cannot please God" (Ro.8:8).
> "She that liveth in pleasure is dead while she liveth" (1 Tim.5:6).

However, the glorious truth is this. The Spirit of God can transform the mind of man. The Spirit of God can pull the mind to spiritual things. (Cp. Ro.12:2; Eph. 4:22-24.)

APPLICATION:

Most carnal minds are influenced heavily by their environment—people, places, and things. If their friends are materialistic or immoral, they focus upon the same. If their environment offers films and literature, they fill their minds with such, whether X-rated or educational or philosophic. Few carnal minds ever break away from their environment and friends. Only the Spirit of God can penetrate the human mind to set it free from the flesh and its carnal passions.

QUESTIONS:

1. What is the certain fate of the carnal mind? How do people become trapped on this path? Can they be freed from this fate?
2. How much choice has God given you between having a carnal mind and a spiritual mind?
3. What are some of the promised consequences for those who have a spiritual mind?
4. What counsel would you give a person who needs to be freed from a carnal mind?

4. THE SPIRIT DWELLS WITHIN THE BELIEVER (v.9).

There is so much meat in verses 9 and 10 that it cannot all be outlined beside the verses due to lack of space.

1. The power of the Spirit is seen in the word "dwell." The Holy Spirit dwells within the believer: He makes His home, takes up residence, and lives within the believer just as we live in our homes.

2. The power of the Spirit creates the glorious truth of the *indwelling presence* of God within the believer and of the believer within God.
⇒ The believer is said to be "in the [Holy] Spirit" (v.9).
⇒ The Spirit of <u>God</u> is said to "dwell" in the believer (v.9).
⇒ The believer is said to have "the Spirit of Christ" (v.9).
⇒ Christ is said to be in the believer (v.10).

> **"And I will pray the Father, and he shall give you another Comforter, that he may abide with you for ever; even the Spirit of truth; whom the world cannot receive, because it seeth him not, neither knoweth him: but ye know him; for he dwelleth with you, and shall be in you" (Jn.14:16-17).**

Note how the deity of Christ is being proclaimed. The "Spirit of Christ" is said to indwell the believer the same as the "Spirit of God." Both are said to be equally within the believer. (Cp. Gal.4:6; Ph.1:10; 2 Cor.3:18; 1 Pt.1:11.)

3. The power of the Spirit removes the believer from being "in" the flesh and places him within <u>Himself</u>, within the Spirit of God. Very simply...
- the believer is no longer *positioned* in the flesh: not in God's eyes and not in God's accounting. The believer no longer dwells in the flesh: he is no longer at home, that is, no longer comfortable, with the things of the flesh.
- the believer is *positioned* in the Spirit of God. God sees and counts the believer as being placed and positioned in His Spirit; therefore, the believer dwells in the Holy Spirit, makes his home in the Spirit, takes up his residence in the Spirit. He is at home and comfortable only with the things of the Spirit.

4. The power of the Spirit identifies the believer as being "in" Christ. This is easily seen. Whatever spirit dwells within a man, it is *that spirit* to whom man belongs. If he has the spirit of selfishness within, he belongs to the spirit of selfishness and is known as being selfish. If he has the spirit of complaining, he belongs to the spirit of complaining and is known as being a complainer. If he has the spirit of evil, he belongs to evil and is known as an evil person. If he has the spirit of caring, he belongs to the spirit of caring, and he is known as a caring person. If he has the Spirit of Christ, he belongs to Christ and is known as a follower of Christ.

> **"I am crucified with Christ: nevertheless I live; yet not I, but Christ liveth in me: and the life which I now live in the flesh I live by the faith of the Son of God, who loved me, and gave himself for me" (Gal.2:20).**

A person is driven to live according to the spirit that is within him. The Holy Spirit has the power to drive the believer to live as Christ lived. We can look at the spirit of a person and tell if he has the Spirit of Christ. If he does, then he bears the fruit of Christ's Spirit. The true believer *proves* that he is in Christ by the life which he lives.

<u>**ILLUSTRATION:**</u>
For anyone who is not handy around the house, or "mechanically challenged," it is a blessing to have a friend who will help when things break down, things like...
- the car that quits running
- the washer that will not wash
- the lawnmower that runs over, but does not cut, the grass
- the leaky pipe that will not stop dripping

Some of us will jump in there, trying our best to fix it. Others go into denial, hoping the problem will fix itself. The smart ones have learned to call professional help.

The leak behind the refrigerator started out to be small. Dan saw the problem and, not wanting to pay for a service call, took immediate action himself. He turned off the water supply to the ice maker, replaced a bad washer, and turned the water back on. But the leak was worse than before. He tried a variety of washers and plumber's tapes, but to no avail. After every attempt to fix the problem, his frustration grew worse and the leak did too!

"Honey, why don't you just make things easy on yourself and call someone to help you?" his wife asked. Finally, Dan listened to her pleas and called a plumber. But not until they were both fed up and a steady trickle of water ran across the kitchen floor!

Believers are much the same: we try to do things on our own until we realize that only God's presence, the Holy Spirit, can get us through the trial. The ministry of the Holy Spirit is available to believers—if we can get beyond our pride and the desire to do things without His help.

QUESTIONS:
1. The Holy Spirit has promised to dwell or to *be at home* in every believer. Have you done everything in your power to make Him feel at home? Or is He often an unwelcome guest?
2. If your heart could be described as a house, what rooms would be off-limits to the Holy Spirit? Would He be allowed...
   - in the cluttered closet that holds your dirty laundry?
   - in the attic where you store a lot of old memories of your past life?
   - in the tool shed where your spiritual gifts are stowed away and rarely used?
   - in the family room where the television screen pours in a message of filth and ungodliness?
   - in the kitchen where your food and drink are stored? Do you have an abundance of the Bread of Life? The Fruit of the Spirit?

5. THE SPIRIT GIVES LIFE TO THE SPIRIT OF THE BELIEVER (v.10-11).

The idea of the Greek makes this verse clear: "If Christ be in you, *although* the body is to die because of sin, the spirit shall live because of righteousness." Very simply stated, the body of man does die, but his spirit can live forever if Christ is "in" him. Note two points.

1. The Spirit of Christ gives life to the *spirit of man* now, the very moment a person believes. Man's body is to die because of sin: the body is corruptible, aging, deteriorating, decaying, and dying. It is in a process of dying—in such a rapid movement toward death—that it can actually be said to be *dead*. The body is dying; therefore, its death is inevitable. However, it is in the midst of death that the Spirit of Christ enters. He enters and converts the spirit of man from death to life. How?

   a. The spirit of man lives because of the righteousness and death of Jesus Christ.

   "That if thou shalt confess with thy mouth the Lord Jesus, and shalt believe in thine heart that God hath raised him from the dead, thou shalt be saved. For with the heart man believeth unto righteousness; and with the mouth confession is made unto salvation" (Ro.10:9-10).

   b. The spirit of man lives by living a righteous and godly life.

   "Not every one that saith unto me, Lord, Lord, shall enter into the kingdom of heaven; but he that doeth the will of my Father which is in heaven" (Mt.7:21).

2. The Spirit of Christ quickens the mortal body *in the future*, in the great day of redemption. Note two things.
   a. The word "quicken" means to make alive, to give life, to cause to live, to renew and remake life.
   b. The "mortal body" shall be quickened and made alive.
      ⇒ The mortal body is the same body that died. The person is the very same person.
      ⇒ The mortal body is given a totally new life; its elements are recreated and remade into a perfect and eternal body. The new body is to be given the power and energy of eternal elements. All will be arranged so that the mortal body becomes an immortal body.

> **"And this is the will of him that sent me, that every one which seeth the Son, and believeth on him, may have everlasting life: and I will raise him up at the last day" (Jn.6:40).**
>
> **"Blessed be the God and Father of our Lord Jesus Christ, which according to his abundant mercy hath begotten us again unto a lively hope by the resurrection of Jesus Christ from the dead" (1 Pt.1:3-4).**

   c. There are two great assurances of the believer's resurrection.
      ⇒ The assurance of Jesus' resurrection.
      ⇒ The assurance of the Holy Spirit who dwells in the believer. The very same Spirit who raised up Christ, who is the power and energy of life, shall raise up the believer (2 Cor.4:14).

> **"[Jesus Christ] declared to be the Son of God with power, according to the spirit of holiness, by the resurrection from the dead" (Ro.1:4).**

QUESTIONS:

1. Most people think of eternity as being only in the future. How does the Holy Spirit give eternal life to the believer now? When does the Spirit of life become real to the believer?
2. What will happen to the believer's mortal body in the future? How can you use verses 10 and 11 to witness to a lost soul?

A CLOSER LOOK # 3

(8:11) **Resurrection, of Believers—Jesus Christ, Resurrection of**: the resurrection of Jesus Christ assures the believer that he too shall be raised from the dead.

1. The resurrection of Christ proves that *God is*: that He does exist and care for the earth. There is no power on earth that can raise a man from the dead. Only a Supreme, Eternal Power and Person can do that. Only God can give life to dead matter and to the dust of the earth. The very fact that Jesus Christ was raised from the dead proves that God exists and cares for this earth.

2. The resurrection of Christ proves that Jesus Christ is who He claimed to be, the Son of God Himself. It proves that Jesus Christ was sent to earth to secure the ideal righteousness for man, to die and arise from the dead for man.

> **"And declared to be the Son of God with power, according to the spirit of holiness, by the resurrection from the dead" (Ro.1:4).**

3. The resurrection of Christ proves that Jesus Christ is the Savior of the world. It proves that Christ is the very One whom God sent to earth to save men from death, giving them eternal life.

> "Who was delivered for our offences, and was raised again for our justification" (Ro.4:25).
>
> 4. The resurrection of Christ proves that He is "the Spirit of life." It proves that Christ is the very Energy and Force of life, the very Power and Being of life, and that He can give the same "Spirit of life" to men. He can raise men from the dead, even as He arose from the dead.
>
> "For if we believe that Jesus died and rose again, even so them also which sleep in Jesus will God bring with him" (1 Th.4:14).

QUESTIONS:
1. If there were no resurrection, what would be your eternal fate?
2. There are many people who are skeptical of the resurrection of Jesus Christ. What can you say that would cause them to change their minds?

6. THE SPIRIT GIVES THE POWER TO MORTIFY—TO PUT TO DEATH—EVIL DEEDS (v.12-13).

Note two points.

1. Believers are in debt to the Spirit, not to the flesh. The word "debtors" means to be obligated, to owe, to be bound by some duty.
   a. Believers are not in debt to the flesh. The flesh does nothing for man, nothing of real value. Note what the flesh does:
      ⇒ It is sinful flesh, contaminated by sin (v.3).
      ⇒ It is carnal or fleshly minded (v.5).
      ⇒ It causes man to die (v.6, 13).
      ⇒ It is the opposite of life and peace (v.6).
      ⇒ It has a mind that is at enmity with God (v.7).
      ⇒ It cannot please God (v.8).

   A man owes the flesh nothing. He is not in debt or obligated to the flesh, for the flesh brings nothing but misery and suffering to man.

APPLICATION:
   A man is a fool to focus his life upon such a weak thing as the flesh, a fool to live as though he were in debt and obligated to something that *caves in*...
   - to sickness and disease so often
   - to sin and shame so often
   - to death much too quickly

   "So then they that are in the flesh cannot please God" (Ro.8:8).
   "For if ye live after the flesh, ye shall die" (Ro.8:13).
   "For the flesh lusteth against the Spirit, and the Spirit against the flesh: and these are contrary the one to the other: so that ye cannot do the things that ye would" (Gal.5:17).

   b. Believers are in debt to the Spirit. It is the Spirit who has done so much for man, the Spirit to whom we are so indebted. The Spirit of God...
      - is the "Spirit of life" (v.2)
      - has freed us from sin and death (v.2)
      - fulfills righteousness in us (v.4)

- pulls our minds to spiritual things (v.5)
- gives us life and peace (v.6)
- dwells within us, removing us from the flesh and identifying us as being "in" Christ (v.9)
- gives life to our spirits now and assures us that He will give life to our mortal bodies in the great day of redemption (v.10-11)

2. Believers determine their own fate. The point is clearly seen: if a man lives after the flesh, he shall die because the flesh dies. The flesh is doomed; it dies, and there has never been an exception. Therefore, if a man chooses to live after the flesh, he experiences what the flesh experiences. If the flesh stumbles and falls, the man stumbles and falls. If the flesh kills itself, then the man dies with the flesh. Scripture clearly teaches this.

"For the wages of sin is death; but the gift of God is eternal life through Jesus Christ our Lord" (Ro.6:23).

However, if a man mortifies or puts to death the deeds of his body, he shall live. Note four facts.
  a. "The deeds of the body" mean the evil deeds, the evil lusts and passions, the desires and urges that lead to sin and shame, destruction and death.
  b. To "mortify" means to put to death. The idea is that of denying, subjecting, subduing, deadening, destroying the strength of.
  c. The power to mortify the evil deeds of the body comes "through the Spirit." However, note this: we must deny the evil deeds, and then the Spirit gives the strength to *deaden* and to *subdue* their strength. We are involved just as the Spirit is involved. He cannot destroy the strength of sin unless we exercise our will and work to destroy it ourselves, and we cannot will and work at it apart from Him. Both the Spirit and ourselves have to be involved, each doing part if we wish the evil deeds of the body to be put to death. To repeat the point above: we exercise our will to deny the evil deeds, and then the Spirit immediately steps in to *deaden* the pull and strength of the evil deed. If we do not want the evil deeds of our body destroyed, if we want to continue living in the sins of the flesh, if we want nothing to do with the Spirit—then the Spirit can do nothing for us. God loves us too much to force us; He will not override our choices. But if we honestly *will* to follow the Spirit and honestly *desire* to destroy the evil deeds of our body, the Spirit will step in to give the power to do so. He will break the power of sin: He will deaden and subdue the strength of it.
      ⇒ Our part is to *will* to follow the Spirit: to mortify the evil deeds and begin to deny them.
      ⇒ The Spirit's part is to subdue, deaden, and eventually destroy the strength of evil deeds.

      Now note: the conquest of evil deeds is not an immediate, once-for-all thing. It is a continuous struggle as long as we live in the flesh. This is actually brought out in the tense of the verb "live." The tense is a continuous and habitual action. We must *continue* to follow the Spirit and *continue* to mortify the evil deeds of the body. It is a day-by-day experience just as living is a day-by-day experience. We are to *live* by developing the habit of living in the Spirit and conquering the evil deeds of the body. The believer *cannot destroy* his flesh while on earth, but he *can break* the strength of evil deeds in his flesh. He can destroy evil deeds in his body.
  d. The person who puts the evil deeds of his body to death shall live. A man dies because of evil, and he lives because of righteousness. If he destroys the evil deeds and follows the Spirit of righteousness, he will not die. He will live.

> **"Knowing this, that our old man is crucified with him, that the body of sin might be destroyed, that henceforth we should not serve sin" (Ro.6:6).**

QUESTIONS:

1. There is no eternal value in the flesh for the Christian believer. Why do so many foolishly place their trust in the flesh?
2. What does it really mean to be in debt to the Spirit?
3. What part do you have in determining your own fate? Do you take that role as seriously as you should?
4. What is the only way for you to put to death the deeds of the body?

7. THE SPIRIT LEADS THE BELIEVER, IDENTIFYING HIM AS A SON OF GOD (v.14).

There are several ideas in the Greek word *lead* or *led*.

⇒ There is the idea of *carrying and bearing along*. The Spirit leads the believer and carries him through the trials of this life. He bears the believer up, carrying him over the corruptions of this world.

⇒ There is the idea of *leading and guiding along*. The Spirit leads and guides the believer along the way of righteousness and truth. He guides the believer by moving in advance and going ahead of him. He blazes the path, making sure the believer knows where to walk (cp. Jn.16:13; cp. Gal.5:18; 2 Pt.1:21).

⇒ There is the idea of *directing on a course and of bringing along to an end*. The Spirit directs the believer where to go and how to get there, directing him to live righteously and conforming him to the image of Christ. The Spirit becomes involved in the life of the believer, bringing the believer to his destined end, that is, to heaven, to live eternally in the presence of God Himself.

This is one of the great powers of the Holy Spirit, the power to lead the believer and to become involved in his life.

APPLICATION:

Whether you are a parent or child or both, you can relate to the above functions of the Holy Spirit.

⇒ There are times when a parent must carry a child, when the child needs the total support of the parent.

⇒ There are times when a parent walks ahead of the child to show the way, or even holds the hand of the child to gently lead him.

⇒ There are times when a parent directs the child, telling the child where to go or how to get there, allowing the child to take the steps himself to arrive at the proper destination or goal.

Likewise, the Holy Spirit will do for us what a parent would do for a child, and so much more. He will meet us where our needs are—whether the need is to be carried, led, or directed.

Now note a crucial point. The evidence or proof that a person is a son of God is just this: Is the person led by the Spirit of God?

⇒ Is the person being carried through the trials of life victoriously, acknowledging God and rejoicing in His strength and eternal security?

⇒ Is the person being led along the way of righteousness and truth?

⇒ Is the person being directed and brought along on the course to heaven, to spend eternity with God?

Very simply, is the person living for God and talking about the things of God? The person who is truly led by the Spirit is wrapped up in the things of God, for he is a son of God. He rejoices in his Father and seeks to please His Father in all that he does.

> **"Howbeit when he, the Spirit of truth, is come, he will guide you into all truth: for he shall not speak of himself; but whatsoever he shall hear, that shall he speak: and he will show you things to come" (Jn.16:13).**

ILLUSTRATION:
The commandment is clear and pointed: the Christian believer is to be led by the Spirit of God, not just some of the time (e.g. on Sunday morning) but all of the time. Just imagine what would happen to your community if you were to make a total commitment to be continually led by the Holy Spirit.

> *"The Kurku, a hill tribe in India of some 98,000 people, have as their supreme desire and objective in life to be filled with demons. When filled, they believe, their lives will be immune to attack or harm from the evil forces. Oh yes, they believe in God, a good spirit, who created the world and created them. But he does them no harm, so they worship the evil spirits.*
> *"But what would happen if 98,000 of God's people in this land had as their supreme aim in life to be filled with the Holy Spirit? The Church of Christ would awaken, and before very long a veritable stream of missionaries would be going forth that such poor souls as the demon worshippers of India might hear of our Saviour."*[1]

QUESTIONS:
1. What would happen if...
   * the people in your home had as their supreme aim to be led by the Holy Spirit?
   * the believers in your church desired more than anything else to be filled and led by the power of the Holy Spirit?
   * the leaders in your community lived and governed as the Holy Spirit would?
   * you were personally and continually led by the Holy Spirit?
2. What differences would it make in each instance?

8. THE SPIRIT ADOPTS (v.15).

Note two very significant points.
   1. The Spirit delivers man from a terrible spirit—"the spirit of bondage." Note what the bondage is: fear. Man frequently experiences apprehension, anxiety, tension, dread, alarm, danger, terror. Man frequently senses some subjection, some enslavement to a form of fear. The one spirit with which all men are familiar is the *spirit of fear*. What causes fear? Almost everything and anything can arouse fear. The list could go on and on. A few of the more prominent things are...

• suffering	• disapproval	• loss of spouse
• disease	• blame	• falling short
• unemployment	• death	• punishment
• loss of livelihood	• traumatic trials	• condemnation
• not measuring up	• loss of position	• rejection
• failure		

---

[1] *Student Foreign Missions Fellowship.* Walter B. Knight. *Knight's Master Book of 4,000 Illustrations*, p.290.

The point is this: the Holy Spirit delivers the believer from the bondage of fear. How? By adoption, by actually adopting the believer as a son of God.

> **"But as many as received him, to them gave he power to become the sons of God, even to them that believe on his name" (Jn.1:12).**

2. The Spirit gives access into God's presence. The believer has access to God because he has been adopted as a son of God. Note: the Spirit is called "the Spirit of adoption." Adoption is such a significant work of the Holy Spirit that it is called "the Spirit of adoption." The believer actually receives the sense—the consciousness, the awareness, the knowledge—that he is a son of God. The believer is a son of God with all the privileges of sonship, especially the privilege of access—of entering God's presence anytime and anyplace. It is this wonderful privilege that enables the believer to break the bondage of fear and to conquer the spirit of fear.

No matter what faces the believer, the believer is able...

- to enter the presence of God
- to lay his fear before God
- to cry out, "Father, Father—help me!"
- to know that God will help him, for God loves him as His adopted son

> **"I am the door: by me if any man enter in, he shall be saved, and shall go in and out, and find pasture" (Jn.10:9).**

Every *genuine believer* knows what it is to fear in this life, and he knows what it is to experience God's delivering him through the fear. He knows what it is to have the "Spirit of adoption" surge through his being, giving assurance and confidence that God is in control and looking after him. He knows what it is to be a true son of God, a son whom God loves so much that He will move the world in order to meet the need of His dear child. God's love for His adopted child is as great as God's sovereign power. God will do anything for the believer who is His adopted son.

> **"And we know that all things work together for good to them that love God, to them who are the called according to his purpose" (Ro.8:28).**

<u>**QUESTIONS:**</u>
1. Before God saved you, you were without hope, bound to the spirit of bondage and fear. Have you truly taken advantage of the freedom God has offered you through His Spirit? Do you sense His love, protection, and presence? If not, how can you go about experiencing it?
2. What was your life like before you became a child of God?
3. What is the key to being able to come into the presence of God?

9. THE SPIRIT BEARS WITNESS WITH OUR SPIRIT (v.16-17).

He bears witness to four glorious truths.

1. The Holy Spirit bears witness that we are the children of God. Very simply stated, the Holy Spirit *quickens* our hearts with the perfect knowledge and the complete confidence that we are children of God.

Note how clearly Scripture proclaims this glorious truth, the truth which every believer longs for the world to know.

a. The Spirit sheds abroad the love of God in our hearts. He spreads the knowledge that God loves us and spreads it all through our beings.

"And hope maketh not ashamed; because the love of God is shed abroad in our hearts by the Holy Ghost which is given unto us" (Ro.5:5).

b. The Spirit is the guarantee (earnest) that we are children of God.

"Who hath also sealed us, and give the earnest of the Spirit in our hearts" (2 Cor.1:22).

c. The Spirit is the seal or the guarantee that we are children of God.

"In whom ye also trusted, after that ye heard the word of truth, the gospel of your salvation: in whom also after that ye believed, ye were sealed with that holy Spirit of promise" (Eph.1:13).

2. The Holy Spirit bears witness that we are the heirs of God. If God is truly our Father, then we inherit what He possesses.
   a. We are heirs of eternal life.

"That being justified by his grace, we should be made heirs according to the hope of eternal life" (Tit.3:7).

b. We are heirs of salvation.

"Are they not all ministering spirits, sent forth to minister for them who shall be heirs of salvation?" (Heb.1:14).

c. We are heirs of the promises made to Abraham, that is, the promises to inherit the world and to become the citizens of a great nation of people. The heirs of God shall inherit a great kingdom, called the new heavens and earth.

"For the promise, that he should be the heir of the world, was not to Abraham, or to his seed, through the law, but through the righteousness of faith" (Ro.4:13).

d. We are heirs of glory.

"Giving thanks unto the Father, which hath made us meet to be partakers of the inheritance of the saints in light" (Col.1:12).

e. We are heirs of righteousness.

"By faith Noah, being warned of God of things not seen as yet, moved with fear, prepared an ark to the saving of his house; by the which he condemned the world, and became heir of the righteousness which is by faith" (Heb.11:7).

f. We are heirs of the grace of life.

"Likewise, ye husbands, dwell with them according to knowledge, giving honour unto the wife, as unto the weaker vessel, and as being heirs together of the grace of life; that your prayers be not hindered" (1 Pt.3:7).

3. The Holy Spirit bears witness that we are joint-heirs with Christ. However, this does not mean that we will receive an equal amount or quantity with Christ. (See A Closer Look # 4, Inheritance—Ro.8:17 for discussion.)

4. The Holy Spirit bears witness that we are conquerors over suffering. All men suffer; and as long as man lives in a sinful and corrupt world, he will continue to suffer; he will be unable to escape suffering. Sin and corruption take their toll upon his body and spirit, pulling him ever onward toward the grave. However, this is not the suffering being spoken about in this passage. There is a suffering that is distinct to the true Christian believer, a suffering that can be called *godly persecution*. *Godly persecution* means more than being persecuted for some great cause or purpose. Many men in the world suffer persecution by fellow citizens because of their dedication to some great purpose. However, not all men within the world oppose them. It is this that makes *godly persecution* different and distinctive. Every person in the world who is not godly opposes the *genuine* Christian believer. The world and its citizens oppose the believer by their very nature. The believer stands for and proclaims righteousness and self-denial, the sacrifice of all one is and has. The world opposes such a life and message, and they desire to stamp it out.

It is suffering for the Kingdom of God and His righteousness that is the point of the Scripture. If we suffer with Christ in the great cause of God and His righteousness, then we will be glorified with Him eternally.

The point is clearly seen. The person who is a true follower of Christ proclaims and stands for Christ; therefore, he suffers the persecution of the world even as Christ did. And because he does suffer with Christ, he will share in the glory of Christ as well.

> **"Blessed are ye, when men shall revile you, and persecute you, and shall say all manner of evil against you falsely, for my sake" (Mt.5:11).**

ILLUSTRATION:

One of the most misunderstood experiences in this life is why God allows suffering. People are quick to accept the good from God but are just as quick to blame Him for their troubles.

> *"In the midst of the movie 'The Hiding Place', there is a scene set in the Ravensbruck concentration camp in Germany. Corrie ten Boom and her sister, Betsy, are there, along with ten thousand other women, in horrible, degrading, hideous conditions. They are gathered with some of the women in the barracks in the midst of the beds, cold and hungry and lice-ridden, and Betsy is leading a Bible class. One of the other women calls out derisively from her bunk and mocks their worship of God. They fall into conversation, and this woman says what so frequently is flung at Christians: 'If your God is such a good God, why does he allow this kind of suffering?' Dramatically she tears off the bandages and old rags that binds her hands, displaying her broken, mangled fingers and says, 'I'm the first violinist of the symphony orchestra. Did your God will this?'*
>
> *"For a moment no one answers. Then Corrie ten Boom steps to the side of her sister and says, 'We can't answer that question. All we know is that our God came to this earth, and became one of us, and he suffered with us and was crucified and died. And that he did it for love.'"[2]*

The next time you suffer for Christ, remember that...
- He became one of us
- He suffered with us
- He was crucified and died for us
- He did it for love

...and through Him you too can conquer suffering.

---

[2] Michael P. Green. *Illustrations for Biblical Preaching*, p.365-366.

1. How can you really know for sure that you belong to God? How can you relate that to an unbeliever?
2. What promise can you claim the next time you have to endure suffering because of persecution? In what ways have you been persecuted in the past? Has someone...
   - made fun of your relationship with Christ?
   - used words to destroy your faith?
   - shunned you, making you a social outcast?
   - physically hurt you because of your convictions?
3. Has your attitude toward suffering been a positive one, one that would stand up and be a good testimony to others?

A CLOSER LOOK # 4

(8:17) **Inheritance**: the believer is a joint-heir with Christ. This is an astounding truth and promise. We shall inherit all that God has and all that Christ is and has. We will be given the privilege of sharing in all things with the Son of God Himself.

However note this: to be a joint-heir with Christ does not mean that believers will receive an equal amount of the inheritance with Christ. Rather, it means that believers are fellow-heirs with Christ; that is, believers will *share* Christ's inheritance with Him.

Being a fellow-heir with Christ means at least three glorious things: it means that we will share in the *nature*, *position*, and *responsibility* of Christ. The following chart shows this with a quick glance.

FELLOW HEIRS BY NATURE

Christ is the Son of God, the very being
and energy of life and perfection. Therefore,
we share in the inheritance of His nature.
We receive...

- the adoption as a son of God (Gal.4:4-7; 1 Jn.3:1)
- the sinless nature of being blameless (Ph.2:15)
- eternal life (Jn.1:4; 10:10; 17:2-3; Jn.3:16; 1 Tim.6:19)
- an enduring substance (Heb.10:34)
- a glorious body (Ph.3:21; 1 Cor.15:42-44)
- eternal glory, honor, and peace (Ro.2:10)
- eternal rest and peace (Heb.4:9; Rev.14:13)
- an incorruptible body (1 Cor.9:25)
- a righteous being (2 Tim.4:8)

FELLOW HEIRS BY POSITION

Christ is the exalted Lord, the Sovereign
Majesty of the universe, the Lord of lords
and King of kings. Therefore, we share in
the inheritance of His position. We receive...

- the position of exalted beings (Rev.7:9-12)
- a citizenship in the Kingdom of God (Jas.2:5; Mt.25:34)
- enormous treasures in heaven (Mt.19:21; Lk.12:33)
- unsearchable riches (Eph.3:8)
- the right to surround the throne of God (Rev.7:9-13; 20:4)
- the position of a king (Rev.1:5; 5:10)
- the position of a priest (Rev.1:5; 5:10; 20:6)
- the position of glory (1 Pt.5:4)

FELLOW HEIRS BY RESPONSIBILITY

Christ is the Sovereign Majesty of the Universe, the One who is ordained to rule and oversee all. Therefore, we share in the inheritance of His responsibility. We receive...

- the rulership over many things (Mt.25:23)
- the right to rule and hold authority (Lk.12:42-44; 22:28-29)
- eternal responsibility and joy (Mt.25:21, 23)
- rule and authority over cities (Lk.19:17, 19)
- thrones and the privilege of reigning forever (Rev.20:4; 22:5)

These passages will give some idea of what Scripture teaches when it speaks of the believer being a fellow-heir with Christ. There are a large number of Scriptures that could be added to these. As Paul declares:

"Eye hath not seen, nor ear heard, neither have entered into the heart of man, the things which God hath prepared for them that love him" (1 Cor.2:9).

"O the depth of the riches both of the wisdom and knowledge of God! how unsearchable are his judgments, and his ways past finding out! For who hath known the mind of the Lord? or who hath been his counsellor? Or who hath first given to him, and it shall be recompensed unto him again? For of him, and through him, and to him, are all things: to whom be glory for ever. Amen" (Ro.11:33-36).

SUMMARY:

One of the best kept secrets in the church is the believer's right to use the power of the Holy Spirit. Instead of doing things in the flesh, in your own might, God has given you a wonderful gift: life in the Spirit. This life is yours because...

1. Christ has now come (v.1).
2. The Spirit gives life (v.2-4).
3. The Spirit pulls the mind to spiritual things (v.5-8).
4. The Spirit dwells within the believer (v.9).
5. The Spirit gives life to the spirit of the believer (v.10-11).
6. The Spirit gives the power to mortify—to put to death—evil deeds (v.12-13).
7. The Spirit leads the believer, identifying him as a son of God (v.14).
8. The Spirit adopts (v.15).
9. The Spirit bears witness with our spirit (v.16-17).

PERSONAL JOURNAL NOTES:
(Reflection & Response)

1. The most important thing that I learned from this lesson was:

2. The thing that I need to work on the most is:

3. I can apply this lesson to my life by:

4. Closing Prayer of Commitment: (put your commitment down on paper).

	B. The Whole Creation Shall Be Freed from Struggling and Suffering, 8:18-27		& struggles for deliverance from corruption
1. In this life a. The believer suffers & struggles b. The future glory will be worth the agony	18 For I reckon that the sufferings of this present time are not worthy to be compared with the glory which shall be revealed in us.	but ourselves also, which have the firstfruits of the Spirit, even we ourselves groan within ourselves, waiting for the adoption, to wit, the redemption of our body. 24 For we are saved by hope: but hope that is seen is not hope: for what a man seeth, why doth he yet hope for?	a. The first-fruits (presence & fruit) of the Spirit deliver & save him b. Hope delivers & saves him
2. The creation suffers & struggles for deliverance from corruption a. Creation is subject to corruption	19 For the earnest expectation of the creature waiteth for the manifestation of the sons of God. 20 For the creature was made subject to vanity, not willingly, but by reason of him who hath subjected the same in hope.	25 But if we hope for that we see not, then do we with patience wait for it. 26 Likewise the Spirit also helpeth our infirmities: for we know not what we should pray for as we ought: but the Spirit itself maketh intercession for us with groanings which cannot be uttered.	c. Prayer & the Spirit deliver & save him
b. Creation will be delivered	21 Because the creature itself also shall be delivered from the bondage of corruption into the glorious liberty of the children of God.		
c. Creation groans in labor for deliverance	22 For we know that the whole creation groaneth and travaileth in pain together until now.	27 And he that searcheth the hearts knoweth what is the mind of the Spirit, because he maketh intercession for the saints according to	d. God delivers & saves him
3. The believer suffers	23 And not only they,	the will of God.	

Section VI
DELIVERANCE AND REDEMPTION: THE BELIEVER SHALL BE FREED FROM STRUGGLING AND SUFFERING BY THE SPIRIT
Romans 8:1-39

Study 2: **The Whole Creation Shall Be Freed from Struggling and Suffering**

Text: **Romans 8:18-27**

Aim: To understand the role and purpose of suffering.

Memory Verse:
> **"Likewise the Spirit also helpeth our infirmities: for we know not what we should pray for as we ought: but the Spirit itself maketh intercession for us with groanings which cannot be uttered" (Romans 8:27).**

INTRODUCTION:
What do you need to help you get up, get started, and make it through another day?
Some people need...
- an irritating alarm clock
- a cup of hot coffee
- a long, hot shower

Then after that, the challenge is to make it through the rest of the day, and the day after that, and the day after that.
⇒ They cannot wait until it's Friday.
⇒ They stare at the clock as if their eyes could make the hands move faster.
⇒ They endure one task after another and one ritual after another until it is time to start the day all over again.
Such is the existence of the person who simply endures life.

On the other hand, there are those who have discovered that the secret to life rests not in their own power, but in the power of the Holy Spirit of God. It is the Holy Spirit...
- who awakens them for a brand new day
- who causes them to live for the future, not just for the weekend
- who allows them to look at every circumstance, even the hard ones, as an opportunity for personal growth

The mature Christian believer has come to learn that struggling and suffering are a part of life. It is a part of life that is not to be shunned but to be embraced. How can anyone live like this? There is only one way, the way of the power of the Holy Spirit. Through the ministry of the Holy Spirit, God will preserve His people with a great hope. The man who has hope will *always* overcome any trial or tribulation. This is one of the most glorious promises in all of Scripture. God is going to free *all creation* from struggling and suffering.

OUTLINE:
1. In this life (v.18).
   a. The believer suffers and struggles.
   b. The future glory will be worth the agony.
2. The creation suffers and struggles for deliverance from corruption (v.19-22).
3. The believer suffers and struggles for deliverance from corruption (v.23-27).

1. IN THIS LIFE THE BELIEVER SUFFERS AND STRUGGLES (v.18).

The word "suffering" here means all the forms of suffering which the believer experiences throughout life. It means...
⇒ the suffering that comes from persecution
⇒ the suffering that comes from the struggle of his spirit to overcome the flesh and the world

Very simply, suffering means the struggle waged by our spirits to overcome all that is experienced in this life, all that is involved in the flesh and the world. It is the spiritual struggle discussed in Romans Chapters 5-8, and so descriptively illustrated in Chapter 7. It is the weight and agony of fighting to overcome...
- sin and corruption
- disease and pain
- abuse and persecution
- unregulated urges and desires
- weaknesses and shortcomings
- aging and loss
- deterioration and decay

The genuine believer struggles against everything that keeps him from living abundantly and eternally. His sole passion is to bring everything under the control of Christ and to be conformed to the image of Christ. Therefore, he struggles to overcome the flesh and the world with their aging and corruption, sin and death. No matter what suffering is required, the believer bears it in order to overcome, gaining the victory of eternal life and its glory.

Note that the believer is to suffer with Christ "in order that" he may be glorified with Christ (Ro.8:17). Suffering prepares the believer to participate in the glory of Christ. It is the necessary condition for exaltation. Suffering and struggling are a refining process through which the believer must pass (1 Pt.1:6-7). It refines the believer by forcing him to expand his trust in God more and more. Suffering drives a believer to cast himself more and more upon the care of God; therefore, the believer moves closer and closer to that perfect trust. Although he will never achieve perfect trust and care in God, he will come to know it when God transports him into the very Kingdom of Heaven itself. Suffering enlarges, purifies, expands, and ennobles the believer. It makes him more and more like what he will be when he actually lives face to face with God. This future glory *transcends immeasurably* the suffering and struggling of this present world.

a. The future glory shall be revealed "in" us; it shall become part of our very nature and being. Glory shall radiate and shine forth from our resurrected bodies.

"When Christ, who is our life, shall appear, then shall ye also appear with him in glory" (Col.3:4).

b. The future glory shall be an *eternal weight* of glory (just imagine such a weight, a weight beyond all measure, surpassing all measurements and calculations).

"For our light affliction, which is but for a moment, worketh for us a far more exceeding and eternal weight of glory; while we look not at the things which are seen, but at the things which are not seen: for the things which are seen are temporal; but the things which are not seen are eternal" (2 Cor.4:17-18).

c. The future glory shall far exceed anything we have seen or heard or longed for in our hearts.

"But as it is written, Eye hath not seen, nor ear heard, neither have entered into the heart of man, the things which God hath prepared for them that love him" (1 Cor.2:9).

d. The future glory shall be so glorious it will reflect through us to others, making us *ministers* of glory.

"They are the messengers of the churches, and the glory of Christ" (2 Cor.8:23).

e. The future glory shall make us just like Jesus in all that He is.

"Beloved, now are we the sons of God, and it doth not yet appear what we shall be: but we know that, when he shall appear, we shall be like him; for we shall see him as he is" (1 Jn.3:2).

ILLUSTRATION:

When things are going well, we all tend to be a little bit nonchalant about life. Suffering, however, causes all of us to look deep inside and ask the hard questions of life. "What does my suffering mean? Why is this happening to me? What do I need to learn from my suffering?" Sometimes when we are placed in the grip of suffering, the answers to these questions become a little bit clearer.

"When Jewish psychiatrist Victor Frankl was arrested by the Nazis in World War II, he was stripped of everything—property, family, possessions. He had spent years researching and writing a book on the importance of finding meaning in life—concepts that later would become known as logotherapy. When he arrived in Auschwitz, the infamous death camp, even his manuscript, which he had hidden in the lining of his coat, was taken away.

"'I had to undergo and overcome the loss of my spiritual child,' Frankl writes. 'Now it seemed as if nothing and no one would survive me; neither a physical nor a spiritual child of my own! I found myself confronted with the question of whether under such circumstances my life was ultimately void of any meaning.'

"He was still wrestling with that question a few days later when the Nazis forced the prisoners to give up their clothes.

"'I had to surrender my clothes and in turn inherited the worn out rags of an inmate who had been sent to the gas chamber,' says Frankl. 'Instead of the many pages of my manuscript, I found in the pocket of the newly acquired coat a single page torn out of a Hebrew prayer book, which contained the main Jewish prayer, <u>Shema Yisrael</u> (Hear, O Israel! The Lord our God is one God. And you shall love the Lord your God with all your heart and with all your soul and with all your might.)

"'How should I have interpreted such a <u>coincidence</u> other than as a challenge to live my thoughts instead of merely putting them on paper?'

"Later, as Frankl reflected on his ordeal, he wrote in his book <u>Man's Search for Meaning</u>, 'There is nothing in the world that would so effectively help one to survive even the worst conditions, as the knowledge that there is a meaning in one's life....He who has a <u>why</u> to live for can bear almost any <u>how</u>.'"[1]

It is crucial for you to remember that while you are suffering, God has given you a great reason, a great purpose, and a great future. A great reason to live. A great purpose to share. A great future with Him. What suffering would be so great to cause you to give up this kind of hope?

<u>QUESTIONS:</u>
1. What comfort does God offer you while you are suffering?
2. Why does God want you to suffer with Christ? Is it fair? Is it reasonable?
3. What would you say to a believer who thought he would be exempt from suffering when he became a Christian?
4. How often do you thank God for what awaits you in the future?

2. THE CREATION SUFFERS AND STRUGGLES FOR DELIVERANCE FROM CORRUPTION (v.19-22).

The word "creation" refers to everything *under* man: animal, plant, and mineral. All creation is pictured as living and waiting expectantly for the day when the sons of God shall be glorified. The words "earnest expectation" mean to watch with the neck outstretched and the head erect. It is a persistent, unswerving expectation, an expectation that does not give up, but keeps looking until the event happens. Note three facts revealed about the universe in which man lives.

1. *Creation is subject to corruption.* This is clearly seen by men; and what men see is constantly confirmed by such authorities as the botanist, zoologist, geologist, and astronomers of the world. All of creation, whether mineral, plant, or animal, suffers just as men do. All creation suffers hurt, damage, loss, deterioration, erosion, death, and decay—all creation struggles for life. It is full of "vanity," that is, condemned to futility

---

[1]   Craig B. Larson. *Illustrations for Preaching and Teaching*, p.250-251.

and frustration, unable to realize its purpose, subject to corruption. Note the two things said about creation in this verse (v.20).

    a. Creation was condemned to vanity—futility and frustration—by God because of man's sin. Creation did not willingly choose to be condemned to corruption. The world was made to be the home of man, the place where he lived. Therefore, when man sinned, his world was doomed to suffer the consequences of sin with him. Man's world was cursed right along with him.

"Cursed is the earth for thy sake" (Gen.3:17).

APPLICATION:

    Just picture the enormous hurt, damage, and decay that take place every day in our world. Think about...

- the disease and savagery of the animal world
- the hurt and damage that so easily happens in the plant world
- the destruction and deterioration that takes place in the mineral world

Think about the earthquakes, tornadoes, storms, floods, droughts, diseases, famines, attacks, and struggles for survival that take place. And these are only a few of the myriad happenings that show the corruption of the world.

    b. Creation has been subjected to corruption "in hope." The news of Scripture is glorious: the situation of the world is neither hopeless nor final. Creation has the same *hope of redemption and of renovation* as man. The world was made for man; therefore, all creation shall be ultimately delivered from corruption just as man shall be delivered from corruption.

2. *Creation shall be delivered from corruption.* This is the wonderful news of the glorious gospel. Note a most significant point: whatever happens to man is bound to happen to his world. Man is the summit of God's creation; therefore, all that is under man is intertwined, interwoven, and interrelated to him. Man and his world are one and the same; they are dependent upon each other. This is enormously significant: since man and his world are interrelated, it means that the world will experience whatever man experiences. When man fell, his world was bound to fall with him. But this is the glorious news as well. When man is liberated from corruption, his world shall be liberated as well. God had to subject man's world to man's fate, but God also had to subject man's world to man's hope. Creation will experience the glorious hope of *living forever* with man, of being completely and perfectly renovated. There will be a "new heavens and a new earth" (cp. Ps.96:11-13; 98:7-9; Is.11:6-9; Rev.5:13).

> **"But the day of the Lord will come as a thief in the night; in the which the heavens shall pass away with a great noise, and the elements shall melt with fervent heat, the earth also and the works that are therein shall be burned up. Seeing then that all these things shall be dissolved, what manner of persons ought ye to be in all holy conversation and godliness, looking for and hasting unto the coming of the day of God, wherein the heavens being on fire shall be dissolved, and the elements shall melt with fervent heat? Nevertheless we, according to his promise, look for new heavens and a new earth, wherein dwelleth righteousness" (2 Pt.3:10-13).**

3. *Creation groans in labor for deliverance.* Note that all creation suffers together: all creation is interrelated, intertwined, and interconnected. The whole universe is dependent upon its various parts for survival. The earth could not survive without the heavens, and the heavens would have no purpose apart from God's creation of man and his earth. This does not mean that man is to be egocentric or egotistical. It simply means that man and his earth are the focal point of God's unbelievable creation, of His

eternal plan and purpose. Being the center of creation *before God* is not a truth to make man proud, but to make him humble—a truth to cause him to bow in worship and praise, appreciation and thankfulness. Being the summit of God's creation is not a gift of privilege, not presently, but of enormous responsibility.

Note the words "groaneth and travaileth." The picture is that of a woman giving birth. Creation experiences *birth pangs* under its struggle to survive. And note: it has been experiencing the *birth pangs* until now, that is, from the fall of man up until this present moment.

In conclusion, the whole scene of these four verses is that creation awaits a renovated world. Creation resents evil and struggles against decay and death. It fights for survival. It struggles against the bondage of being slaughtered or changed.

The idea expressed is that creation awaits the Day of Redemption: anxiously, expectantly, longingly, and eagerly awaits for its deliverance from corruption. Creation moans and groans and cries for the unveiling of the Son of God.

> "Nevertheless we, according to his promise, look for new heavens and a new earth, wherein dwelleth righteousness" (2 Pt.3:13).

QUESTIONS:
1. In what ways have you observed creation's corruption? What does this tell you about people who worship nature (e.g. the spirits in trees, animals, stars, the sun, the moon, etc.)?
2. Considering what God has promised to do with creation, what is your responsibility to creation now?
3. Have you been as respectful and responsible toward all of God's creation as you should be? How can you be more so?

3. THE BELIEVER SUFFERS AND STRUGGLES FOR DELIVERANCE FROM CORRUPTION (v.23-27).

Note four facts.

1. It is the first-fruit of the Holy Spirit that delivers and saves man. The term first-fruit means either the presence of the Holy Spirit or the fruit of the Holy Spirit: life, love, joy, peace (Gal.5:22-23). When a believer is truly saved, he possesses the Holy Spirit and bears the fruit of the Spirit. He actually begins to live abundantly and eternally, and he experiences the fulness of God's Spirit: His love, joy, and peace. Experiencing these causes the believer to groan and ache...
- for the perfection of the Spirit's presence and fruit
- for the day of adoption, the day when he will actually move into the perfect presence of God
- for the redemption of his body

The believer is stirred by the taste of the Spirit and of His first-fruits, stirred to groan for their perfection. He groans and aches to be delivered from the sufferings of this world and released into the glorious *liberty of perfection* with God.

> "It is sown a natural body: it is raised a spiritual body. There is a natural body, and there is a spiritual body" (1 Cor.15:44).

2. It is hope that delivers and saves man. Hope saves us, for it is hope that keeps us seeking after God and His redemption. We hope for redemption; therefore, "with patience we wait for it" (see A Closer Look # 1, Hope—Ro.8:24-25 for discussion).

3. It is prayer and the Holy Spirit that delivers and saves a man. As the believer faces the sufferings of this life, he has the greatest resource imaginable: prayer. He has the right to approach God whenever needed and to ask God for the strength to walk through and to conquer the suffering. That is what prayer is all about.

Two significant things are said about prayer.

    a. Believers do not know how to pray *as they should.* Note the word "we." Paul includes himself in this, which is to say no believer knows how to pray. By nature we are weak, lacking the power...

- for prolonged concentration
- to avoid distractions
- to stop all wandering thoughts
- to prevent emotional changes
- to govern varying affections
- to know what lies in the future, even one hour from now
- to know what is really best for us and our growth in any given situation

    b. The Holy Spirit helps our infirmities. It is true that He helps us in *all* our infirmities, but the point of the present passage deals only with prayer. Note: it is assumed that we are praying in this verse. The Spirit is not going to force us to pray. It is our responsibility to pray, to take the time to get alone and pray. When we do this, the Spirit begins to act both *upon* and *for* us.

    Note this also: the Spirit "helpeth our infirmities." Whatever our particular weakness is, it is that weakness which He helps. If we are truly sincere and are wrestling to pray, then the Spirit helps us to control concentration, distractions, wandering thoughts, emotional changes, and affections. How? As we struggle to pray by controlling our flesh and its weakness, the Holy Spirit takes our mind and emotions and...

- quiets and silences them
- stirs and excites them
- draws and pulls them
- directs and guides them

    He leads us to pray as we should, controlling and subjecting the flesh and concentrating upon the prayer.

    Note another fact: the Holy Spirit makes "intercession for us with groanings which cannot be uttered." Sometimes the struggles and sufferings of life become so heavy we just cannot bear them. At other times, matters of such importance grip our hearts to the extent that words are impossible. Emotions become too much for words. We become lost in the presence of God. Every genuine believer knows what it is to be speechless before God and left groaning in the Spirit. Every believer has experienced...

- God's unspeakable gift

    "Thanks be unto God for his unspeakable gift" (2 Cor.9:15).

- joy unspeakable

    "Whom having not seen, ye love; in whom, though now ye see him not, yet believing, ye rejoice with joy unspeakable and full of glory" (1 Pt.1:8).

- words which are unspeakable

    "How that he was caught up into paradise, and heard unspeakable words, which it is not lawful for a man to utter" (2 Cor.12:4).

    The point to note is that the Holy Spirit takes these great moments of prayer and helps us in our "groanings" before the Lord. We are not able to utter words; therefore, the Spirit intercedes for us with groanings that cannot be uttered.

> **"Praying always with all prayer and supplication in the Spirit, and watching thereunto with all perseverance and supplication for all saints" (Eph.6:18).**

APPLICATION:

The believer's great need is to come before God—and to come often—in such intense prayer.

> **"Seek the LORD and his strength, seek his face continually" (1 Chron.16:11).**
> **"Ask, and it shall be given you; seek, and ye shall find; knock, and it shall be opened unto you" (Mt.7:7).**

ILLUSTRATION:

There is a great gospel song that says, "No one ever *cared* for me like Jesus." But here Scripture is saying, "No one ever *prayed* for me like the Holy Spirit." How many times have you cried out to God but were at a loss for words? God plainly says there is hope even in those times: the Holy Spirit not only knows what needs to be said, He says it for you. Here is one man's story on bridging the language gap.

> *One day Sue's television quit working properly. She called the repair shop to find out what to do. In trying to explain the problem, Sue was unable to clearly communicate the facts. All she knew was that her television was not working properly and needed fixing.*
>
> *When the repairman arrived, he took off the back of the television and said, "Maam, what you've got here is...[and rattled off a string of strange terms] I'm going to call the store to see if we have these parts in stock." And so the repairman called and talked with the parts manager. Sue overheard him say, "Do we have any 'blaah, blaah, blaah' in stock? Great! I'll pick up the parts and fix it this afternoon."*
>
> *In no time at all, Sue's television was as good as new. She had no idea what parts her television needed. It all sounded too technical for her. But she was glad that the repairman and the parts manager knew what they were talking about. Sue's need was taken care of because these two men knew the problem and what it would take to fix it. This is exactly what the Holy Spirit does for believers. When we do not know how to pray, He not only knows the problem, He has the unique ability to tell our Heavenly Father in a language that only He understands.*

The next time words fail you in prayer, remember that the Holy Spirit is right there with you—interceding in prayer for you.

4. It is God who delivers and saves a man. Note the three things said in this verse.
   a. God searches the hearts of us all. There is no exception. He knows exactly what is within our hearts. He can read and understand what our groanings and needs are. Not a need will be missed.

> **"And thou, Solomon my son, know thou the God of thy father, and serve him with a perfect heart and with a willing mind: for the LORD searcheth all hearts, and understandeth all the imaginations of the thoughts: if thou seek him, he will be found of thee; but if thou forsake him, he will cast thee off for ever" (1 Chron.28:9).**

b. God knows the mind of the Holy Spirit. The Holy Spirit prays for us according to the will of God; therefore, God knows exactly what the Spirit is requesting for us. There is perfect agreement between the Holy Spirit and God the Father.

> **"Howbeit when he, the Spirit of truth, is come, he will guide you into all truth: for <u>he shall not speak of himself</u>; but whatsoever he shall hear, that shall he speak: and he will show you things to come" (Jn.16:13).**

c. God will answer our prayer and meet our need. He will deliver and save us, causing the very best thing to happen.

> **"Whatsoever ye shall ask of the Father in my name, he may give it you" (Jn.15:16).**
> **"And we know that all things work together for good to them that love God, to them who are the called according to his purpose" (Ro.8:28).**

QUESTIONS:

1. What is your only true hope of being delivered from corruption? In what ways does man try to deliver himself?
2. The world hopes in a lot of things, things such as...
   - man's wisdom
   - man's wealth
   - man's political power
   - man's religious traditions

   When are you most tempted to place your hope in one of these things instead of in the Lord? How can you cultivate your hope in the Lord?
3. The Holy Spirit knows best how to pray for you. Can you think of a time when you sensed the Holy Spirit was praying for you? How are His prayers beneficial to you?

A CLOSER LOOK # 1

(8:24-25) <u>Hope</u>: assured expectation, confident knowledge, inward possession, spiritual surety. Note the statements of definition again, for they are packed full of meaning. The believer's hope cannot be defined as the world defines hope. The believer's hope is entirely different from the world's hope or desire or wish. The world desires and wishes for what it can see, and they may or may not be able to get what they long for.

The believer's hope is entirely different in that it deals with spiritual things, and the believer will unquestionably get what he hopes for. The believer's hope is based on the *inward experience and witness of God's Spirit.* The believer knows that God's Spirit lives within him, and he actually experiences the things of the Spirit *now.* Granted, his experience is only a taste; the things of the Spirit are *not yet perfected* in his life, *but they do exist,* and they are present in his body. Man already possesses the things of God while in the flesh. His hope of salvation is a present experience—he is saved now—he already has a taste of salvation. Therefore, his hope is a *sure* hope. To the genuine believer, hope is the absolute assurance of things promised but not yet seen.

He has absolute assurance because he already experiences the things of God. They are already an *inward possession,* a *spiritual surety,* an *assured expectation,* a *confident knowledge.* Note four facts about hope.

1. God has chosen for us to be saved by hope and not by sight. If we were saved by sight, we would not hope in God. If we could actually see and experience perfect redemption and salvation now, then there would be nothing more for which to hope. The result would be catastrophic: we would not be drawing close to God, believing and trusting Him, nor looking to Him to provide a perfect salvation for us. There would be *no liberty and freedom between God and man, no love and trust established.* There just

would be no relationship and no fellowship between God and man, not based on a *free moral love, trust, and belief.*

2. God is after one thing: our being patient in hope, that is, our persevering in hope. Why? The more we *hope* for salvation and redemption, the closer we draw to God. And, above all else, God wants us to draw near Him: fellowshipping, believing, trusting, loving, and hoping in Him.

3. The path of hope is the only way God could choose for salvation. For only as a man hopes in God will he draw near to God. The more he hopes, the more he will trust, believe, love, and depend upon God. And this is exactly what God is after; it is His plan and purpose for man and his world.

4. The believer's hope is expressed in several glorious ways. Note that God Himself is called "the God of hope" (Ro.15:13).

   a. The hope of "the resurrection of the dead" (Acts 23:6).
   b. The hope of the promise (Acts 26:6-7).
   c. The hope of Israel (Acts 28:20).
   d. The hope that is the object of faith (Ro.4:18; cp. Acts 26:6-7).
   e. The hope of the glory of God (Ro.5:2; Col.1:27; Tit.2:13).
   f. The hope that saves us (Ro.8:24).
   g. The hope that causes believers to endure afflictions (Ro.8:25; 1 Th.1:3).
   h. The hope of believers that comes through the Scripture (Ro.15:4).
   i. The hope which is a gift of the Holy Spirit (Ro.15:13).
   j. The hope that is one of the three essential traits of the believer (1 Cor.13:13).
   k. The hope in Christ (1 Cor.15:10; 1 Tim.1:1).
   l. The hope of righteousness (Gal.5:5).
   m. The hope of God's calling (Eph.1:18; 4:4).
   n. The hope which the lost do not have (Eph.2:12).
   o. The hope of the gospel (Col.1:23).
   p. The hope of salvation (1 Th.5:8).
   q. The "good hope" which God gives (2 Th.2:16).
   r. The hope of eternal life (Tit.1:2; 3:7; cp. Acts 2:26).
   s. The "blessed hope" of the Lord's return (Tit.2:13).
   t. The hope that stirs diligence and gives full assurance (Heb.6:11).
   u. The hope set before believers (Heb.6:18).
   v. The hope which anchors the believer's soul (Heb.6:19).
   w. The hope that stirs belief (Heb.11:1).
   x. The "living hope" of the believer (1 Pt.1:3).
   y. The hope that stirs believers to purify themselves (1 Jn.3:3).

QUESTIONS:

1. Think of a practical example of the world's concept of hope compared to God's hope. Why would man choose what the world offers?
2. When are you most filled with God's hope? When is hope lacking in your life?
3. How patient are you in hope? When are you most likely to lose your patience in God's plan?
4. Why is hope such a tremendous witnessing tool when sharing with the lost?

SUMMARY:

Every person suffers. Eventually, we all suffer some pain or loss. Suffering is just as much a part of life as is breathing and eating. The bad news is that suffering is not a pleasant experience. Suffering hurts. But the good news is that you do not have to go through it alone. God has graciously offered the power of the Holy Spirit to help you make it through each day, every day. Remember, the next time you want to give up and quit:

1. In this life you will suffer and struggle, but the future glory will be worth the agony.
2. The creation suffers and struggles for deliverance from corruption.
3. The believer suffers and struggles for deliverance from corruption.

PERSONAL JOURNAL NOTES:
(Reflection & Response)

1. The most important thing that I learned from this lesson was:

2. The thing that I need to work on the most is:

3. I can apply this lesson to my life by:

4. Closing Prayer of Commitment: (put your commitment down on paper).

	C. God Assures Deliverance (Freedom) from Struggling & Suffering, 8:28-39	that justifieth. 34 Who is he that condemneth? It is Christ that died, yea rather, that is risen again, who is even at the right hand of God, who also maketh intercession for us.	**5. Assurance 5: Christ does not condemn the believer** a. He died for us b. He arose for us c. He was exalted for us d. He intercedes for us
1. Assurance 1: God works things out for those who love Him	28 And we know that all things work together for good to them that love God, to them who are the called according to his purpose.	
2. Assurance 2: God has determined to fulfill His purpose for the believer a. To conform him to Christ b. To honor Christ	29 For whom he did foreknow, he also did predestinate to be conformed to the image of his Son, that he might be the first-born among many brethren.	35 Who shall separate us from the love of Christ? shall tribulation, or distress, or persecution, or famine, or nakedness, or peril, or sword? 36 As it is written, For thy sake we are killed all the day long; we are accounted as sheep for the slaughter.	**6. Assurance 6: Christ delivers the believer through the severest circumstances**
3. Assurance 3: God has assured the glorification of the believer—once-for-all	30 Moreover whom he did predestinate, them he also called: and whom he called, them he also justified: and whom he justified, them he also glorified.	37 Nay, in all these things we are more than conquerors through him that loved us.	
4. Assurance 4: God has acted for the believer, not against him a. He is our Savior b. He is our Provider c. He is our Justifier	31 What shall we then say to these things? If God be for us, who can be against us? 32 He that spared not his own Son, but delivered him up for us all, how shall he not with him also freely give us all things? 33 Who shall lay any thing to the charge of God's elect? It is God	38 For I am persuaded, that neither death, nor life, nor angels, nor principalities, nor powers, nor things present, nor things to come, 39 Nor height, nor depth, nor any other creature, shall be able to separate us from the love of God, which is in Christ Jesus our Lord.	**7. Assurance 7: Christ delivers the believer through the most extreme experiences & forces**

(Note: Because of the length of this outline and commentary, you may wish to split this passage into two or more studies.)

Section VI
DELIVERANCE AND REDEMPTION: THE
BELIEVER SHALL BE FREED FROM STRUGGLING
AND SUFFERING BY THE SPIRIT
Romans 8:1-39

Study 3: **God Assures Deliverance (Freedom) through Struggling and Suffering**

Text: **Romans 8:28-39**

Aim: To be assured of one great truth: God works all things out for good; He does it for those who truly love Him

Memory Verse:
> "And we know that all things work together for good to them that love God, to them who are the called according to his purpose" (Romans 8:28).

INTRODUCTION:

You might remember the tender words from this chorus:
> God is so good
> God is so good
> God is so good
> He's so good to me

Do you believe in your mind that God is good? Do you believe in your heart, in the deepest recesses of your emotions, that God is good to *YOU*? There are many believers who feel that God is good...

- to those who do good works
- to those of a certain race or nation
- to those who are from a certain economic class
- to those who are from a certain church or denomination
- to those who go to church all the time
- to those who know how to pray with big words
- to anyone but themselves

But what does the Bible have to say about God's goodness? Why is God good to people? It is not because people are good. It is not because people belong to a certain race or nation. It is not because a man is rich or poor. It is not because someone gets an award for perfect church attendance. It is not because someone speaks with great eloquence when he prays. And God is not good to everyone but you. The Bible teaches that God is good to those who are His own children, to those who belong to Him.

What a tremendous blessing for the believer. We can know with absolute assurance that no matter what happens, God will work things out for good and will bring good into our lives. It is crucial that the believer have this knowledge and understanding down deep in his heart, for it will sustain him during the difficult days of life: *God is good. God is so good to me.*

The glorious message of Romans is that God assures deliverance (freedom) from struggling and suffering—through Christ. This is the whole point of all that has been written before. Man desperately struggles against the pressures and forces both within himself and alien to himself. He struggles against the weight and discouragement of trials; against the pollution and corruption of life; against the relentless accusations and bombardments of conscience and law; against the pain and decay of his body; against the striking fear and hopelessness of an eternal judgment hereafter. He struggles against the unknown and against pain, hurt, sorrow, loneliness, alienation, aging, death, and hell (cp. Gal.5:17). And somehow, through his suffering and struggle throughout life, he feels that his suffering and struggling are *due to a wrong relationship with God.*

Therefore, man views his many problems as *really* being one supreme problem: how to get right with God. He feels sure if he can establish the right relationship with God, God will hereafter help him through his trials and take care of his future.

This is the very message of Romans. Man needs to get right with God, for he is under the condemnation and wrath of God (Ro.1:18-3:20). Man needs a right relationship with God; he needs to be justified, that is, declared righteous by God (Ro.3:21-5:21). Man needs to be freed from the struggle of sin, for sin corrupts and leads to death (Ro.6:1-23). Man needs to be freed from the bondage of law (spiritual legalism); for the law enslaves, accuses, condemns, and strikes hopelessness within the heart (Ro.7:1-25).

"O wretched man that I am! who shall deliver me from the body of this death?" (Ro.7:24).
"I thank God [that] Jesus Christ our Lord" shall free me from struggling and suffering (Ro.7:25ᵃ; cp.Ro.8:1-39).

All of the discussion in Chapter 8 up to this point now moves to a climax. Those who love God and are called by Him will definitely be freed from the bondages and corruptions of this life; they will be ushered into glory. God assures this. Nothing, absolutely nothing, shall prevent God's settled plan and purpose from coming about in the life of the believer. God's settled plan and purpose for the universe shall be consummated. He has determined two supreme things (Ro.8:29):

⇒ Believers shall be conformed to the image of His dear Son (v.29).
⇒ His Son shall have many brothers, among whom He is to be honored as the first (the most preeminent) Person (v.29).

OUTLINE:

1.	Assurance 1:	God works things out for those who love Him (v.28).
2.	Assurance 2:	God has determined to fulfill His purpose for the believer (v.29).
3.	Assurance 3:	God has assured the glorification of the believer—once-for-all (v.30).
4.	Assurance 4:	God has acted for the believer, not against him (v.31-33).
5.	Assurance 5:	Christ does not condemn the believer (v.34).
6.	Assurance 6:	Christ delivers the believer through the severest circumstances (v.35-37).
7.	Assurance 7:	Christ delivers the believer through the most extreme experiences and forces (v.38-39).

1. ASSURANCE 1: GOD WORKS THINGS OUT FOR THOSE WHO LOVE HIM (v.28).

This is the first assurance of deliverance. What a comforting declaration! Scripture actually declares that "all things work together for good" for the believer. Think about it: nothing could assure the believer any more than God's working all things out for his good. Note four things.

1. The words "all things" go well beyond the great events of the world. God does control the events of the world, but He controls much more. He rules over "all things"—all the events and happenings that occur in the life of the believer. He works "all things" out for good in behalf of His dear child.

2. The words "work together" mean to create and eliminate, place and replace, connect and group, interrelate and intermingle, shape and forge, press and stretch, move and operate, control and guide, arrange and influence. The words "work together" are also present action which means that all things *are continually* working together for good. God is in control of the believer's life. Daily, moment by moment, God is arranging and rearranging all things for the believer's good.

3. The word "good" here means for the ultimate good. We cannot see the future; we cannot take a single event and see all the lines and ramifications that run from it. We cannot see all the things that result from one single event, much less see the results of every event. But God does; therefore, God takes all the events of our lives and works them out for our ultimate good.

4. There is, however, a limitation on this glorious promise, a limitation that desperately needs to be noted. God works all things out for good *only* for those who *love God* and are *called* according to His purpose.

a. This fact is graphically seen in the Greek. The clause "to those who love God" is placed first in the sentence: "But we know that for those who love God all things work together for good." Scripture makes sure the point is not missed. God *only* looks after the affairs of the person who loves Him.

APPLICATION:
Think about it for a moment, for it is the only reasonable conclusion. If a man does not love God—does not place his life into the hands of God—how can God take care of Him? If the man turns his back and walks away from God, how can God look after him? God is not going to force His care upon any of us. He is not going to make mechanical robots out of us, forcing us to live at His beck and call. Such is not love; it is only mechanical behavior. What God wants is love that flows from a heart that *chooses* to love Him. The choice is ours: we either turn our lives over to Him in love, or we continue to take our lives into our own hands.

b. Note the words, "called according to his purpose." The believer's deliverance is designed and planned by God. God calls him for the glorious purpose of being saved from the struggles and sufferings of this life.
   ⇒ Note a significant fact. The believer's *position* and *behavior* are both involved in the call of God.
   ⇒ *Positionally*, God chooses the believer by setting him apart through the Holy Spirit and through belief of the truth.

> **"God hath from the beginning chosen you to salvation through sanctification of the Spirit and belief of the truth: whereunto he called you by our gospel, to the obtaining of the glory of our Lord Jesus Christ" (2 Th.2:13-14).**

   ⇒ *Behaviorally*, God calls the believer to a life of purity and holiness.

> **"For God hath not called us unto uncleanness, but unto holiness" (1 Th.4:7).**

The point is this: God delivers the person who is positioned in Christ and who lives a pure and holy life. The person who truly *loves God* and is living a godly life is the person who experiences all things being worked out for his good. It is the godly person who loves God who will be delivered from the struggling and suffering of this corrupt world.

> **"There hath no temptation taken you but such as is common to man: but God is faithful, who will not suffer you to be tempted above that ye are able; but will with the temptation also make a way to escape, that ye may be able to bear it" (1 Cor.10:13).**
> **"Many are the afflictions of the righteous: but the LORD delivereth him out of them all" (Ps.34:19).**

APPLICATION:
Contrast the carnal attitude of Jacob and the spiritual attitude of Paul.
   ⇒ Jacob said, "All these things are against me" (Gen.42:36).
   ⇒ Paul said, "All things work together for good to them that love God" (Ro.8:28).

ILLUSTRATION:
How is it that God can take the bad things that happen to us and somehow, some way, bring good about? No man can do this, but God can and does because He has the whole picture in mind.

Drew was a young child who loved to put puzzles together. One day Drew's father bought a puzzle in a box marked "Map of the United States"—that was all, just the words with no picture. At home, Drew opened the box and excitedly poured out the brightly colored, multi-shaped pieces. But he was stumped. He had no idea where to begin. In his mind, all he saw were a lot of pieces that made absolutely no sense. After several frustrating minutes, Drew said, "Dad, would you help me put this together? There must be something missing." His father got on the floor with him and within a few minutes the puzzle began to take shape. "Dad, how did you do this so quickly? How did you know which pieces went where?"

"Son, you only saw the blank box and all the pieces. I've been fortunate enough to see the whole picture. I knew what our country looked like even before we started this puzzle."

God, too, sees the whole picture. God is the only One who knows what our lives will look like even before we realize that life is a puzzle. It is not our responsibility to figure life out or even to put the pieces together. But we can be assured that God is able to put our lives together in a most wonderful way.

QUESTIONS:
1. Do you really trust God to put all the pieces of your life together and work them out for good? How can you show your trust?
2. Think for a moment. What bad things in your life has God taken and used to bring about good? How has this been a testimony to those who are close to you?
3. What kind of person has God promised to deliver from the struggling and suffering of this world? How can you be sure you are this kind of person?

2. ASSURANCE 2: GOD HAS DETERMINED TO FULFILL HIS PURPOSE FOR THE BELIEVER (v.29).

Note three significant points.
1. This passage is often abused and misused. It is not dealing so much with theology or philosophy but more with the spiritual experience of the Christian believer. If the pure logic of philosophy and theology are applied, then the passage says that God chooses some for heaven and others for a terrible hell. But this is simply not the meaning God intends for the passage. What God wants believers to do is to take heart, for He has assured their salvation.

God knows the suffering that believers go through daily (cp. Ro.8:28-39). God "did foreknow" even before the foundation of the world (v.29). But no matter how great the suffering, no matter how great the opposition, no matter how great the struggle, God is going to complete His purpose for believers. God has "predestinated [believers] to be conformed to the image of His Son," and absolutely nothing can change that. Why? "That Christ might be the firstborn [have the preeminence] among many brethren" (Ro.8:29).

God loves His Son in the most supreme way possible. God has ordained that His Son shall have many brothers (adopted brothers) who will love and serve Him as the firstborn, that is, as the first Person or the most preeminent Person of the universe. God has ordained that Jesus Christ shall hold the highest rank and position: that He be the exalted Head of all creation and the One to whom all men look (cp. Col.1:15, 18). Therefore, God is going to allow nothing to permanently defeat believers. God is going to allow no fallen child of His ever to remain down permanently. God is going to fulfill His purpose in every child of His, and nothing can stop His purpose. Jesus Christ, His

Son, will have a *multitude of brothers and sisters* who worship and serve Him throughout eternity.

2. Believers will be conformed to the image of God's dear Son. The words "conformed to the image" mean both an inward and an outward likeness.

    a. "Conformed" means the very same form or likeness as Christ. Within our nature—our being, our person—we shall be made just like Christ. As He is perfect and eternal—without disease and pain, sin and death—so we shall be perfected just like Him. We shall be transformed into His very likeness.

    b. "Image" means a derived or a given likeness. The image of Christ is not something which believers merit or for which they work; it is not an image that comes from their own nature or character. No man can earn or produce the perfection and eternal life possessed by Christ. The image of Christ, His perfection and life, is a gift of God. To be conformed to the image of God's Son means...

- to become a partaker of the divine nature (2 Pt.1:4)
- to be adopted as a son of God (Eph.1:5)
- to be holy and without blame before Him (Eph.1:4; 4:24)
- to bear the image of the heavenly: which is an incorruptible, immortal body (1 Cor.15:49-54; cp. 1 Cor.15:42-44)
- to have one's body fashioned (conformed) just like His glorious body (Ph.3:21)
- to be changed (transformed) into the same image of the Lord (2 Cor.3:18)
- to be recreated just like Him (1 Jn.3:2-3)

3. Note what it is that assures the believer's deliverance from the suffering and struggling of this world. It is two things.

    a. The foreknowledge of God. The word "foreknow" is used three different ways in Scripture. It means...

- to know something beforehand, ahead of time
- to know something intimately by loving, accepting, and approving it
- to elect, foreordain, and predetermine something

The present passage is interpreted differently by different scholars. Note that the second and third meanings are much the same. When a person is loved and approved, selection or election is involved. The person becomes a very special or select person.

Again, the point to see is not the pure logic of the theological or philosophical argument. This is not God's purpose in this passage. God's purpose is to assure the believer: the believer is going to be conformed to the image of Christ, and nothing can stop the glorious process. God *foreknew* the fact, saw it even before the world was ever founded. He has always loved and approved the believer, electing and ordaining him from the very beginning.

"Known unto God are all his works from the beginning of the world" (Acts 15:18).

    b. The predestination of God. The word *predestination* means to destine or appoint before, to foreordain, to predetermine. The basic Greek word means to *mark off or to set off* the boundaries of something. The idea is a glorious picture of what God is doing for the believer. The boundary is marked and set off for the believer: the boundary of being conformed to the image of God's dear Son. The believer shall be made just like Christ, conformed to His very likeness and image. Nothing can stop God's purpose for the believer. It is predestinated, set, and marked off. The believer may struggle and suffer through the sin and shame of this world; he may even stumble and fall, become discouraged and downhearted. But if he is a genuine child of God, he will not be defeated, not totally. He will soon arise from his fall and begin to follow Christ again. He is predestinated to be a brother of Christ, to worship and serve Christ throughout all eternity. And Christ will not be disappointed. God loves His Son too much to allow Him to be disappointed by losing a single brother. Jesus Christ will have His joy fulfilled; He will see every brother of His face to face, conformed perfectly to His image. He will have the worship and service of every brother chosen to be His by God the Father. The believer's eternal destiny, that of being an adopted brother to the Lord Jesus Christ, is determined. The believer can rest assured of this glorious truth. God has predestinated him to be delivered from the suffering and struggling of this sinful world.

"According as he hath chosen us in him before the foundation of the world, that we should be holy and without blame before him in love: having predestinated us unto the adoption of children by Jesus Christ to himself, according to the good pleasure of his will" (Eph.1:4-5).

QUESTIONS:
1. Where do you think you are right now in the process of being conformed to the likeness of Christ?
   - I'm well on the way with the finish line in sight.
   - I'm breathing heavy but feel good about my pace.
   - I feel like I'm running in circles.
   - I'm sorry. Did you mention a race?
   Are you satisfied with your progress? Could you be doing better?
2. To what purpose has God called you? How faithful have you been to that purpose? Could you be more faithful?
3. How would you explain the term "predestination" to a new believer or an unbeliever? Why is this such an important doctrine for every believer to understand?

3. ASSURANCE 3: GOD HAS ASSURED THE GLORIFICATION OF THE BELIEVER—ONCE-FOR-ALL (v.30).

This is the third assurance of deliverance. It must be remembered throughout this passage that Scripture is talking about the genuine believer. A genuine believer is a person who sincerely believes in Jesus Christ and diligently seeks to please Him by living soberly, righteously, and godly in this present world (Tit.2:11-13). It is the genuine believer whose glorification is predestinated, set and assured forever and ever by God. The true believer can rest in this glorious truth, for God has done three wonderful things for him. God has *called, justified, and glorified him.* Note that all three steps are in the past tense; all three steps are something already accomplished. The believer's glorification has already taken place in the plan and mind of God. God already sees believers glorified; He already sees believers in His presence. It is assured and predestinated—already written down in the annals of heaven, never to be erased.

Again, does this mean that some are destined to hell and some to heaven? No, a thousand times, no! This is not the purpose of this Scripture. God's purpose is to give enormous assurance to the true believer: he shall be delivered from the struggling and suffering of this sinful world. He is going to be freed—if he is a true believer—freed from all the sin and shame, failure and shortcoming, pain and death. He is going to be glorified right along with God's dear Son, the Lord Jesus Christ.

1. God has *called* the true believer. Some time ago the Spirit called and stirred the heart of the true believer to come to Christ. The believer responded to the call. Scripture definitely teaches that the believer had a choice. He could have chosen to respond or not to respond. (Cp. Rev.22:17.) Thank God he responded and came to Christ. Therefore, the call was *effective*; the call worked. The believer did respond to Christ.

> **"Come unto me, all ye that labour and are heavy laden, and I will give you rest" (Mt.11:28).**

2.   God has *justified* the believer. Again, note the past tense. Justification has *already taken place* for the true believer. It is *just as if* he had never sinned.

APPLICATION:
The point is clear. If the believer has been truly *called*, if he has been truly saved, then his deliverance from struggling and suffering is assured. His deliverance is a past fact, and it is set eternally by God. No matter how deeply the believer senses his shortcoming and failure, his struggle with the sin and suffering of this world, he is a child of God. Every time he comes short or stumbles and falls, he needs to get up and begin all over again. He must not become discouraged and defeated, self-accusing and incriminating, feeling unworthy and undeserving, unwanted and rejected. Such a state of mind is one of the most useful strategies of the devil—a strategy which he uses to defeat believers by the multitudes. God *has called* the believer, so he must arise and begin to diligently follow Christ once again. Every believer who is walking about defeated—no matter how great his fall—should arise right now and turn back to Christ. This is our call, our duty.

> **"And such were some of you: but ye are washed, but ye are sanctified, but ye are justified in the name of the Lord Jesus, and by the Spirit of our God" (1 Cor.6:11).**

Paul the apostle, who was a converted murderer, is a dynamic example of this victorious attitude, the very attitude needed so desperately by all believers.

> **"Brethren, I count not myself to have apprehended: but this one thing I do, forgetting those things which are behind, and reaching forth unto those things which are before, I press toward the mark for the prize of the high calling of God in Christ Jesus" (Ph.3:13-14; cp. Job 17:9; Ps.84:7; Pr.4:18; Heb.12:4).**

3.   God has *glorified* the believer. This, too, is past tense: the glorification of the believer is an accomplished fact, a fact that has already taken place in God's mind and plan. God already sees and counts the believer as *glorified* in His presence for eternity.

> **"For I reckon that the sufferings of this present time are not worthy to be compared with the glory which <u>shall be</u> revealed in us" (Ro.8:18).**
> **"For our light affliction, which is but for a moment, worketh for us a far more exceeding and eternal weight of glory" (2 Cor.4:17).**

QUESTIONS:
1. Do you believe every believer is called by God? If so, what role do you or did you play in responding to God's call of salvation?
2. As a believer, your justification has already taken place. Does this mean you can now do whatever you want to do with no consequences? Why or why not?

4. ASSURANCE 4: GOD HAS ACTED FOR THE BELIEVER NOT AGAINST HIM (v.31-33).

This is the fourth assurance of deliverance. This is the greatest truth in all the world. God did not have to act for man, but He did. God loves every man, no matter his condition or sin and shame. Therefore, believers can rest assured that nothing, absolutely nothing, shall ever separate them from the plan and purpose of God. God's love is absolute. It is perfect. And God shall have His perfect love expressed by completing His perfect plan and purpose for each life. The believer can have absolute assurance that God will work all things out for his good, even things that fail and are painful to the heart. God shall deliver the believer from the struggling and suffering of this world. The true believer shall be conformed to the image of Christ and glorified with Him (v.29-30).

The point is this: God Himself is the believer's assurance. God Himself has acted for the believer; He has done everything necessary and then more: "If God be for us, who can be against us?"

1. *God is our Savior.* It was God who "spared not His own Son, but delivered Him up for us all" (v.32). The words "spared not" mean that God did not hold back or refrain from giving up His Son; He did not refuse or even hesitate to give up His Son. The picture is that of God's weighing man's eternal separation from Him against the sacrifice of His Son. He had a choice to make, and He made it; He deliberately chose to sacrifice His Son for us. God knew exactly what He was doing. He wanted man delivered from this struggling and suffering world, and there was only one way for man to be saved:

⇒ Someone had to bear man's penalty for transgression and sin; the penalty was the judgment of death.

Therefore, God handed His own Son over to die *for* us—in our behalf, in our stead, in our place, as our substitute. God *spared not* His own Son; He delivered Christ Jesus up for us all. What a glorious, marvelous, wonderful love! And just how wonderful His love is can be clearly seen in this: it was while we were sinners, acting and rebelling against God, that He gave His Son to die for us.

> **"But God <u>commendeth</u> his love toward us, in that, while we were yet sinners, Christ died for us" (Ro.5:8).**
>
> **"For when we were yet without strength, in due time Christ died <u>for the ungodly</u>" (Ro.5:6).**

2. *God is our Provider.* Since God has done such a great and glorious thing, "how shall He not also give us all things?" Giving His own Son for us was the greatest gift in all the world; therefore, He is bound to give us everything else. Nothing could ever cost God anything close to the price He has paid in giving up His Son; therefore, God shall give us everything else. Note three points.

a. God's provision includes spiritual, eternal, and material gifts.
⇒ The spiritual provision is the fruit of the Spirit.

> **"But the fruit of the Spirit is love, joy, peace, longsuffering, gentleness, goodness, faith, meekness, temperance: against such there is no law" (Gal.5:22-23).**

⇒ The eternal provision is deliverance from the struggling and suffering of this sinful world. It is the gift of eternal life, of living gloriously conformed to the image of His dear Son, Jesus Christ.

> **"That in the ages to come he might show the exceeding riches of his grace in his kindness toward us through Christ Jesus" (Eph.2:7).**

⇒ The material gifts are the necessities of life.

> **"Therefore take no thought, saying, What shall we eat? or, What shall we drink? or, Wherewithal shall we be clothed?...But seek ye first the kingdom of God, and his**

righteousness; and all these things shall be added unto you"
(Mt.6:31, 33).

b. The provision is *freely* given. God's gift of His Son was freely given; therefore, all that God provides for man is freely given. No man can merit or earn
God's provision. God provides and meets the need of the believer because He
loves the believer.

"For by grace are ye saved through faith; and that not of
yourselves: it is the gift of God: not of works, lest any man
should boast" (Eph.2:8-9).

c. The provision of God comes through Christ and through Him alone. Note the
words "with Him." It is *with Christ* that God gives us all things. If we are *with
Christ*, then all things are given to us. We shall be delivered from struggling
and suffering. Believers can rest assured of this. No matter how much we
struggle and suffer through the sin and shame of this world, God will see us
through it all. He is going to conform us to the glorious image of His Son.

"Jesus answered and said unto her, If thou knewest the
gift of God, and who it is that saith to thee, Give me to drink;
thou wouldest have asked of him, and he would have given
thee living water" (Jn.4:10).

3. *God is our Justifier*. This is the most glorious truth: God does not charge us
with sin. In fact, He does not *lay anything* to our charge; He justifies. Remember: it is
just as if we had never sinned.
Note the question: Who shall lay anything to the charge of God's elect? It is God;
only God can charge us with sin and shame. But note: if we have truly trusted Jesus
Christ as our Savior, if we are God's elect, He does not charge us with sin. He justifies
us. He forgives our sin and counts us righteous in Christ Jesus. If we are God's children, no one can charge us with anything; no one can doom us to be...

- a failure
- a detriment
- a shame
- an embarrassment

- hopeless
- helpless
- defeated
- lost

- unusable
- unworthy
- of no value

Man is not our judge; therefore, man cannot judge these things to be true of us—only
God can. God is our Judge, and this is the glorious truth: God does not judge His elect.
He does not lay sin and shame against His children; He justifies His children. No matter how much we have struggled and suffered through the sin and shame of this world,
God delivers us. No matter how far we have fallen, no matter how discouraged we
have become, if we are truly God's children, He picks us up and justifies us in Christ
Jesus, continuing to conform us to the image of His dear Son. God does not leave us
down and defeated, nor does He go around charging us with sin and shame. God justifies us and continues His work of forgiveness and grace in our lives.

"Know ye not that the unrighteous shall not inherit the kingdom of God? be not deceived: neither fornicators, nor idolaters,
nor adulterers, nor effeminate, nor abusers of themselves with
mankind, nor thieves, nor covetous, nor drunkards, nor revilers,
nor extortioners, shall inherit the kingdom of God. And such were
some of you: but ye are washed, but ye are sanctified, but ye are
justified in the name of the Lord Jesus, and by the Spirit of our
God" (1 Cor.6:9-11).

QUESTIONS:

1. Could God have given any better proof of His love for you than to sacrifice His own Son? Put yourself in a position of having to make a great sacrifice. Could you give up the one being you love more than anything or anyone in the world? Does this make you better appreciate God's sacrifice?
2. God is our Provider. Why, then, do so many men refuse to acknowledge and accept His provision of spiritual, eternal, and material gifts? How can you be sure you are receiving all that God has to offer?
3. Why is it better for God, rather than your fellow man, to be your judge ?

5. ASSURANCE 5: CHRIST DOES NOT CONDEMN THE BELIEVER (v.34).

This is the fifth assurance of deliverance. Note how direct and forceful the question is: "Who is he that condemneth?" It is Christ; only Christ can condemn us for our sin and shame. But the glorious news is that Christ does not condemn us. On the contrary, the very opposite is true. Christ does four wonderful things for us.

1. *Christ has died for us.* Christ is our glorious Savior. We deserve to be condemned by God and put to death for sin. Our sins are a shame, for sin is rebellion against God. But we do not have to face condemnation. Christ has already paid the penalty for sin. Christ has already been condemned and executed for our transgression against God. This is the glorious love of Christ. He has already died *for us*: in our place, in our stead, as our substitute. Therefore when we sincerely come to Christ, He does not condemn us; He loves us and forgives our sin and shame. This is the very purpose of His death—to free us from sin, from its penalty and condemnation.

> **"Who his own self bare our sins in his own body on the tree, that we, being dead to sins, should live unto righteousness: by whose stripes ye were healed" (1 Pt.2:24).**

2. *Christ has risen from the dead for us.* Christ is our risen Lord. His resurrection does two marvelous things for the believer.
   a. The resurrection of the Lord proves that God was perfectly *satisfied* with the death of Jesus Christ. What Christ did—His dying for our sins—was *acceptable* to God; therefore, God has *accepted* Jesus' death *for us*.

   > **"And declared to be the Son of God with power, according to the spirit of holiness, by the resurrection from the dead" (Ro.1:4).**

   b. The resurrection of the Lord gives the believer a new life, making the believer a *new creature* and a *new man*.

   > **"Therefore we are buried with him by baptism into death: that like as Christ was raised up from the dead by the glory of the Father, even so we also should walk in <u>newness of life</u>" (Ro.6:4).**

3. *Christ has been exalted for us.* He is our exalted Lord. He sits face to face with God at His right hand. This gives two assurances to the believer.
   a. The believer shall also be exalted into the presence of God. Just as Christ lives face to face with God, the believer shall also live face to face with God throughout all eternity.

   > **"Now if we be dead with Christ, we believe that we shall also live with him: knowing that Christ being raised from the dead dieth no more; death hath no more dominion over him.**

For in that he died, he died unto sin once: but in that he liveth, he liveth unto God" (Ro.6:8-10).

b. The Lord Jesus Christ is exalted as the Sovereign and majestic Lord of the universe. He is the Ruler who reigns and rules over all, who possesses all might and power, who is full of all wisdom and truth. He is the One who is going to destroy and utterly eliminate sin and evil in the world. He is the One who is going to establish a kingdom of righteousness and justice, love and truth in the new heavens and earth.

> "Which he wrought in Christ, when he raised him from the dead, and set him at his own right hand in the heavenly places, far above all principality, and power, and might, and dominion, and every name that is named, not only in this world, but also in that which is to come" (Eph.1:20-21).

Note: it is Jesus Christ (and not another) who rules and reigns over the universe. This stirs enormous assurance in the hearts of genuine believers. Why? Because Jesus Christ has demonstrated His glorious love and care for the world. He not only can, but He will look after us and work all things out for good until He returns (v.28). The *control of evil* in the world and our lives is under His care. He is working all things out for good to those of us who truly love Him and are called according to His purpose (v.28).

> "But even the very hairs of your head are all numbered. Fear not therefore: ye are of more value than many sparrows" (Lk.12:7).

4. *Christ makes intercession for us* before the throne of God. He is our great Intercessor, our Mediator and Advocate who stands between God and man. It is Christ Jesus who brings us to God and who makes redemption, the forgiveness of our sins, possible (Eph.1:7).

⇒ It is His advocacy, the advocacy of His death and resurrection for us, that forgives our sins.

> "My little children, these things write I unto you, that ye sin not. And if any man sin, we have an advocate with the Father, Jesus Christ the righteous: and he is the propitiation for our sins: and not for ours only, but also for the sins of the whole world" (1 Jn.2:1-2).

⇒ It is His intercession, the intercession of His death and resurrection for us, that saves us.

> "Who was delivered for our offences, and was raised again for our justification" (Ro.4:25).

⇒ It is His presence in heaven and His plea, the *plea* of His death and resurrection *for us*, that opens the door of heaven to us.

> "For Christ is not entered into the holy places made with hands, which are the figures of the true; but into heaven itself, now to appear in the presence of God for us" (Heb.9:24).

The point is this. The believer has the greatest assurance imaginable: he shall be delivered from the struggling and suffering of this world. No matter the sin and shame of his life, if he truly comes to Christ, he is not condemned. He is not judged for sin, no matter how terrible or how far he has fallen. If he will only come to Christ, Christ will deliver him. Christ will not leave him down and discouraged and defeated. Christ will not even scold or reproach him. Christ will receive His dear child with open arms.

"In whom we have redemption through his blood, the forgiveness of sins, according to the riches of his grace" (Eph.1:7).

QUESTIONS:
1. Have you ever willingly taken the blame for something you did not do? Why did you do it? This is what Christ did for you. How can you thank Him for His great sacrifice?
2. Jesus Christ makes intercession for you before the throne of God. What does this mean? What kind of assurance should this give you when you are suffering? Do you think Christ can ever pray a prayer for you that your Heavenly Father will not answer? Why or why not?

6. ASSURANCE 6: CHRIST DELIVERS THE BELIEVER THROUGH THE SEVEREST CIRCUMSTANCES (v.35-37).

This is the sixth assurance of deliverance, and it is the most wonderful assurance imaginable. "Who [or what] can separate us from the love of God?" Too many people, even believers, feel that God does not love them, that He just could not love them. They feel unworthy of His love, for they come too short, are too disobedient, and fail too often. How could God possibly love them when they go against His will so much? The results of such feelings are...

- a sense of unworthiness
- a downing of oneself
- a sense of discouragement
- an accusing of oneself
- a low self-esteem
- a defeated life

Note a crucial point: such feelings totally contradict Scripture. Look at the verse: "Who [or what] can separate us from the love of Christ?" There is no circumstance, no situation, no event that can cause Christ to turn away from us. No matter how terrible or severe the situation, it cannot separate the true believer from the love of Christ. Christ loves the believer regardless of the circumstance, and He longs to be reconciled to the believer. No more severe circumstance can be imagined than the ones given:

⇒ *Tribulation*: to undergo struggles, trials, temptation, suffering, or affliction.
⇒ *Distress*: to suffer anguish, trouble, strain, agony; not knowing which way to turn or what to do.
⇒ *Persecution*: to be abused, mocked, ridiculed, shamed, mistreated, ignored, neglected, harassed, attacked, or injured.
⇒ *Famine*: to have no food, to be starving and to have no way to secure food.
⇒ *Nakedness*: to be stripped of all clothes and earthly comforts; to be bare, having all earthly possessions taken away.
⇒ *Peril*: to be exposed to the most severe risks; to be confronted with the most terrible dangers to one's body, mind, soul, property, family, and loved ones.
⇒ *Sword*: to be killed; to suffer martyrdom.

Just imagine a person's experiencing all this. What would his thoughts be? Would he feel that he had been forsaken by God? In the midst of so much dark trouble, would he believe that God loved him?

Scripture declares loudly and clearly that God does love him. There is absolutely nothing—no matter how dark and depressing, no matter how severe—that can separate the believer from the love of Christ. Circumstances are not evidence that God does not love us. God loves us no matter what the circumstances may be.

But believers must always remember: they are going to suffer while they are in this world. In fact, the world is going to count them as sheep for the slaughter, rejecting and persecuting them (Ps.44:22). The world is going to persecute believers as long as believers continue to live for Christ. Their lives of godliness convict the world, and the world rejects godliness.

However, note what is said. No matter the circumstances, we are more than conquerors through Christ who has loved us (v.37). No matter the circumstances and their severity, Christ will carry us through all, strengthening and encouraging us. We cannot lose, no matter the severity of the situation. Christ loves us and is going to look after and take care of us. The believer can rest assured; Christ protects him from the severest circumstances:

⇒ Christ meets all the material necessities of life.

"**Therefore, take no thought, saying, What shall we eat? or, What shall we drink? or, Wherewithal shall we be clothed?...But seek ye first the kingdom of God, and his righteousness; and all these things shall be added unto you**" (Mt.6:31, 33).

⇒ Christ gives us rest.

"**Come unto me, all ye that labour and are heavy laden, and I will give you rest**" (Mt.11:28).

⇒ Christ gives us peace.

"**Peace I leave with you, my peace I give unto you: not as the world giveth, give I unto you. Let not your heart be troubled, neither let it be afraid**" (Jn.14:27).

⇒ Christ provides an escape from temptation.

"**There hath no temptation taken you but such as is common to man: but God is faithful, who will not suffer you to be tempted above that ye are able; but will with the temptation also make a way to escape, that ye may be able to bear it**" (1 Cor.10:13).

⇒ Christ comforts us through all trials.

"**Blessed be God, even the Father of our Lord Jesus Christ, the Father of mercies, and the God of all comfort; who comforteth us in all our tribulation, that we may be able to comfort them which are in any trouble, by the comfort wherewith we ourselves are comforted of God**" (2 Cor.1:3-4).

⇒ Christ supplies all our needs.

"**I can do all things through Christ which strengtheneth me**" (Ph.4:13).

⇒ Christ delivers us through persecution.

"**For consider him that endured such contradiction of sinners against himself, lest ye be wearied and faint in your minds**" (Heb.12:3).

⇒ Christ delivers us into His very presence, giving us eternal life if we are martyred.

"**And the Lord shall deliver me from every evil work, and will preserve me [transport, take me] unto his heavenly kingdom: to whom be glory for ever and ever**" (2 Tim.4:18).

⇒ Christ cares for us no matter the situation.

"Casting all your care upon him; for he careth for you"
(1 Pt.5:7).

Christ enables us to overcome the world.

"For whatsoever is born of God overcometh the world: and
this is the victory that overcometh the world, even our faith"
(1 Jn.5:4).

⇒ Christ shows Himself strong in our behalf.

"For the eyes of the LORD run to and fro throughout the
whole earth, to show himself strong in the behalf of them whose
heart is perfect toward him" (2 Chron.16:9).

⇒ Christ delivers us from fear.

"Fear thou not; For I am with thee: be not dismayed; for I
am thy God: I will strengthen thee; yea, I will help thee; yea, I
will uphold thee with the right hand of my righteousness"
(Is.41:10).

⇒ Christ sustains and supports the aged believer.

"And even to your old age I am he; and even to hoar [gray]
hairs will I carry you: I have made, and I will bear; even I will
carry, and will deliver you" (Is.46:4).

QUESTIONS:
1. As a true believer, can you do anything or go through anything that would cause Christ to reject or turn away from you?
2. We often are tempted to equate our trials with being punished by God. This is just not true. God loves His people. When have you felt as if God were punishing you by allowing suffering into your life? What has Christ promised to do for you when the circumstances become overwhelming?
3. What is the most difficult thing you have ever had to endure? How did Christ work in your life to assure you of His faithfulness?

7. CHRIST DELIVERS THE BELIEVER THROUGH THE MOST EXTREME EXPERIENCES AND FORCES (v.38-39).

This is the seventh assurance of deliverance. There is nothing in the universe that can separate the believer from the love of God which is in Christ Jesus our Lord. The believer can be fully persuaded of this glorious fact. Just consider the experiences and forces mentioned by Scripture:

⇒ Not death: confronting death and leaving this world cannot separate us from Christ and His love (Jn.5:24).
⇒ Not life: no trial or pleasure or comfort of life, not any person nor any thing in this life can separate us from Christ and His love.
⇒ Not angels, principalities, or powers: no heavenly or spiritual creature, no being from any other dimension can separate us from Christ and His love.
⇒ Not anything present or anything to come: neither present events, beings, or things, nor future events, beings, or things can cut us off from Christ and His love.
⇒ Not height or depth: nothing from outer space nor from the depths of the earth can separate us from Christ and His love.

Note the *grand finale*: if there be any creature other than the ones named, that creature cannot separate us from "the love of God, which is in Christ Jesus our Lord."

> **"The LORD thy God in the midst of thee is mighty; he will save, he will rejoice over thee with joy; he will <u>rest in his love</u>, he will joy over thee with singing" (Zeph.3:17).**
>
> **"For God so loved the world, that he gave his only begotten Son, that whosoever believeth in him should not perish, but have everlasting life" (Jn.3:16).**

ILLUSTRATION:

It is important for every believer to remember that no matter what comes his way, God is in control of the situation; God is still going to take care of us.

> *"The story has been told of a believer, Frederick Nolan, who was fleeing from his enemies during a time of persecution in North Africa. Pursued by them over hill and valley with no place to hide, he fell exhausted into a wayside cave, expecting his enemies to find him soon.*
>
> *"Awaiting his death, he saw a spider weaving a web. Within minutes, the little bug had woven a beautiful web across the mouth of the cave. The pursuers arrived and wondered if Nolan was hiding there, but on seeing the unbroken and unmangled piece of art, thought it impossible for him to have entered the cave without dismantling the web. And so they went on. Having escaped, Nolan burst out and exclaimed:*
>
> *"'Where God is, a spider's web is like a wall,*
>
> *"'Where God is not, a wall is like a spider's web.'"*[1]

There is no need to wonder *how* God will take care of you; just be assured that He *will*.

QUESTIONS:

1. God has placed you firmly in His hand. But do you sometimes feel as if you are falling out of control? How can you overcome this fear?
2. A familiar saying is this: God will not allow anything to come into your life without first passing through His hand of love and care. What is the worst thing that could happen to you? What has God promised you, even in your worst circumstance?

SUMMARY:

God is good, and if you are His child, He is good to you. In a world full of suffering and agony, God has given you, the believer, great assurance that He has *everything* under control. How has He done this?

Assurance 1:	God works things out for those who love Him.
Assurance 2:	God has determined to fulfill His purpose for the believer.
Assurance 3:	God has assured the glorification of the believer—once-for-all.
Assurance 4:	God has acted for the believer not against him.
Assurance 5:	Christ does not condemn the believer.
Assurance 6:	Christ delivers the believer through the severest circumstances.
Assurance 7:	Christ delivers the believer through the most extreme experiences and forces.

---

[1] Michael P. Green. *Illustrations for Biblical Preaching*, p.295.

PERSONAL JOURNAL NOTES:
(Reflection & Response)

1. The most important thing that I learned from this lesson was:

2. The thing that I need to work on the most is:

3. I can apply this lesson to my life by:

4. Closing Prayer of Commitment: (put your commitment down on paper).

	CHAPTER 9 VII. ISRAEL & THE GOSPEL OF RIGHTEOUS-NESS, 9:1-11:36 A. The Privileges of Israel & Their Tragic Failure, 9:1-5 I say the truth in Christ, I lie not, my conscience also bearing me witness in the Holy Ghost, 2 That I have great heaviness and continual sorrow in my	heart. 3 For I could wish that myself were accursed from Christ for my brethren, my kinsmen according to the flesh: 4 Who are Israelites; to whom pertaineth the adoption, and the glory, and the covenants, and the giving of the law, and the service of God, and the promises; 5 Whose are the fathers, and of whom as concerning the flesh Christ came, who is over all, God blessed for ever. Amen.	c. The unbelievable willingness of a man to be sacrificed for his people 2. A man's great respect for his people a. Were Israelites b. Had the adoption c. Had the glory d. Had the covenants e. Had the law f. Had the true worship g. Had the promises h. Had the fathers i. Had the Messiah
1. A man's great love for his people a. The plea of a distressed man to be trusted b. The heart of a distressed man			

(Note: Because of the length of this outline and commentary, you may wish to split this passage into two studies.)

Section VII
ISRAEL AND THE GOSPEL OF RIGHTEOUSNESS
Romans 9:1-11:36

Study 1:   **The Privileges of Israel and Their Tragic Failure**

Text: **Romans 9:1-5**

Aim: To sense a heavy burden for the lost, especially for those whom you love the most (family and friends).

Memory Verse:
   "For I could wish that myself were accursed from Christ for my brethren, my kinsmen according to the flesh" (Romans 9:3).

SECTION OVERVIEW: (9:1-11:36)

The change from Chapter 8, from deliverance and redemption, is abrupt and striking. Chapters 9-11 have to do with the place of the Jews in world history. The church faces this bewildering problem because the Jews were God's chosen people with a unique and special place in God's purposes. However, when God sent His Son into the world, the Jews rejected Him. How can this tragic and terrible paradox be explained? Why would God's people choose to reject and crucify God's very own Son? This is the problem Paul begins to deal with in the next three chapters. Two things need to be noted throughout this section.

First, the Jews were the special chosen people of God. Paul never questioned this. The Jews had a very special place in God's plan for the salvation of man down through human history.

Second, the real chosen people, the real Israel, always lay in a righteous remnant (a small group of believers who genuinely kept the faith, who really believed in the coming Messiah or Savior), not in the whole nation (cp. Ro.9:25-27).

ROMANS 9:1-5

INTRODUCTION:
When everything is on the line, and the difference between success and failure rests on you, can your...
- family and close friends depend on you?
- fellow believers depend on you?
- co-workers depend on you?
- teammates depend on you?

One of the most striking stories that came out of the 1996 Summer Olympic Games was when Kerri Strug, a young American gymnast, helped her team win the gold medal. With the competition on the line, she attempted her first vault and suffered a serious ankle injury. Knowing that her ankle was injured did not keep her from continuing on with the competition. Instead, she bravely ran down the ramp a second time and performed an almost perfect vault. After landing on her injured ankle, she maintained her composure long enough to satisfy the judges. Then, she collapsed in pain.

Sometimes in order for others to win, it requires a personal sacrifice on our part. But society teaches us to look out for "#1." In so doing we might feel good, but we often neglect the needs of others. It is even easy for a Christian believer to be comfortable and complacent in his or her own salvation, sensing no burden, no willingness to sacrifice for the lost. But in this life, there is a whole lot more at stake than a gold, silver, or bronze medal. At stake is a crown, the very crown of life. Are you willing to sacrifice, to help the lost receive their crown?

Paul bears his heart in this passage, revealing a deep evangelistic fervor for his people, the Jews. It is a rare glimpse of the burning compassion that every servant of God should possess for his own loved ones and kinsmen.

OUTLINE:
1. A man's great love for his people (v.1-3).
2. A man's great respect for his people (v.4-5).

1. A MAN'S GREAT LOVE FOR HIS PEOPLE (v.1-3).

This is the picture of a man's great love and concern for his people, a love and concern for their salvation.

1. Paul pleads for his people to trust him. The Jews had called Paul a false prophet and a liar. Why? Because he was now proclaiming God's love and salvation for *all* men instead of just for the Jews. Man no longer had to become a proselyte of Jewish religion in order to know God (cp. Ro.10:12-13). To the traditional Jew, Paul was a heretic. He was a man who was to be utterly distrusted. They hated and despised him, wanting to kill him and do away with his message.

2. Note how distressed Paul's heart is. Despite the rejection and ill treatment from the Jews, Paul still loved his kinsmen, and he sensed a deep urgency for them to grasp the truth. Their salvation was of such concern that he swore his concern by three things: Christ, his conscience, and the Holy Spirit. Paul was forcibly saying, "I am not lying...
- "I say the truth *in Christ*...
- "*my conscience* also bears me witness...
- "my conscience bears witness in the *Holy Spirit*...

"I do have a great concern and love for my kinsmen. But my concern is not that their sinful ways be approved, but that they come to know the truth; for without the truth, they will be lost and doomed."

Just how deeply Paul's heart was distressed over his kinsmen is clearly seen in the description of his heart.

⇒ "I have great heaviness": pain, grief, mourning.

⇒ "I have...continual sorrow": intense pain, anguish, torment. And note: it is continuous and unceasing. Paul was always bearing pain for the salvation of his kinsmen. The depth of Paul's love and concern is graphically seen in what he said.

3. Paul is the picture of a man who had an unbelievable willingness to be sacrificed for his people. He was willing to be accursed, that is, separated from Christ, if it would save his people. He was willing to swap his salvation for their doom if it would lead to their salvation. Paul felt the deepest emotion, love, and concern for his people.

Note: the words of Paul must not be stretched too far. Paul was speaking from an evangelistic fervor not from a theological view. He was immersed in emotion, just as so many of God's people become over loved ones who are lost. Many have been so immersed in emotion that they have offered to swap their salvation for a loved one. Sometimes the Spirit of God works in the hearts of God's people to strain and suffer through intense prayer for the salvation of lost souls, and sometimes the strain and intensity of prayer is so deep that a believer could wish one extreme (his own salvation) for the other extreme (the salvation of loved ones).

APPLICATION:

The point is forceful: God's people should be willing to suffer the ultimate pain for the salvation of souls.

"Hereby perceive we the love of God, because he laid down his life for us: and we ought to lay down our lives for the brethren" (1 Jn.3:16).

ILLUSTRATION:

Do you really believe that unsaved men, women, boys, and girls will go to hell if they die without Christ? In the busyness of our lives, there is a great temptation to "get used to the idea" of people's dying and going to hell. But it is up to the believer to do everything in his power to provide a bridge to the lost—even if it costs something. Dr. James Kennedy reminds us of a time where a father gave up his son in order that others might live.

"Back in the days of the Great Depression a Missouri man named John Griffith was the controller of a great railroad drawbridge across the Mississippi River. One day in the summer of 1937 he decided to take his eight-year-old son, Greg, with him to work. At noon, John Griffith put the bridge up to allow ships to pass and sat on the observation deck with his son to eat lunch. Time passed by quickly. Suddenly he was startled by the shrieking of a train whistle in the distance. He quickly looked at his watch and noticed it was 1:07—the Memphis Express, with four hundred passengers on board, was roaring toward the raised bridge! He leaped from the observation deck and ran back to the control tower. Just before throwing the master lever he glanced down for any ships below. There a sight caught his eye that caused his heart to leap poundingly into his throat. Greg had slipped from the observation deck and had fallen into the massive gears that operate the bridge. His left leg was caught in the cogs of the two main gears! Desperately John's mind whirled to devise a rescue plan. But as soon as he thought of a possibility he knew there was no way it could be done.

"Again, with alarming closeness, the train whistle shrieked in the air. He could hear the clicking of the locomotive wheels over the tracks. That was his son down there—yet there were four hundred passengers on the train. John knew what he had to do, so he buried his head in his left arm and pushed the master switch forward. That great massive bridge lowered into place just as the Memphis Express began to roar across the river. When John Griffith lifted *his head with his face smeared with tears, he looked into the passing windows of the train. There were businessmen casually reading their afternoon papers, finely dressed ladies in the dining car sipping coffee, and children pushing long spoons into their dishes of ice cream. No one looked at the control house, and no one looked at the great gear box. With wrenching agony, John Griffith cried out at the steel train: 'I sacrificed my son for you people! Don't you care?' The train rushed by, but nobody heard the father's words, which recalled Lamentations 1:12: 'Is it nothing to you, all who pass by?'"*[1]

There are few men who could have done what John Griffith felt he had to do. It would be a fair guess that none of us could have sacrificed our own child for anyone, much less to those who were so indifferent to our great act of love and sacrifice. But God did. Our loving heavenly Father allowed His dear Son to be placed in the throes of sin and death. At the cross is where sin and death met to claim Jesus Christ in order that we might not die but have eternal life. His willing sacrifice provided for us a bridge over certain damnation and eternal separation from God.

QUESTIONS:
1. When is the last time you pleaded with a lost person to accept Christ? How does the possibility of being rejected affect the passion with which you share the gospel?
2. When you share the gospel, how convinced are you about...
   - its power to save the lost?
   - its ability to change the habits of sinners?
   - its real need in today's modern society?
3. What sacrifices would you be willing to make in order to see the lost members of your family come to Christ?

2. A MAN'S GREAT RESPECT FOR HIS PEOPLE (v.3-5).

Paul had just declared his great love for Israel; now he assures them of his respect. He did not deny their place in the plan and purposes of God. He knew they were a greatly privileged people, a people who had been highly favored by God.

The Jews were Israelites. Their very name, Israel, meant *a prince with God* or *one who rules with God* or *one who contends with God*. And their name had been given them from the very founding of their nation. It had come from Jacob, whose name had been changed by God to Israel. The name was later adopted by the descendants of Jacob (Gen.32:28; 34:7; Jn.1:47).

APPLICATION:
In the providence of God, believers have been highly privileged just as Israel was. Believers have been given the name of God's own Son, *Christian*, which means *a follower* or *a disciple of Jesus Christ*. What we must guard against is bringing shame to the Lord's name. Too many profess His name but do not really follow Him.

> **"Not every one that saith unto me, Lord, Lord, shall enter into the kingdom of heaven; but he that doeth the will of my Father which is in heaven" (Mt.7:21).**
> **"This people draweth nigh unto me with their mouth, and honoureth me with their lips; but their heart is far from me" (Mt.15:8; cp. Is.29:13).**

---

[1] Dr. D. James Kennedy. *Is It Nothing to You?* (Coral Ridge Presbyterian Church, Ft. Lauderdale, Florida. March 19, 1978).

QUESTIONS:
1. What obligations does bearing the name "Christian" have upon you?
2. How can you overcome the negative concept so many people have associated with being a Christian?

The Jews had the privilege of being adopted by God. They were chosen in a very special sense to be the children of God.

"You are the children of the Lord your God" (Dt.14:1).
"Israel is my son, even my firstborn" (Ex.4:22).

Note a crucial point: this does not mean that the whole nation of Israel was saved. Not all citizens of Israel *believed* God, and being adopted into God's family has always been by genuine faith. In order to be a true child of God, it has always been necessary for a *person* to believe in God, entrusting his whole being into God's keeping. (Cp. Ro.9:6-8, 27, 29; 2:28-29; 4:13.)

APPLICATION:
The word "adoption" means *to place as a son*. The picture of adoption is a beautiful picture of what God does for the Christian believer. In the ancient world, the family was based on a Roman law called "patria potestas," the father's power. The law gave the father absolute authority over his children so long as the father lived. He could work, enslave, sell, and if he wished, pronounce the death penalty. Regardless of the child's adult age, the father held all power over personal and property rights.

Therefore, adoption was a serious matter. Yet, adoption was a common practice to ensure that a family would not become extinct by having no male children. And when a child was adopted, three legal steps were taken.
1) The adopted son was adopted permanently. He could not be adopted today and disinherited tomorrow. He became a son of the father—forever. He was eternally secure as a son.
2) The adopted son immediately had all the rights of a legitimate son in the new family.
3) The adopted son completely lost all rights in his old family. The adopted son was looked upon as a new person—so new that old debts and obligations connected with his former family were canceled and abolished as if they never existed.

The Bible says several things about the believer's adoption as a son of God.
1. The believer's adoption establishes a new relationship with God—forever. He is eternally secure as a child of God. But the new relationship is established only when a person comes to Christ through faith (Gal.3:26; 4:4-5).
2. The believer's adoption establishes a new relationship with God as father. The believer has all the rights and privileges of a genuine son of God (Ro.8:16-17; 1 Jn.3:1-2).
3. The believer's adoption establishes a new dynamic experience with God as father, a moment-by-moment access into His very presence (Ro.8:14, 16; Gal.4:6).
4. The believer's adoption gives him a very special relationship with other children of God—a family relationship that binds him with others in an unparalleled spiritual union.
5. The believer's adoption makes him a new person. The believer has been taken out from under the authority and power of the world and its sin. The believer is *placed as a son* into the family and authority of God. The old life with all of its debts and obligations is canceled and wiped out (2 Cor.5:17; Gal.3:23-27; 2 Pt.1:4).
6. The believer's adoption is to be fully realized in the future at the return of Jesus Christ (Ro.8:19; Eph.1:14; 1 Th.4:14-17; 1 Jn.3:2).

7. The believer's adoption and its joy will be shared by all creation on a cosmic scale (Ro.8:21). There is to be a new heavens and earth (2 Pt.3:12-14; Rev.21:1-7).

> **"For ye have not received the spirit of bondage again to fear; but ye have received the Spirit of adoption, whereby we cry, Abba, Father" (Ro.8:15).**

QUESTIONS:
1. Have you ever really thought of yourself as being adopted by God? What more could anyone offer you than what God has offered?
2. God has offered you total security as His adopted child. If you are feeling insecure, who or what needs to be changed?
3. Once God has adopted you into His family, what kind of relationship are you to have with His other adopted children? Is this relationship all that it can be right now? What can you do to improve it?

The Jews had the privilege of the glory of God, that is, the Shekinah Glory. The Shekinah Glory was the brilliant light which descended into the midst of God's people when God was visiting His people. It symbolized God's glorious presence and was revealed in the form of a cloud. The cloud of God's glory and presence was revealed in two very special ways.

1. It was the glorious presence of God in the cloud that led Israel through the wilderness wanderings.

> **"And the LORD went before them by day in a pillar of a cloud, to lead them the way; and by night in a pillar of fire, to give them light; to go by day and night" (Ex.13:21).**

2. It was the glorious presence of God in the cloud that filled the tabernacle and came to rest over the ark.

> **"Then a cloud covered the tent of the congregation, and the glory of the LORD filled the tabernacle" (Ex.40:34).**

APPLICATION:
Believers have seen "the glory of God in the face of Jesus Christ" (2 Cor.4:6); believers are the light of the world (Mt.5:14). This means two significant things.
1) It is a terrible thing to possess the light and the glory of God and not to share it with those in darkness.

> **"Let your light so shine before men, that they may see your good works, and glorify your Father which is in heaven" (Mt.5:16).**

2) It is a terrible thing to be in darkness and to see light off in the distance and not follow after it. There is absolutely no excuse for seeing the glory of God and failing to follow it.

> **"While ye have light, believe in the light, that ye may be the children of light" (Jn.12:36).**

QUESTIONS:
1. Can you remember a time when you regretted *not* shedding God's light in a situation? What was the outcome? What could you have done differently?
2. Can you remember a time when you saw the light (the right way) but did not follow it? What was the outcome? What could you have done differently?

The Jews had the privilege of the covenants. A covenant is an agreement made between two parties, a contract drawn up between two or more people, a special relationship set up and established between persons. Note the plural is used: covenant**s**. God made several covenants with Israel. There was...

- the covenant with Noah after the flood (Gen.9:9f)
- the covenant with Abraham (Gen.12:1f; 15:18; 17:4f)
- the covenant of law made at Mount Sinai (Ex.19:5; 24:8; 34:10; Dt.29:1f)
- the covenant with David (2 Sam.7:16)
- the covenant of grace (Heb.8:8-13)

The point to note is the great love of God. He did not reach out for man only once and then leave man to his doom. God reached out to man time and again. God sought man at every opportunity, seeking to establish a relationship with him.

> **"Yea, I have loved thee with an everlasting love: therefore with lovingkindness have I drawn thee" (Jer.31:3).**

QUESTIONS:
1. What covenants has God made with you? Has He ever broken any of them?
2. What covenants have you made with God? Have you ever broken any of them? Do you need to be more sincere when you make a promise to God? To anyone?

The Jews had the privilege of the law. They had not only the Ten Commandments given to Moses on Mount Sinai, but they also had the whole law of God. By law is simply meant *the will of God written down*. Through the centuries, God simply had Moses and His messengers write out His will so that man would always know exactly how to live.

APPLICATION:
One of the great tragedies of human life is for a person to know that something is right and not do it. Yet, this is the daily occurrence of man. It may be a simple matter of consuming something that damages his body or the more serious matter of cursing God's name. No matter what the transgression is, man stands guilty. He is inexcusable, for he has the law of God, and he has had God's law for centuries. Man knows how to live in love and justice. No greater indictment could exist than the charge: "There is none righteous, no, not one" (Ro.3:10; cp. Ro.3:9-18).

> **"And that servant, which knew his lord's will, and prepared not himself, neither did according to his will, shall be beaten with many stripes" (Lk.12:47).**
> **"Cursed be he that doeth the work of the LORD deceitfully [negligently]" (Jer.48:10).**

The Jews had the privilege of true worship and of the true service of God. They had...

- the true temple
- the true ordinances of God
- the true priests, prophets, and messengers of God
- the true approach to God

The Jews had been given every opportunity and privilege to approach God, and even more, to understand and grasp the person of God Himself. The Jews were greatly privileged. While other people stumbled and wandered about in the darkness of false worship, creating *gods* within their own imaginations, the Jews had access to God Himself, access to the only true and living God. They had the opportunity to establish a personal relationship with God.

APPLICATION:

What an indictment! To have the opportunity to know God personally, but to turn one's back and walk away. However, there is an even greater offense than this. How much greater is the offense when a person knows the true approach to God and does not share it.

Believers know the truth; they know the way to God. Therefore, they must share the glorious message of the *only* living and true God. Note two significant facts.

1) Many know the truth; they know the true approach to God, yet they refuse to enter His presence. The tragic fact is this: God does not close the door to them; they shut the door upon themselves.

> **"For the heart of this people is waxed gross, and their ears are dull of hearing, and their eyes have they closed; lest they should see with their eyes, and hear with their ears, and understand with their heart, and should be converted, and I should heal them" (Acts 28:27).**

2) The blood of the lost is upon the hands of the believer. Why? Because the way to God and the means to proclaim the message to the world has existed for some time. Yet, we have failed to go into the world and share the life-saving news. There is no one to blame but us. Note the severe warning of God to His people:

> **"But if the watchman see the sword come, and blow not the trumpet, and the people be not warned; if the sword come, and take any person from among them, he is taken away in his iniquity; but his blood will I require at the watchman's hand. So thou, O son of man, I have set thee a watchman unto the house of Israel; therefore thou shalt hear the word at my mouth, and warn them from me. When I say unto the wicked, O wicked man, thou shalt surely die; if thou dost not speak to warn the wicked from his way, that wicked man shall die in his iniquity; but his blood will I require at thine hand" (Ezk.33:6-8).**

The only way for us to be freed from the judgment is to share the message of God and warn men.

QUESTIONS:

1. How many days go by without your showing a lost person the way to God?
2. Can God really hold you accountable for a person's not hearing about Him? Why? What more can God say to make you take His charge more seriously?

The Jews had the promises of God. God had shared with them all of His blessings and He had given them the hope for which a man's soul craves. He had shared with them the plan and destiny for which He had created man. When man sinned and turned away from God, it was to the Jews whom God gave...

- the promise of the Savior (See Lk.3:24-31; Jn.1:45 for most of the prophecies concerning the first coming of Jesus Christ.)
- the promise of the world as an inheritance (cp. Acts 13:23, 32-33)
- all the glorious promises stretching from Genesis to Revelation

APPLICATION:

Three things are essential when dealing with the promises of God, three things which so many within Israel failed to do.

1) We must not stagger at the promises of God.

> **"He staggered not at the promise of God through unbelief; but was strong in faith, giving glory to God" (Ro.4:20).**
> **"But without faith it is impossible to please him: for he that cometh to God must believe that he is, and that he is a rewarder of them that diligently seek him" (Heb.11:6).**

2) We must fear lest we come short of His promises.

> **"Let us therefore fear, lest, a promise being left us of entering into his rest, any of you should seem to come short of it" (Heb.4:1).**

3) We must steadfastly look for the promise of the new heavens and earth.

> **"Knowing this first, that there shall come in the last days scoffers, walking after their own lusts, and saying, Where is <u>the promise of His coming</u>? for since the fathers fell asleep, <u>all things continue</u> as they were from the beginning of the creation....But the day of the Lord will come as a thief in the night; in the which the heavens shall pass away with a great noise, and the elements shall melt with fervent heat, the earth also and the works that are therein shall be burned up. Seeing then that all these things shall be dissolved, what manner of persons ought ye to be in all holy conversation and godliness, looking for and hasting unto the coming of the day of God, wherein the heavens being on fire shall be dissolved, and the elements shall melt with fervent heat? Nevertheless, we, <u>according to his promise</u>, look for new heavens and a new earth, wherein dwelleth righteousness" (2 Pt.3:3-4, 10-13).**

ILLUSTRATION:

Living the Christian life is fairly easy if everything is going our way. But add a little stress, a little hardship, a little bit of despair, and we quickly find ourselves at a mental fork in the road: to rest in the promises of God or to go our own way. God's promises are for you, even when He seems to be so far away.

"It is not difficult to sing when all is going well. But often God gives a special song to one of his hurting children during the night times of their life. Believers find new joys in their nights of sorrow and despair, and they discover a greater closeness with their Lord during times of deep need. The apostle John wrote the book of Revelation while on the barren island of Patmos; John Bunyan completed the classic Pilgrim's Progress while in the Bedford jail; Beethoven composed his immortal 9th Symphony while totally deaf; and Fanny Crosby once remarked, 'If I had not lost my sight, I could never have written all the hymns God gave me.'

"Charles Weigle's song, 'No One Ever Cared For Me Like Jesus,' was the product of one of the darkest periods of his life. Weigle spent most of his life as an itinerant evangelist and gospel songwriter. One day after returning home from an evangelistic crusade, he found a note left by his wife of many years. The note said she had had enough of an evangelist's life. She was leaving him. Weigle later said that he became so despondent during the next several years that there were even times when he contemplated suicide. There was the terrible despair that no one really cared for him anymore. Gradually his spiritual faith was restored, and he once again became active in the Christian ministry. Soon he felt compelled to write a song that would be a summary of his past

tragic experience. From a heart that had been broken came these choice words that God gave to Charles Weigle:
> *No one ever cared for me like Jesus; there's no other friend so kind as He;*
> *No one else could take the sin and darkness from me—*
> *O how much He cared for me!"*[2]

And even in *your* darkest moments, *God has promised* to care for you.

QUESTIONS:
1. What is the greatest promise God has given you?
2. What promises has God made that He has failed to keep?
3. Do you truly rest in the promises of God? Do you know what all His promises are? How can you learn more about His promises?

The Jews had the privilege of the fathers and their heritage. Their ancestors had been the primary recipients of the promises between God and man. They had the tradition and the history. Why did Jesus Christ come to the Jewish nation and come to earth as a Jew? Very simply stated, the Jews were God's special people. They had been born by a special act of God. It all started long, long ago. God had wanted four things.

1. He wanted a people who would love Him supremely and give Him their first loyalty. (Cp. Gen.17:7; Is.43:10.)
2. He wanted a people who would witness to all other nations that He and He alone was the one true and living God. (Cp. Gen.12:3; 22:18; Acts 13:26, 47.)
3. He wanted a people through whom He could send the promised Seed, the Savior and Messiah, Jesus Christ, to all men everywhere. (Cp. Gen.3:15; 17:7; 22:18; Gal.3:16; Jn.4:22.)
4. He wanted a people through whom He could send His written Word, the Holy Bible, and preserve it for all generations. (Cp. Ro.9:4-5; 1 Pt.2:10-12.)

APPLICATION:
It is a sad thing for a person to have a godly heritage (parents, friends, teachers, schooling, etc.) and go astray. The Bible is full of examples.
⇒ There were the two who began denying the resurrection (2 Tim.2:16-19).
⇒ There was Demas, who turned back to the world (2 Tim.4:10).
⇒ There was Judas, who forsook Christ (Mt.26:14-16).

> **"For it is impossible for those who were once enlightened, and have tasted of the heavenly gift, and were made partakers of the Holy Ghost, and have tasted the good word of God, and the powers of the world to come, if they shall fall away, to renew them again unto repentance; seeing they crucify to themselves the Son of God afresh, and put him to an open shame"** (Heb.6:4-6).

QUESTIONS:
1. Some people look at their godly heritage and feel it will make them acceptable to God. Is a godly heritage a free ticket into heaven? Why or why not?
2. Other people accept the godly life and then turn their back on it. Have you ever known someone who did this? What does Scripture say is their fate?

The Jews had the privilege of the Messiah's coming from their roots. This was the most glorious privilege of the Jews. It involved being the very people...
- through whom God was to send His Son
- through whom God was to bless the world

---

[2] Kenneth W. Osbeck. *Amazing Grace: 366 Inspiring Hymn Stories for Daily Devotions.* (Grand Rapids, MI: Kregel Publications, 1990), p.193.

ROMANS 9:1-5

Note that Paul declares both the humanity and the deity of Jesus Christ. He came in the "flesh," but He "is over all, <u>God</u> blessed forever."

APPLICATION:
A person's attitude and response toward Jesus Christ determine his eternal destiny.

> **"Whosoever therefore shall confess me before men, him will I confess also before my Father which is in heaven. But whosoever shall deny me before men, him will I also deny before my Father which is in heaven" (Mt.10:32-33).**

QUESTIONS:
1. By bearing the name "Christian," you have made a claim to be *of Christ* or *like Christ*. When are you the most aware of being a Christian? Is it...
   * when you are around other believers?
   * when a strong temptation is sent your way?
   * when you go to church?
   * when you sin and need God's forgiveness?
   * when you are being persecuted for your faith or beliefs?
   * when you meet with God in prayer and you study His Word?
   * when you get into a predicament and need a miracle from God?
2. Your attitude and response toward Christ determine your eternal destiny. Are you satisfied that your attitude is what it should be?

SUMMARY:

The only way to get a burning passion for the souls of the lost is not...
   * by attending a seminar on evangelism
   * by reading all of the latest "how to" books on evangelism
   * by memorizing a way to share the gospel

The only way that you will ever have a deep desire for the salvation of your lost family and friends is to have your heart broken by God. As He breaks your heart, it will drive you to prayer. As God breaks your heart, you will know His heart for the lost. As God breaks your heart, you will never get used to the idea of seeing people go to hell. Like the apostle Paul, you will have a deep burden for the lost: Paul was marked by...

1. A man's great love for his people.
2. A man's great respect for his people.

PERSONAL JOURNAL NOTES:
(Reflection & Response)

1. The most important thing that I learned from this lesson was:

2. The thing that I need to work on the most is:

3. I can apply this lesson to my life by:

4. Closing Prayer of Commitment: (put your commitment down on paper).

	B. The True Israel or Children of God, 9:6-13	9 For this is the word of promise, At this time will I come, and Sarah shall have a son.	
1. God's Word, His promise, has not failed	6 Not as though the word of God hath taken none effect. For they are not all Israel, which are of Israel:	10 And not only this; but when Rebecca also had conceived by one, even by our father Isaac;	b. Proof 2: Scripture—God's Word & God's promise to Isaac
2. They are not members of a particular race or institution			
3. They are not of any particular parentage or heritage	7 Neither, because they are the seed of Abraham, are they all children: but, In Isaac shall thy seed be called.	11 (For the children being not yet born, neither having done any good or evil, that the purpose of God according to election might stand, not of works, but of him that calleth;)	1) The promise was before the children's birth
4. They are the believers of God's promise	8 That is, They which are the children of the flesh, these are not the children of God: but the children of the promise are counted for the seed.	12 It was said unto her, The elder shall serve the younger. 13 As it is written, Jacob have I loved, but Esau have I hated.	2) The promise was by election not by the goodness of the children
a. Proof 1: Scripture—God's Word & God's promise to Abraham			

Section VII
ISRAEL AND THE GOSPEL OF RIGHTEOUSNESS
Romans 9:1-11:36

Study: **The True Israel or Children of God**

Text: **Romans 9:6-13**

Aim: To gain a true understanding of your relationship to God.

Memory Verse:
> "In this the children of God are manifest (obvious), and the children of the devil: whosoever doeth not righteousness is not of God, neither he that loveth not his brother" (1 John 3:10).

INTRODUCTION:
It has been said that life is nothing more than a glorified beauty contest that chooses between the ugly and the beautiful. Think about it for a moment. What controls your choice when you select between...
- a colorful flower or a plain plant?
- an attractive person or an homely person?
- a rich and famous person or a poor person down on his luck?
- a well-dressed person or a person dressed in outdated and ill-fitting clothing?

To be perfectly honest, all of us have been *trained or geared to favor* what looks the best. Thankfully, God has not bound Himself to this kind of thinking. If He chose what was the *best*, none of us would stand a chance of being saved. On what basis does God offer salvation to man? If you are a true believer, why on earth did He save you? This is a startling passage, a passage that should awaken many a person to his true relationship with God. In no uncertain terms, this passage declares just who the children of God are.

OUTLINE:
1. God's Word, His promise, has not failed (v.6).
2. They (the children of God) are not members of a particular race or institution (v.6).
3. They (the children of God) are not of any particular parentage or heritage (v.7).
4. They (the children of God) are the believers of God's promise (v.7-13).

1. GOD'S WORD, HIS PROMISE, HAS NOT FAILED (v.6).

God made a glorious promise to Abraham, a promise that had two major points. If Abraham would follow God...

- then God would give him a seed, a son through whom a great nation would be born. He would become the father of a great host of people.
- then God would cause all nations to be blessed through his seed.

Scripture says that Abraham did exactly as God said. He believed God with all his heart and followed God, not knowing where God would lead him (Heb.11:8. Think how this is true of every follower of God.)

Note a significant point: all the promises in Scripture are based upon this single promise to Abraham; that is, if the promise made to Abraham is voided and done away with, then all the promises of God's Word are invalid. God's Word and His promises will have failed. In light of this, there are two things that make some people think the Word of God has failed.
1. Israel rejected God's Son, Jesus Christ, when God sent Him to earth. Ever since that day, very few Jews have turned and followed Christ. Where is the nation that God promised Abraham?
2. The Gentiles are the ones who are following God through His Son Jesus Christ, not the Jews. Therefore, it looks as though God has turned from Israel to the Gentiles.
These two facts cannot be denied. They are facts of history. How, then, can God's Word and promise to Abraham ever be fulfilled? Have God's Word and promise failed? Is God's Word now invalid?
Forcefully, Paul declares that God's Word has not failed. God's Word and the promises of it are effective and still valid. God is fulfilling His promise to Abraham: a nation is being born to Abraham, a nation which is the true Israel and the true children of God.

"The Word of God shall stand forever" (Is.40:8).

ILLUSTRATION:
In a world where promises are easily made and just as easily broken, the believer can have the firm assurance that God's promises are everlasting. He is true to His Word!

> "Daddy, will you play with me?" is the universal cry of children everywhere. And David's son was no exception. David heard this cry from his own son just about every day. A hard-working man, David would leave the house early and get home late in the day. Understandably, the last thing David felt like doing was going back outside to play catch with his son. Most fathers would have just made an excuse, but not David.
> He remembered his own childhood, especially the times he played alone. His father was a very busy man who seldom took time to play. David would ask him again and again, but to no avail. "Son, we'll play tomorrow" was usually the answer. However well-intentioned, tomorrow never came. And eventually David learned not to even bother asking.

When David's own son was born, he determined he would not make the same mistake his father had made with him. He made up his mind that he would make the time to play with his son.

As the darkness came at the end of one particular day, David threw the ball to his son one more time. After catching the ball, the young boy ran up to his father and said, "Daddy, do you know what I wish? When I grow up and have my own little boy, we want you to be on our team!"

This father's promise reached not only to his own son, but also to his future grandson and beyond. In the same sense, God's promise to Abraham touched even the sons of Abraham (including you). It is a promise that is not inhibited by generations or time. Your Father has promised to spend time with you. Are you willing to spend time with Him?

QUESTIONS:
1. When is the last time you failed to keep a promise you made? What impact did that failure have on others? What value do you place on the fact that God has *never* broken a promise He has made?
3. What is the most precious promise God has given you? Why?

2. THEY (THE CHILDREN OF GOD) ARE NOT MEMBERS OF A PARTICULAR RACE OR INSTITUTION (v.6).

"They are not all Israel, which are of Israel." Many Jews believed they were children of God because they were...
- born in the nation of Israel as an Israelite
- reared in the Jewish religion

The Jewish people reverenced God and His law and were known as a God-fearing and religious people. Therefore, a Jew felt he was a child of God by being a citizen of Israel and a circumcised member of Judaism. Many Jews felt that God's promise to Abraham meant that every citizen of the nation of Israel was a child of God as long as he was circumcised and more or less practiced the religion of Judaism.

APPLICATION 1:
The same thoughts have always prevailed among people of the world. Many believe they are Christians because they are citizens of a so-called Christian nation or Christian institution. They think they are acceptable to God because they profess belief in God and have been baptized, becoming a full-fledged member of some church. Such, of course, is just not so. A person *does not* become a child of God by being...
- a citizen of a particular nation, no matter what nation it is nor how good and benevolent the nation is
- a member of a particular religion or institution, no matter how true and godly the religion or institution may be

APPLICATION 2:
Being a citizen of a Christian nation or being a member of a great church does not make a person a child of God. It is not an earthly nation nor a material church that makes a person acceptable to God.

"But as many as received him, to them gave he power to become the sons of God, even to them that believe on his name: which were born, not of blood [heritage], nor of the will of the flesh, nor of the will of man, but of God" (Jn.1:12-13).

1. It was Billy Graham who once said "just because you were born in a garage does not make you a car." A lot of people wrongly believe they are saved by being born in a certain country. Why can your earthly citizenship not save you? What is the only way a man can be saved?
2. What effect does the color of your skin have upon your salvation? The language you speak? Your economic status? Your denominational affiliation? The faith of your parents and grandparents? The church in which you are a member?

3. THEY (THE TRUE CHILDREN OF GOD) ARE NOT OF ANY PARTICULAR PARENTAGE OR HERITAGE (v.7).

"Neither because they are the seed of Abraham, are they all children." As stated, many Jews felt they were children of God because they were children of Abraham, one of the great servants of God (cp. Mt.3:9; Jn.8:38-39). They rested...
* in the godliness of Abraham, feeling that his godliness would cover them
* in the promises made to Abraham, thinking that the promises made to him would include them

Many Jews believed that they were children of God because of their godly heritage. They trusted in the fact that their parents and so many others in their roots (genealogies) worshipped the God of Judaism. They considered themselves to be children of godly forefathers; therefore, they professed to believe in God no matter what kind of lives they lived.

APPLICATION:
Throughout the centuries, many have trusted their godly heritage to save them. Too many are trusting godliness to rub off on them—to rub off from...
* their godly parents
* their godly brothers and sisters
* their godly minister
* their godly spouse
* their godly friends
* their godly co-workers

Few think that God will really reject them. They think that in *the final analysis* God will accept them. They think that enough godliness will rub off on them from some godly heritage, person, or institution for God to accept them.

> **"Not every one that saith unto me, Lord, Lord, shall enter into the kingdom of heaven; but he that doeth the will of my Father which is in heaven" (Mt.7:21).**

QUESTIONS:
1. It is an easy thing to place your trust in some godly person, hoping to "ride their coat-tails" all the way to heaven. If someone were placing their trust in you, what would you tell them?
2. Why is it impossible for someone to become a child of God through someone else's godliness?

4. THEY (THE CHILDREN OF GOD) ARE THE BELIEVERS OF GOD'S PROMISE (v.7-13).

Note two proofs.
1. There is the proof of Scripture, of God's Word and promise to Abraham: "In Isaac shall thy seed be called" (v.7; cp. Gen.21:12). When God gave this promise to Abraham, Abraham had two sons, Ishmael and Isaac. Ishmael had been born through a slave-girl, Hagar. For decades Abraham's wife, Sarah, had been unable to bear a child. Sometime after her child-bearing years had passed, Sarah insisted Abraham attempt to

have a son for her through her personal slave Hagar. It was from this physical union that Ishmael was born. However, it was only a few years later that God appeared to Abraham, telling him that Sarah was to bear the child of promise, the very child whom God had promised to Abraham when He first called Abraham (cp. Gen.18:1f).

The point is twofold.

   a. The children of the flesh are not the children of God's promise. The birth of Ishmael was due to man's effort. He was born because Sarah and Abraham were trying to secure the "promise" by their own works. Ishmael was entirely the product of natural, human, carnal, and fleshly plans. Abraham and Sarah were trying to bring about the promise of God by their own efforts and works. God had absolutely nothing to do with Ishmael's birth.

APPLICATION:

   Ishmael represents all who seek the promise of God—that is, to become children of God—by their own fleshly works and efforts.

> **"But as many as received him, to them gave he power to become the sons of God, even to them that believe on his name: which were born, not of blood [heritage], nor of the will of the flesh [sexual desire], nor of the will of man [a human father], but of God" (Jn.1:12-13).**

ILLUSTRATION:

   How many times have we missed God's best for us because of a lack of patience or a disregard for His Word? God's promises are always reliable—but only if we believe them.

> *"The story has been told of a man who was crossing a desert in the days of the pioneers. He ran into trouble and was dying of thirst when he spotted a pump near an abandoned shack. He had no water to prime the pump, but he noticed a jug of water near the pump with a note attached. It read: 'There is just enough water in this jug to prime the pump, but not if you drink some first. This well has never gone dry, even in the worst of times. Pour the water in the top of the pump and pump the handle quickly. After you have had a drink, refill this jug for the next man who comes along.'*
>
> *"What would the man dying of thirst do? To follow the instructions and prime the pump without first taking a drink would be an exercise of the kind of belief the Bible speaks of. Biblical belief requires that one stake his life on the truth of the promise. If the man follows the instructions, he takes the chance of pouring out all the water and getting none to drink if the pump fails. So he must trust that the message is right. He must act in belief, without first receiving, and must trust in the truth of the promise."*[1]

   When it comes to God's promises, do you trust Him enough to wait on Him? Or do you do things your way?

   b. The children of the promise are counted for the seed. Isaac was the child whom God had promised to Abraham (v.8-9). This means three things.

     ⇒ The promised child is the "seed" through whom the promise was to be fulfilled.

     ⇒ The promised child was born miraculously by the grace of God. Abraham and Sarah were about one hundred years old, well beyond child-bearing years, when Isaac was born (Ro.4:19).

     ⇒ The child of promise was born through faith (Heb.11:11).

---

[1] Michael P. Green. *Illustrations for Biblical Preaching*, p.135-136.

APPLICATION:

A person becomes a child of God through faith in the promises of God. A child of the promise is a person who believes the promise of God, a person who...

- does not seek to secure the promise by his own efforts and works
- follows through on his belief, waiting upon God to fulfill His promise

> **"For ye are all the children of God by faith in Christ Jesus. For as many of you as have been baptized into Christ have put on Christ. There is neither Jew nor Greek, there is neither bond nor free, there is neither male nor female: for ye are all one in Christ Jesus. And if ye be Christ's, then are ye Abraham's seed, and heirs according to the promise" (Gal.3:26-29).**

2. There is the proof of Scripture, of God's Word and promise to Rebecca: "The elder shall serve the younger" (Gen.25:23). (See A Closer Look # 1,2—Ro.9:10-13 for discussion.)

QUESTIONS:

1. Can you think of a time when you had to wait on God for a promise to be fulfilled? Did He keep His promise?
2. Why are men so impatient with God? How can you train yourself to be more patient? To claim God's promises and live by them?
3. What is the most difficult of God's promises for you to believe? Why? Which promise is the easiest to believe? Why?

A CLOSER LOOK # 1

(9:10-13) **Election—Predestination—God, Grace of—Jacob—Esau:** a striking and decisive proof of God's election is seen in the choice of Jacob over Esau. Also, a striking proof that salvation is solely by the grace of God and not by the works and goodness of men is seen in the two sons. Note three facts.

1. The promise to Rebecca was given before Jacob and Esau were born. Jacob's character, behavior, ability, works, and parents had nothing to do with God's choosing him. God and God alone chose Jacob to be the child of promise. Jacob's choice was not by his own personal efforts, but by the grace of God.

2. The promise was by election, not because of "any good or evil" of the children (v.11). Unquestionably, when we accept Scripture for what it says, our minds stagger at this argument. But there is one great truth that must always be remembered: neither Jacob nor Esau *deserved* mercy. Neither one *deserved* being chosen by God for anything. No man *deserves* mercy or purpose from God. God does not have mercy on a man because a man deserves or merits mercy nor because a man wills or runs after God (cp. Jn.1:12; Ro.9:16). God has mercy upon a man because He is a merciful God.

3. Election, being children of the promise, is *not of works but of God who calls men to salvation*. The point is this. Paul is using the two children to get across the same point he stressed with Isaac: a true child of God is not a person who...

- belongs to a particular race or institution
- belongs to a particular family or heritage
- works to secure the promise through his own plans and efforts

God is merciful and He is love—absolutely so. Therefore, God has predestined a line of people to receive His promise of glory. Back in antiquity God chose Jacob, showing His mercy to Jacob. He chose Jacob to continue the line through whom He could send the Savior into the world and through whom He could fulfill all the promises of God to man. The fact that God chose Jacob for the line does not mean in any sense of the word that He condemned Esau to hell.

> **"For God so loved the world, that he gave his only begotten Son, that <u>whosoever believeth</u> in him should not perish, but have everlasting life" (Jn.3:16).**

QUESTIONS:

1. Using simple terms, how would you describe the concept of *election* to a new believer?
2. If God has elected you for salvation, what role do you play in the process?

A CLOSER LOOK # 2

(9:11-13) <u>God—Purpose—Predestination</u>: "Esau I hated." This does not mean to hate in the sense of despising. It is merely a deliberate decision on the part of God for Jacob to be the child of promise instead of Esau. There is *no personal feeling* involved. Esau had done no wrong to merit God's disapproval. Neither had Jacob done any good to merit God's approval. It is merely the right of God to choose Jacob over Esau. It is critical to note that God was always choosing the younger son over the oldest son throughout the Old Testament. He did so for a specific purpose: God was illustrating that man was to receive His promises by grace. Man's law and efforts gave the inheritance to the oldest son; therefore, God chose the younger son over the oldest. God overruled man's law and efforts by giving the promise and inheritance to the younger son, for the younger son was not appointed by men to receive it nor did he deserve it. He received the promise and the inheritance *only by the mercy and grace of God*. Note this also: God's choice of Jacob was not a question of personal salvation but of *God's purpose* being settled before they were born (cp. Mal.1:2-3. Also cp. Gen.29:33; Mt.6:24; Lk.14:26; Jn.12:25.)

QUESTIONS:

1. What practical or personal comparison can you make to relate to God's choice of Jacob over Esau? Did Jacob deserve to be chosen?
2. What did you do that caused God to reach down and save your soul? Did you deserve it?

SUMMARY:

One of life's greatest mysteries is this: God did not save you on the basis of your earthly citizenship nor the color of your skin. He did not save you because of a godly parent or friend. Salvation was not given because of anything you did nor anything you had to offer God. God sent Jesus Christ to save you because He wanted to call you His son or daughter. It was a sovereign choice made by a sovereign God for an eternal purpose?

1. God's Word, His promise, has not failed.
2. The children of God are not members of a particular race or institution.
3. The children of God are not of any particular parentage or heritage.
4. The children of God are the believers of God's promise.

ROMANS 9:6-13

PERSONAL JOURNAL NOTES:
(Reflection & Response)

1. The most important thing that I learned from this lesson was:

2. The thing that I need to work on the most is:

3. I can apply this lesson to my life by:

4. Closing Prayer of Commitment: (put your commitment down on paper).

C. The Rejection of Israel: God's Right to Show Mercy & Justice as He Wills, 9:14-33

1. Is God righteous, that is, just?

2. God has the right to be merciful & just
  a. He shows mercy as He wills

  b. He shows justice as He wills

3. God has the right to do as He wills

  a. Man has no right to reply against God
  b. God's right is as the potter's right over clay

14 What shall we say then? Is there unrighteousness with God? God forbid. 15 For he saith to Moses, I will have mercy on whom I will have mercy, and I will have compassion on whom I will have compassion. 16 So then it is not of him that willeth, nor of him that runneth, but of God that showeth mercy. 17 For the scripture saith unto Pharaoh, Even for this same purpose have I raised thee up, that I might show my power in thee, and that my name might be declared throughout all the earth. 18 Therefore hath he mercy on whom he will have mercy, and whom he will he hardeneth. 19 Thou wilt say then unto me, Why doth he yet find fault? For who hath resisted his will? 20 Nay but, O man, who art thou that repliest against God? Shall the thing formed say to him that formed it, Why hast thou made me thus? 21 Hath not the potter power over the clay, of the same lump to make one

vessel unto honour, and another unto dishonour? 22 What if God, willing to show his wrath, and to make his power known, endured with much long-suffering the vessels of wrath fitted to destruction: 23 And that he might make known the riches of his glory on the vessels of mercy, which he had afore prepared unto glory, 24 Even us, whom he hath called, not of the Jews only, but also of the Gentiles? 25 As he saith also in Osee, I will call them my people, which were not my people; and her beloved, which was not beloved. 26 And it shall come to pass, that in the place where it was said unto them, Ye are not my people; there shall they be called the children of the living God. 27 Esaias also crieth concerning Israel, Though the number of the children of Israel be as the sand of the sea, a remnant shall be saved: 28 For he will finish the work, and cut it short in righteousness: because a short work will the Lord make upon the earth. 29 And as Esaias said before, Except the Lord of Sabaoth had left us a seed, we had been as Sodoma, and been made like unto Gomorrha.

4. God has the right to put up with evil (unbel.) men in order to share His glory with some (bel.) men
  a. God is willing to suffer long with evil
  b. God's purpose
    1) To make known His glory
    2) To prepare some for glory
    3) The subjects of His glory: Both Jews & Gentiles

5. God has identified the chosen people long ago in prophecy
  a. They are from other nations as well as from Israel

  b. They are the small remnant of Israel
    1) God will finish the work—fulfill His promise to Israel

    2) God will leave a seed of believers in Israel

c. They are the pursuers of righteousness by faith d. They are not the pursuers of righteousness by the works of the law—as Israel was	30 What shall we say then? That the Gentiles, which followed not after righteousness, have attained to righteousness, even the righteousness which is of faith. 31 But Israel, which followed after the law of righteousness, hath not attained to the law of righteousness.	32 Wherefore? Because they sought it not by faith, but as it were by the works of the law. For they stumbled at that stumblingstone; 33 As it is written, Behold, I lay in Sion a stumblingstone and rock of offence: and whosoever believeth on him shall not be ashamed.	e. They are not those who stumble over the Stone (Jesus Christ) as Israel did f. They are the persons who believe in Christ

(Note: Because of the length of this outline and commentary, you may wish to split this passage into two studies.)

Section VII
ISRAEL AND THE GOSPEL OF RIGHTEOUSNESS
Romans 9:1-11:36

Study 3: **The Rejection of Israel: God's Right to Show Mercy and Justice as He Wills**

Text: **Romans 9:14-33**

Aim: To gain a better understanding of God's sovereignty.

Memory Verse:
> **"As it is written, Behold, I lay in Sion a stumblingstone and rock of offence: and whosoever believeth on him shall not be ashamed" (Romans 9:33).**

INTRODUCTION:
When was the last time you got into an argument with God...and won? It is silly, but men argue with God every day. Over the course of time men have accused God...
- of not being fair ("How could a loving God ever send someone to hell?")
- of holding back His love ("If God really loved me, He would never have allowed this to happen to me.")
- of being out of control ("Where is God when nations are at war?")
- of being out of touch with modern society ("Times have changed since Bible days. It is unrealistic to judge men based on ancient, outdated laws.")

Make no mistake about it: God is in control of our world. Despite God's being blamed for many of man's problems, Scripture is painfully true: the problem is not with God. The problem is with man and his sin. This passage discusses two major questions: Is God righteous (v.14-24), and why has Israel been rejected by God as His primary mission force to the world (v.25-33)?

OUTLINE:
1. Is God righteous, that is, just (v.14)?
2. God has the right to be merciful and just (v.15-18).
3. God has the right to do as He wills (v.19-21).
4. God has the right to put up with evil (unbelieving) men in order to share His glory with some (believing) men (v.22-24).
5. God has identified the chosen people long ago in prophecy (v.25-33).

1. IS GOD RIGHTEOUS, THAT IS, JUST (v.14)?

Paul's question is shocking: Is there unrighteousness with God? Remember what it was that caused this question. God went against all the laws of men in the ancient world, the laws governing the inheritance left to children. According to man's law, the oldest son was to receive the inheritance; however, in dealing with Isaac's children, God announced that the oldest son, Esau, would serve the younger son, Jacob. Jacob was God's choice to inherit the promise made to Abraham and Isaac, and note: God chose Jacob even before the children were born (Ro.9:10-13).

The question is this: Can God elect men, favor and disfavor men, and still be righteous and just? Can God choose and reject men even before they are born and still be righteous and just? Is there unrighteousness with God?

God forbid! It could never be! It is utterly impossible for God to be unrighteous and unjust. *Glance quickly* at the five points of the outline, and the answer to the question is immediately seen.

2. GOD HAS THE RIGHT TO BE MERCIFUL AND JUST (v.15-18).

1. God shows mercy as He wills. He has mercy and compassion upon whom He wills. Therefore, if God chooses to show mercy to men, He has the right to do so even when men do not deserve it. Again, if God chooses to show compassion to men, He has the right to do so even when men do not deserve it.

Note when it was that God spoke these words to Moses (Ex.33:19). Israel had just been worshipping the golden calf, committing the most serious offense, that of idolatry; and Moses had just interceded for Israel, asking God to forgive their sin (Ex.32:32). The people did not deserve God's forgiveness. They deserved annihilation in the face of God's holiness. A quick glance at the idolatrous and licentious event will show why. The event demonstrates just how depraved the heart of men can be (Ex.32:1-6). God answered Moses by saying He would not destroy the people, but He would have mercy and compassion. He is God; therefore, if He chooses to be merciful He can be merciful.

"I will have mercy on whom I will have mercy, and I will have compassion on whom I will have compassion" (v.15).

Now note: God had mercy and compassion upon Israel *not* because they...
- willed to receive His mercy (human resolve)
- ran after God (human works, effort, energy)
- deserved God's mercy

Israel received the forgiveness and mercy of God because God desired and intended to be merciful to them. The point is clear: God is not unrighteous if He has mercy upon men. Men do not deserve mercy; they deserve judgment. Therefore, when God gives the unrighteous a gift, it is not unjust or unrighteous; it is merciful and compassionate.

2. God shows justice as He wills. The historical event of Pharaoh is an example. Note five points:

a. Scripture says that God "raised up" Pharaoh. This means that God allowed Pharaoh to appear, brought him forth upon the scene of world history. We must always remember the teaching of Scripture:

"There is no power but of God: the powers that be are ordained of God" (Ro.13:1).

b. Pharaoh was evil, very evil. He was an unbeliever: a harsh, stubborn, and obstinate man who stood against and cursed God as though face to face. Scripture declares that God does not tempt men with evil (Jas.1:13). Therefore, Pharaoh would have been evil, stubborn, harsh, and unbelieving even if he had been a small town vendor in southern Egypt. God did not make Pharaoh sinful and evil. Pharaoh would have been sinful and evil no matter where he had lived.

c. Pharaoh had a unique opportunity; he had something many never receive: Pharaoh heard the truth from one of God's greatest servants, Moses. He had opportunity after opportunity to repent, but he refused. Scripture says time and again that Pharaoh himself hardened his heart (Ex.8:15, 32; 9:34).

d. Scripture also says that God hardened Pharaoh's heart (Ex.4:21; 7:3; 9:12; 10:20, 27; 11:10). What does this mean? On the basis of Scripture...
  * it does not mean that God caused Pharaoh to sin and to be stubborn. God never tempts men to sin (Jas.1:13).
  * it means that God judged Pharaoh the same as He judges all men. Pharaoh hardened his heart; therefore, he was judged and condemned to have a hardened heart. Pharaoh "sowed" a hardened heart; therefore, he "reaped" a hardened heart (Gal.6:7-8); Pharaoh "measured" out a hardened heart; therefore, he was "measured" out a hardened heart (Mt.7:2).

Very simply stated, God's law and nature of justice, of *judicial equity,* took effect upon Pharaoh just as it does upon all men. Pharaoh reaped exactly what he sowed.

e. God overruled Pharaoh's evil and used it for the good of His people (Ro.8:28). God used Pharaoh's evil to demonstrate His own sovereign power and to declare the name of God throughout all the earth.

The point is this: Pharaoh was a very sinful and evil man; therefore, God demonstrated His justice in Pharaoh. God acted righteously toward Pharaoh. Just as men execute justice upon evil men, God executed justice upon Pharaoh because of his evil. God is God; therefore, He has the right to execute justice as He wills.

The conclusion is clearly stated:

"Therefore hath...[God] mercy on whom he will have mercy, and whom he will he hardeneth" (v.18).

APPLICATION:

A man desperately needs to do two things.

1) A man needs to seek the face of God for mercy.

"Let the wicked forsake his way, and the unrighteous man his thoughts: and let him return unto the LORD, and he will have mercy upon him; and to our God, for he will abundantly pardon" (Is.55:7).

2) A man needs to guard ever so diligently against becoming hard toward God.

"Harden not your heart, as in the provocation, and as in the day of temptation in the wilderness" (Ps.95:8).

QUESTIONS:

1. None of us deserve the mercy of God. But why do some men have trouble accepting God's mercy upon certain types of sinners who have lived the most deviant lifestyles?
   * murderers
   * prostitutes
   * child abusers
   * and on and on

2. How can you become more merciful and less judgmental toward others who do not deserve it?
3. Can God's justice ever be unjust? Why do so many people see the bad things that happen to them as coming from God? How can you get across to an unbeliever what God's full justice will mean if he rejects God?

3. GOD HAS THE RIGHT TO DO AS HE WILLS (v.19-21).

Men object to God's sovereignty, to His right to run the world as He wills. The reason men object to God's right to rule and reign is clearly stated: men want the right to determine their own fate, to live as they wish while on earth and still be assured of a good life in the next world. They do not want God or anyone else determining their fate. It is this spirit of self-centeredness and pride that causes men to object to God's sovereignty. Note how the present objection is worded. If God has mercy upon some and hardens others...

- why does He find fault and blame the sinner? Is God not choosing to forgive some and choosing not to forgive others?

Paul gives three answers to this objection, answers that establish the sovereignty of God beyond question. Note that the third answer is set off by itself as a major point because of its significance to the whole subject (pt.4, v.22-24).

1. Man has no right to reply against God, no right to accuse God of being unrighteous and unjust. Any man who replies against God has too low a view of God and too high a view of man. How can a creature who has been formed by God say to God, "Why have You made me like this?" How can a creature question God, a creature...

- who owes his life, all that he is and has, to God?
- who is so frail and so easily subject to destruction?
- who knows so little of the universe and its truth?
- who is so morally undisciplined and sinful?
- who is so limited to the material world and the physical dimension of being?
- who lives only for a few short years?

How can man dare question the Supreme Being who made the universe and all that is therein? Who is man that he thinks he can accuse the God of the universe with being unrighteous and unjust? Who does man think he is in accusing God with being immoral and with showing partiality and favoritism?

The point is this: God is God; therefore, He can do as He wills. As God, He sees the overall view; therefore, He knows what should be done and He does it. Man is foolish to question God and charge Him with wickedness, with being unrighteous and unjust. In fact, when man questions and charges God, man only shows...

- how *finite and foolish* he really is
- how *wicked and depraved* he really is

2. God's right over man is as the potter's right over clay. Now note a crucial point that must not be missed if we are to correctly understand this passage.

- The clay referred to here already exists. This passage is not dealing with God's creation of the clay, but with God's government and rule over creation. Again, God is not creating the clay here; He is taking a lump that He has already created and is now using it for His purposes.

Paul is not speaking of God's creating some men to be sinners. God does not purpose or design to condemn men to hell. The fact is, God wills no man to perish; He longs for every man to be saved (2 Pt.3:9). What, then, is this verse saying?

Very simply, God uses the clay as He finds it. He takes the clay (man) and molds it, using it for His purposes. All men are sinful, being born into a sinful and depraved world. God knows the hearts of all men even when they are born. He knows a heart is subject to be an honorable vessel or to be a dishonorable vessel.

⇒ All hearts that are subject to honor, God takes and molds into vessels of honor.

⇒ All hearts that are subject to dishonor, God takes and molds into vessels of dishonor.

God is God; therefore, He knows the heart of every man. He knows if the heart is subject to be tender, loving, and responsive to Him. If the heart is responsive to the things of God, then God gets the gospel to that person and quickens it to the person's heart, saving him and beginning the process of making him a vessel of honor.

God also knows if a person's heart is subject to hardness, selfishness, and rejection of God. This person is made into a vessel of dishonor; that is, God uses even the sinner and his rejection to His glory. How the sinner's rejection is used to glorify God is seen in the next major point (see note, pt.6—Ro.9:22).

The point is this: God has the *right* to make and use both honorable and dishonorable men to work all things out for good. He has the right to use both good and evil men to work out His purposes, purposes which are always good. His right is no different than the potter's.

> **"And we know that all things work together for good to them that love God, to them who are the called according to his purpose. For whom he did foreknow, he also did predestinate to be conformed to the image of his Son, that he might be the first born among many brethren" (Ro.8:28-29).**

ILLUSTRATION:
Have you ever wondered why God [the Creator] allows unbelievers [the created] to "talk back" to Him? Some people act like bullies, daring the God of the universe to knock the chip off of their shoulder. God is patient, but one day in the future God will also judge those who are His enemies.

> *"When the infidel Robert G. Ingersoll was delivering his lectures against Christ and the Bible, his oratorical ability usually assured him of a large crowd. One night after an inflammatory speech in which he severely attacked man's faith in the Savior, he dramatically took out his watch and said, 'I'll give God a chance to prove that He exists and is almighty. I challenge Him to strike me dead within 5 minutes!' First there was silence, then people became uneasy. Some left the hall, unable to take the nervous strain of the occasion, and one woman fainted. At the end of the allocated time, the atheist exclaimed derisively, 'See! There is no God. I am still very much alive!'*
> *"After the lecture a young fellow said to a Christian lady, 'Well, Ingersoll certainly proved something tonight!' Her reply was memorable. 'Yes, he did,' she said. 'He demonstrated that even the most defiant sinner cannot exhaust the patience of the Lord in just 5 minutes!' Another man added, 'As I was coming downtown today, a belligerent little fellow came running out of an alley, daring me to hit him. Do you suppose I actually struck him, just because he challenged me to do so? In the same way, our Lord will not strike everyone dead who defies Him. We should be thankful that in this age He is still operating in grace and desires to show His love rather than His wrath.'"*[1]

Remember, God has a right to judge or to forgive...when He wishes.

---

[1] *Bible Illustrator for Windows*. Version 2.0b. Copyright © 1990-1997 by Parsons Technology, Inc.

1. If a man convinces himself that God is not sovereign, not in charge, he gives himself permission to live as he pleases. When are you most prone to ignore God's authority in your life?
2. What does God owe you...
   - if you go to church almost every Sunday?
   - if you never break any traffic laws?
   - if you never kill anyone?
3. What right does man have to tell God how to run His universe? What suggestions do you offer to God? Do you tell Him...
   - to stop the suffering in your life?
   - to make you independently wealthy?
   - to give you everything you want?
   - to wink at your sin?
   - to answer your prayers *now!?*

4. GOD HAS THE RIGHT TO PUT UP WITH EVIL (UNBELIEVING) MEN IN ORDER TO SHARE HIS GLORY WITH SOME (BELIEVING) MEN (v.22-24).

The outline gives an overview of what is said.

God is willing to suffer (tolerate, put up with, endure) evil men for a long time. Why? Why does God not go ahead and do away with evil and with evil men? There is one very powerful reason: God is fulfilling His purpose in the world.
   - ⇒ God is making known the riches of His glory upon believers, the subjects of mercy.
   - ⇒ God is preparing still others for glory (cp. 2 Pt.3:9).
   - ⇒ The ones being prepared for glory include both Jews and Gentiles. (Note how even this fact points toward God's showing no partiality toward any people or person, Jew or Gentile. God does not pick some for sin and hell and some for righteousness and heaven.)

Several significant things need to be noted in these verses.

1. Note the difference between the word "fitted" and the word "prepared." The vessels of wrath are "fitted" for destruction, but the vessels of mercy are "prepared" for glory. The agent that "fitted" the vessels for wrath *is not identified*. Scripture simply says that they are "fitted" for destruction. This allows the interpretation that they fitted themselves for destruction; whereas God is said to *prepare* the vessels of mercy for glory. A different word entirely is used.

APPLICATION:

Scripture is clear about this fact. Men do *fit* themselves for wrath; God does not tempt or lead men into sin (Jas.1:13). The very opposite is true. God saves men and wants all men to be saved, and He prepares all those who come to Him for glory.

> **"For God so loved the world, that he gave his only begotten Son, that <u>whosoever</u> believeth in him should not perish, but have everlasting life. For God sent not his Son into the world to condemn the world; but that the world through him might be saved. He that believeth on him is not condemned: but he that believeth not is condemned already, because he hath not believed in the name of the only begotten Son of God" (Jn.3:16-18).**

2. Note the whole passage has to do with proving that God is just and righteous. If God actually created men to be sinful so that He could condemn them to wrath, He would not be righteous and just. Even in our finite world, to make something evil is

considered unrighteous and unjust. How much more is this so in the infinite world of heaven? God just does not *fit* men to wrath; men fit themselves to wrath.

3. The whole world is sinful and depraved. "There is none righteous, no not one" (Ro.3:10). "All have sinned and come short of the glory of God" (Ro.3:23. Cp. Ro.10:9-18 for a descriptive picture of man's sinful condition.) God knows the heart of every man, even before he is born. He even knows who will be saved and who will not be saved. Why, then, does He not stop the world instead of letting it go on, when He knows some men are going to doom themselves? There is one primary reason: if God stopped the world then there would be...

- no more vessels of mercy, no more believers
- no more believers to be brought and offered as brothers and sisters to Christ (Ro.8:29)
- no more people upon whom God could demonstrate His glorious mercy and love (Ro.9:23; Eph.2:7)

Note what Scripture says, for it clearly states why God does not end the world and keep any more evil men from being doomed: God is willing to put up with evil men in order to shower "the riches of His glory" upon those who believe on His Son (v.23; cp. v.33). God has only one Son, and He loves His Son so much that He wants Him to be glorified and honored beyond imagination.

4. The one thing to be remembered is this: there is nothing inconsistent with God's showing mercy to some while condemning others. God punishes the *wicked* only for their sins. Human experience as well as the Bible prove beyond doubt that all men are sinful. None deserve mercy. No man deserves to be chosen by God for anything. Therefore, there is no injustice done to a wicked man if God chooses to show mercy to another. One thing will happen, however. The vessel of mercy, the man to whom mercy is shown, will fall upon his face in utter adoration and praise; and he will become a willing servant, willingly owned and possessed by his Savior (Ro.9:22-23; cp. Ro.11:33-36).

APPLICATION:

When we truly realize that God has had mercy upon us, it should cause us to fall upon our faces before Him. He has loved us, truly loved us to the point of forgiving our sins through the Lord Jesus Christ. Seeing His love for us should break us in humble adoration and worship. It is the love of Christ for us that constrains us to love God.

> **"For the love of Christ constraineth us; because we thus judge, that if one died for all, then were all dead: and that he died for all, that they which live should not henceforth live unto themselves, but unto him which died for them, and rose again" (2 Cor.5:14-15).**

5. Another point brought out in this passage is this: the "riches of God's glory" are more clearly seen in the lives of the chosen because of the wickedness of all others. The highest good is said to be accomplished in both the wicked and the chosen vessels. The glory of God's love is much more clearly seen by the contrast of a fallen and depraved universe (cp. v.22-23).

6. Still another point to be kept foremost in mind is this: there is nothing inconsistent or unjust if God looks at two undeserving men and chooses to have mercy upon one and not the other. There is no injustice done to a wicked man if God chooses to forgive another man and not forgive him.

Some people say this: there must be something in a man or something done by a man to cause God to choose him. But this just is not so, for that implies that man earns salvation. Such says that salvation is by works, and this is totally against the teaching of Scripture. Salvation is by God's grace alone; it is "not of works lest any man should boast" (Eph.2:8-9). Therefore, as is taught by this passage, God chooses the vessels of mercy out of the depth of His own justice and mercy.

The mind staggers at this whole passage. We can only ponder it and stand in amazement at the depth of the riches both of the wisdom and knowledge of God!

> **"How unsearchable are His judgments, and His ways past finding out! For who hath known the mind of the Lord?" (Ro.11:33-34).**
> **"Now unto the King eternal, immortal, invisible, the only wise God, be honour and glory for ever and ever" (1 Tim.1:17).**

We will understand God's providence and our freedom of choice in the Day of Redemption. Until then, we can only accept the doctrine as two parallel lines that will find their union and explanation in Him. In that day, He will explain them to us face to face. (What a glorious day that will be!)

A final point of paramount importance is the conclusion drawn in verses 25-33. Paul's point is to give weight to this fact: God has judged the rejection of Israel as a nation by choosing persons from the Gentile nations as well. God's people are persons from *all nations* who pursue His righteousness as found in Christ. The conclusion of the whole passage is, "whosoever believes on him [Christ] shall not be ashamed" (Ro.10:11). This conclusion, that the one who believes is the one truly saved, gives balance to the whole argument.

QUESTIONS:
1. Do you ever tire of God's patience with evil men? How about His patience with you? Do you wish He would treat you as you deserved?
2. The whole world is sinful and depraved. What is God's purpose for not destroying the world today? What is your specific role in God's purpose?
3. How vibrant is God's glory in your life? What can you do to show more of God's glory?

5. GOD HAS IDENTIFIED THE CHOSEN PEOPLE LONG AGO IN PROPHECY (v.25-33).

"Salvation is of the Jews" (Jn.4:22). Israel was the chosen people of God, chosen to be God's witnesses to carry the message of salvation to the world. However, Israel failed, keeping the message to itself and excluding all other peoples. Israel even took the lead in killing God's Son, Jesus Christ. This is the whole point of these verses, to point out how *the chosen* people of God come from all nations of the earth. This fact is clearly seen even in the Jewish prophets. "The chosen" are identified in six different statements which are irrefutable to the open and honest mind.

1. The chosen people of God are from other nations as well as from Israel. The Jewish prophet Hosea predicted this fact. Note the three things Hosea said about the Gentiles. The Gentiles...

- *will* be called God's people. They are the very ones who were *not* called God's "people" (Hos.2:23).
- *will* be called beloved. They are the very ones who were *not* called beloved (Hos.2:23).
- were in a place where it was said that they were *not* God's people. The Gentiles were in the very place where they *were* to be called the children of God (Hos.1:10).

APPLICATION:

History has always proven that the Gentiles are as morally depraved and self-righteous as people can be. But despite all, God in His glorious mercy has thrown open the door of salvation to the Gentiles as well as to the Jews. No matter how self-righteous or morally evil a person has been, God reaches out to that person. Neither the most depraved corruption nor the most humanistic self-righteousness can keep God from forgiving a person if that person truly believes in His Son, the Lord Jesus Christ (v.33).

> **"To him [Jesus Christ] give all the prophets witness, that through his name whosoever believeth in him shall receive remission of sins" (Acts 10:43).**
> **"For I am not ashamed of the gospel of Christ: for it is the power of God unto salvation to every one that believeth; to the Jew first, and also to the Greek" (Ro.1:16).**

2. The chosen are the small remnant of Israel. The great prophet Isaiah predicted this.
   a. Isaiah predicted that only a few among Israel would truly believe and love God supremely. The nation would be a great people whose numbers would be as the sand of the sea, but only a *remnant* would be saved (v.27). Note that God would have to fulfill His Word by cutting short His dealings with Israel. That is, so many in Israel would be so sinful, they would be a threat to destroying everyone. Therefore, God would have to cut His work short in dealing with Israel in order to assure a remnant of believers, fulfilling His word to Abraham (cp. Is.10:22-23).
   b. Isaiah also predicted that God would leave a seed of believers in Israel (Is.1:9). Note that Israel's wickedness is compared to Sodom and Gomorrha. Israel has suffered a fate just as terrible as Sodom and Gomorrha, perhaps worse because the nation's sufferings have been the epitome of severity down through the centuries. But note: God has saved a remnant through it all. There are Jews who have trusted God's Son, Jesus Christ of Nazareth (cp. Ro. 11:27-29).

> **"I say then, Hath God cast away his people? God forbid. For I also am an Israelite, of the seed of Abraham, of the tribe of Benjamin....But what saith the answer of God unto him? I have reserved to myself seven thousand men, who have not bowed the knee to the image of Baal" (Ro.11:1, 4).**

3. The chosen are the pursuers of righteousness by faith. Note the contrast between this point and the next. The most unlikely thing happened.
   ⇒ The Gentiles who have always been so base and self-righteous have all of a sudden turned to God for righteousness, the righteousness of faith.
   ⇒ The Jews who have always been so God-centered and religious have missed God's righteousness, the righteousness of faith in Christ.

> **"He answered and said unto them, Well hath Esaias prophesied of you hypocrites, as it is written, This people honoureth me with their lips, but their heart is far from me" (Mk.7:6).**

4. The chosen are not pursuers of righteousness by the works of the law—as Israel was (v.31-32). Note that this begins to answer why God had to turn away from Israel as the primary mission force of His grace. Israel was zealous to secure righteousness, but failed because she sought righteousness by the law.

> **"Many will say to me in that day, Lord, Lord, have we not prophesied in thy name? and in thy name have cast out devils? and in thy name done many wonderful works? And then will I profess unto them, I never knew you: depart from me, ye that work iniquity" (Mt.7:22-23).**

5. The chosen are not those who stumble over the Stone, Christ Himself, as Israel has done (cp. Is.8:14; 28:16).

"Unto you therefore which believe he is precious: but unto them which be disobedient, the stone which the builders disallowed, the same is made the head of the corner, and a stone of stumbling, and a rock of offence, even to them which stumble at the word, being disobedient: whereunto also they were appointed" (1 Pt.2:7-8).

6. The chosen are the persons who believe in Christ.

ILLUSTRATION:

It is comforting to know that God's power to save is not limited to how *good* we are or how *attractive* we might look. The same God who calls the lost choir member to salvation can also reach down into the depravity of humanity and rescue the perishing.

> *"[Evangelist] Luis Palau tells of a woman in Peru whose life was radically transformed by the power of Christ. Rosario was her name. She was a terrorist, a brute of a woman who was an expert in several martial arts. In her terrorist activities she had killed twelve policemen. When Luis conducted a crusade in Lima, she learned of it and, being incensed at the message of the gospel, made her way to the stadium to kill Luis.*
> *"Inside the stadium, as she contemplated how to get to him, she began to listen to the message he preached on hell. She fell under conviction for her sins and embraced Christ as her Savior. Ten years later, Luis met this convert for the first time. She had by then assisted in the planting of five churches; was a vibrant, active witness and worker in the church; and had founded an orphanage that houses over one thousand children."*[2]

Heaven will be filled with converted sinners who do not stumble over the Cornerstone, the Lord Jesus Christ. Is He your stepping stone or stumblingblock?

"That whosoever believeth in him should not perish, but have eternal life" (Jn.3:15).

"Jesus said unto her, I am the resurrection, and the life: he that believeth in me, though he were dead, yet shall he live" (Jn.11:25).

QUESTIONS:
1. Do you know who the chosen people of God are? Can you explain this to an unbeliever?
2. In simplest terms, what qualifies a person to be called "the chosen"?

SUMMARY:

In the final analysis, God is right—always! No matter what you may think, feel, or suspect, *God is never wrong*. Before you get into a situation where you try to rationalize or argue with God, remember these important points that the apostle Paul has highlighted:

1. God is righteous, that is, just (v.14).
2. God has the right to be merciful and just (v.15-18).
3. God has the right to do as He wills (v.19-21).
4. God has the right to put up with evil (unbelieving) men in order to share His glory with some (believing) men (v.22-24).
5. God has identified the chosen long ago in prophecy (v.25-33).

---

[2] Michael P. Green. *Illustrations for Biblical Preaching*, p.81.

ROMANS 9:14-33

PERSONAL JOURNAL NOTES:
(Reflection & Response)

1. The most important thing that I learned from this lesson was:

2. The thing that I need to work on the most is:

3. I can apply this lesson to my life by:

4. Closing Prayer of Commitment: (put your commitment down on paper).

	CHAPTER 10	6 But the righteous-ness which is of faith speaketh on this wise, Say not in thine heart, Who shall ascend into heaven? (that is, to bring Christ down from above:)	4. God's righteousness does not have to seek out a Messiah or a Deliverer (utopia)
	D. The Tragic Mistake of Israel: Missing God's Righteousness, 10:1-11		a. Righteousness is not achieved by trying to climb up to heaven
1. There was Paul's desire & Israel's mistake	**B**rethren, my heart's desire and prayer to God for Israel is, that they might be saved.	7 Or, Who shall descend into the deep? (that is, to bring up Christ again from the dead.)	b. Righteousness is not achieved by descending into the depths to conquer death & hell
a. Paul's desire for Israel's salvation	2 For I bear them record that they have a zeal of God, but not according to knowledge.	8 But what saith it? The word is nigh thee, even in thy mouth, and in thy heart: that is, the word of faith, which we preach;	**5. God's righteousness & salvation are right before a person**
b. Israel's mistake: They have zeal, but it is not based on complete knowledge	3 For they being ignorant of God's righteousness, and going about to establish their own righteousness, have not submitted themselves unto the righteousness of God.		
1) They seek their own righteousness		9 That if thou shalt confess with thy mouth the Lord Jesus, and shalt believe in thine heart that God hath raised him from the dead, thou shalt be saved.	a. By confessing Jesus to be the Lord (from heaven, cp. v.6)
2) They do not submit to God's righteousness	4 For Christ is the end of the law for righteousness to every one that believeth.		b. By believing God raised Jesus from the dead (from the depths, cp. v.7)
2. God's righteousness is Jesus Christ	5 For Moses describeth the righteousness which is of the law, That the man which doeth those things shall live by them.	10 For with the heart man believeth unto righteousness; and with the mouth confession is made unto salvation.	c. By believing with the heart & confessing with the mouth
3. God's righteousness is opposed to man's righteousness, to man's way for reaching God		11 For the scripture saith, Whosoever believeth on him shall not be ashamed.	**6. God's righteousness & salvation deliver a person from shame**

Section VII
ISRAEL AND THE GOSPEL OF RIGHTEOUSNESS
Romans 9:1-11:36

Study 4: The Tragic Mistake of Israel: Missing God's Righteousness

Text: Romans 10:1-11

Aim: To make absolutely sure of one thing: that you have experienced the true righteousness of God.

Memory Verse:
"That if thou shalt confess with thy mouth the Lord Jesus, and shalt believe in thine heart that God hath raised him from the dead, thou shalt be saved" (Romans 10:9).

ROMANS 10:1-11

INTRODUCTION:
⇒ Have you ever headed out on a trip in the wrong direction?
⇒ Have you ever missed your exit on the interstate and kept right on going?
⇒ Have you ever turned left when you should have turned right or north when you should have turned south?

People make honest mistakes every day while traveling. But no matter how sincere they are, if they are headed in the wrong direction, they will not reach their desired destination. Missing a turn while driving is one thing. Missing an opportunity to have a relationship with God Himself is something altogether different.

This passage has two powerful points. It shows the tragic mistake of Israel, and it proclaims the great danger of missing God's righteousness. It is an excellent study on God's righteousness. It shows man exactly what has to be done in order to receive utopia upon earth, exactly what has to be done to make all things right. It reveals how a man can receive righteousness and be saved from death and judgment to live forever.

OUTLINE:
1. There was Paul's desire and Israel's mistake (v.1-3).
2. God's righteousness is Jesus Christ (v.4).
3. God's righteousness is opposed to man's righteousness, to man's way for reaching God (v.5).
4. God's righteousness does not have to seek out a Messiah or a Deliverer (utopia) (v.6-7)
5. God's righteousness and salvation are right before a person (v.8-10).
6. God's righteousness and salvation deliver a person from shame (v.11).

1. THERE WAS PAUL'S DESIRE AND ISRAEL'S MISTAKE (v.1-3).

Paul had a burning desire for Israel's salvation. He loved his people and loved them deeply.
⇒ The word "desire" means longing, willing, yearning, craving. He craved and yearned to see the salvation of his people. If he saw their salvation, his desire would be fulfilled.
⇒ Note that Paul prayed for Israel's salvation. They could be saved; their rejection of Christ was not hopeless. The door of salvation is open to all men, the Jew as well as the Gentile.

APPLICATION:
The fact that Paul prayed for the salvation of the Jews is a lesson to all believers. We too need to be praying for the salvation of the Jews. Why? Because so much of the world's heritage that is good and decent has come from the Jews:
⇒ morality ⇒ the Bible ⇒ the Son of God, Jesus Christ
⇒ law ⇒ the prophets ⇒ the true religion

> **"Ye worship ye know not what: we know what we worship: for salvation is of the Jews" (Jn.4:22).**

Now note Israel's great mistake: they had a zeal for God, but it was not based on complete knowledge.
⇒ The Jews had a great deal of knowledge about God (Ro.2:17f).
⇒ But the Jews did not have a complete knowledge of God, not full and perfect. They did not have an *experiential knowledge* of the truth.

The point is, the Jews knew some things about God, but their knowledge was only partial. What they knew was incomplete; it was not enough. As a result they did not know God personally.

Why did Israel have an incomplete and imperfect knowledge of God? There are three reasons.

1. Israel was ignorant of God's righteousness. They failed to understand...
   - God's true nature: His holiness and perfection and the utter necessity to be perfect in order to be acceptable to Him, to be given the right to live in His presence.
   - man's true nature: his sin and desperate need for *perfect* righteousness in order to be acceptable to God, to be given the right to live in God's presence.
   - God's love: His love in sending His Son to save man by providing a perfect righteousness for him.

Very simply, Israel was ignorant of God's method of justification, ignorant as to how a man really becomes acceptable to God.

> **"Having the understanding darkened, being alienated from the life of God through the ignorance that is in them, because of the blindness of their heart" (Eph.4:18).**

2. Israel went about establishing its own way of righteousness. They sought to make themselves acceptable to God through...
   - rituals
   - ceremonies
   - laws
   - works

They sought to save themselves by being as religious as they could. They felt God would never reject them if they did their best. Therefore, they drew up every rule and regulation they could to make themselves *religiously good* and acceptable, and they worked and worked to follow the rules and regulations. They sought to build their own way and route to God.

> **"He answered and said unto them, Well hath Esaias prophesied of you hypocrites, as it is written, This people honoureth me with their lips, but their heart is far from me" (Mk.7:6).**

3. Israel refused to submit themselves to the righteousness of God. Very simply, they refused to accept Jesus Christ who is God's righteousness.

APPLICATION:
Note a crucial point: zeal and sincerity are not enough in seeking God. No person or group of people could be any more zealous or sincere in seeking God than the Jews. But something else is always needed; zeal and sincerity always require one other ingredient: complete knowledge. Zeal and sincerity by themselves cannot reach a destination. A person can be as zealous and sincere as possible and still be on the wrong road, never reaching his destination. To reach his destination, he must know and travel the right road.

> **"Who [God] will have all men to be saved, and to come unto the knowledge of the truth. For there is one God, and one mediator between God and men, the man Christ Jesus" (1 Tim.2:4-5).**

ILLUSTRATION:
There are many people who sincerely believe that if they do good works they will gain God's acceptance. But those people will miss heaven because they have no knowledge of the true character of a holy God.

> *"Noah's message from the steps going up to the Ark was not, 'Something good is going to happen to you!'*

> *"Amos was not confronted by the high priest of Israel for proclaiming, 'Confession is possession!'*
>
> *"Jeremiah was not put into the pit for preaching, 'I'm O.K., you're O.K.!'*
>
> *"Daniel was not put into the lion's den for telling people, 'Possibility thinking will move mountains!'*
>
> *"John the Baptist was not forced to preach in the wilderness and eventually beheaded because He preached, 'Smile, God loves you!'*
>
> *"The two prophets of the tribulation will not be killed for preaching, 'God is in his heaven and all is right with the world!'*
>
> *"Instead, what was the message of all these men of God? Simple, one word: 'Repent!'"*[1]

No one can force or fake or talk his way into heaven. The only way is God's way—through His Son, Jesus Christ.

QUESTIONS:
1. How deep is your burden for family members who do not know Christ? Do you pray for them regularly, with great fervor?
2. Why do some believers ignore the serious condition of the lost people around them? What do you need to do to ensure that your heart will not become hardened toward the lost?
3. Why is zeal or sincerity not enough to save the lost from their sins? How is zeal displayed by those who are committed to false religions and cults?
4. How can you tell if someone really knows Christ personally?

2. GOD'S RIGHTEOUSNESS IS JESUS CHRIST (v.4).

Jesus Christ is the One who puts an end to man's having to seek righteousness through the law. Man no longer has to work and work to be acceptable to God, to work and work knowing full well that he is coming up ever so short of God's glory and demand. Man no longer has to live under the enslaving power of sin, under its guilt and shame and punishment. Man no longer has to live under the weight and pressure of failing, of being ever so unworthy and hopeless, lonely and alienated. Man can now be set free and know full well that he is acceptable to God. Man can now have a heart that swells with assurance and confidence, the perfect knowledge that he is God's and God is his. Man can know that he is accepted as righteous before God. How? Through the righteousness of Jesus Christ. "Christ is the end of the law for righteousness to every one that believeth." This means at least three things.

1. Christ *ended* the law in that He is the object toward which the law pointed. All the ceremonies, sacrifices, offerings, and purifications led to and pointed toward Christ.

⇒   The law was a schoolmaster to bring us to Christ.

> **"Wherefore the law was our schoolmaster to bring us unto Christ, that we might be justified by faith. But after that faith is come, we are no longer under a schoolmaster" (Gal.3:24-25).**

Very simply, the law was never intended to be the way to become righteous and acceptable to God. The law was given to point to and lead men to Christ, who is the righteousness of God.

⇒   The law was but a shadow of the real substance that was to come.

> **"[The law and its ceremonies] are a shadow of things to come; but the body is of Christ" (Col.2:17; cp. Heb.9:9).**

---

[1]   Michael P. Green. *Illustrations for Biblical Preaching*, p.301.

2. Christ *ended* the law in that He fulfilled and completed the law perfectly. He lived under the law, keeping it perfectly. He was sinless, obeying every rule and requirement of the law. By fulfilling the law, Jesus Christ has become...

- the Ideal Man
- the Perfect Man
- the Representative Man

> **"For he hath made him to be sin for us, who knew no sin; that we might be made the righteousness of God in him" (2 Cor.5:21).**

3. Christ *ended* the law in that he destroyed the penalty and condemnation of the law against man. Christ took the sin of man upon Himself to bear the condemnation for man. Christ died for man; He bore the execution of being separated from God for man.

> **"Blotting out the handwriting of ordinances that was against us, which was contrary to us, and took it out of the way, nailing it to his cross" (Col.2:14).**

However, note a critical point: Christ ends the law for righteousness *only for those who believe*. A man is justified, that is, counted righteous, by God, only if he truly believes that Jesus Christ is the righteousness of God.

APPLICATION:
Jesus Christ is the righteousness of God. The law finds its perfection in Jesus Christ. He is the very embodiment of all that God wants man to be. Therefore, man should no longer look to the law for his righteousness. Man should no longer look to the law as the way to reach God and to secure God's favor. Man should now look to Jesus Christ and approach God through Jesus Christ.

> **"For Christ is the end of the law for righteousness to every one that believeth" (Ro.10:4).**

QUESTIONS:
1. If Christ had not paid the penalty for your sin, what would you (and everyone else) be facing at death?
2. Do you show your appreciation to God for His great sacrifice for you? What is the best way you can show your thankfulness?

3. GOD'S RIGHTEOUSNESS IS OPPOSED TO MAN'S RIGHTEOUSNESS, TO MAN'S WAY FOR REACHING GOD (v.5).

Man tries to reach God by law and works, by simply doing the very best he can. However, there is a terrible flaw in this approach. Moses was the first to point out the flaw: the man who lives by the law must keep the law, and keep it perfectly (cp. Lev.18:5).

> **"The man which doeth those things shall live by them" (Ro.10:5).**
> **"For as many as are of the works of the law are under the curse: for it is written, Cursed is every one that continueth not in all things which are written in the book of the law to do them" (Gal.3:10).**

The point is this. There are only two ways to become righteous. A person can become righteous...

- by keeping the law perfectly, by never sinning in act, word, or thought (if a person could keep the law perfectly—never sinning even once—he could be declared righteous)
- by trusting in the righteousness of a Person who has lived a sinless life and who stands before us as the Ideal Man, the Ideal Man who can represent us before God

QUESTIONS:
1. If you could become righteous by being obedient to the law, would you ever achieve righteousness? Why or why not?
2. What is the ultimate satisfaction or reward for obeying the law? Of believing and obeying Christ?
3. Is it easier to obey the law or Christ? Why do so many men continue to choose the harder road?

4. GOD'S RIGHTEOUSNESS DOES NOT HAVE TO SEEK OUT A MESSIAH OR A DELIVERER (UTOPIA) (v.6-7).

Note the contrast between heaven and the deep or abyss. This is a picture of the summit and the pit, of the very best and the very worst. Men search...

- for the height of heaven: for life and joy and pleasure, for the very best, for their utopia
- for the answer to death and hell: for the release and freedom from death and the sense of judgment—for their utopia

Another way to say the same thing is this: men search for righteousness, that is, for everything to be right. If they can achieve righteousness and make everything right, then they will have their utopia.

The point is this. Man's search for life or for utopia is *really* a search for a deliverer who can do two things: ascend into heaven to bring utopia down to earth and descend into the depths to conquer sin, death, and hell (cp. Dt.30:11-13. Cp. Ps.139:6-9; Pr.24:7; Amos 9:2.) Men are really searching for a true Messiah, for Christ Himself.

APPLICATION:
A person does not have to scale heaven nor fathom the deep to be saved. If he did, he would be lost eternally, for no man can penetrate heaven to secure righteousness or go into the depths to conquer death and hell. No man can work hard enough to climb up into heaven or labor enough to conquer death and hell. No man or combination of men can penetrate the spiritual world and dimension or transform man into a perfect being so that he never has to die and face judgment. Righteousness—man being right and perfect—is beyond the grasp of man's efforts.

> "Who hath ascended up into heaven, or descended? Who hath gathered the wind in his fists? Who hath bound the waters in a garment? Who hath established all the ends of the earth? What is his name, and what is his son's name, if thou canst tell?" (Pr.30:4).

QUESTIONS:
1. Since righteousness is found only in Jesus Christ, what is the hardest thing a person has to do in order to be saved, to become righteous?
2. How can you share the simplicity of God's plan for becoming righteous with an unbeliever?

5. GOD'S RIGHTEOUSNESS AND SALVATION ARE RIGHT BEFORE A PERSON (v.8-10) (cp. Dt.30:14)

Jesus Christ is the Deliverer who has ascended into heaven and brought utopia down to man, and He is the Savior who has descended into the depths to conquer death and hell (Ro.10:9).

> **"Wherefore he saith, When he ascended up on high, he led captivity captive, and gave gifts unto men. (Now that he ascended, what is it but that he also descended first into the lower parts of the earth? He that descended is the same also that ascended up far above all heavens, that he might fill all things)" (Eph.4:8-10).**

Since Christ has come, the gospel does not require man to scale the heavens nor to fathom the great abyss. Such requirements would be impossible. The gospel only demands faith and open confession that Christ has done both. Why would God commission His Son to go to such limits for man? Simply because God loves man that much (Jn.3:16; Ro.5:8).

The means to have all that a man desires—righteousness, salvation, and utopia—are found within man's mouth and heart. Man has to do three simple things to be counted righteous and acceptable by God. He has to do three simple things to be saved from sin, death, and hell, and to receive utopia:

1. Man must confess with his mouth the *Lord Jesus*. He must confess that Jesus Christ is the *Lord from heaven* (cp. v.6.)

> **"And no man hath ascended up to heaven, but he that came down from heaven, even the Son of man which is in heaven" (Jn.3:13).**

2. Man must believe that God raised Jesus from the dead. He must believe that Jesus Christ...
   - died for man
   - was raised up from the dead because He perfectly satisfied God's demand for justice

God's holiness and justice were perfectly satisfied with the death of Jesus Christ. God was perfectly satisfied with Christ's taking man's sin upon Himself and bearing the punishment of sin for man.

> **"Who was delivered for our offences, and was raised again for our justification" (Ro.4:25).**

3. Man must believe with the heart and then confess with the mouth. A man believes unto righteousness; that is, a man believes in Jesus Christ, and God takes that man's faith and counts it *as righteousness*. Then the man confesses Christ *to salvation*; that is, he is saved by openly confessing Christ. No man can deny God's Son and expect God to save him.

> **"Whosoever therefore shall confess me before men, him will I confess also before my Father which is in heaven. But whosoever shall deny me before men, him will I also deny before my Father which is in heaven" (Mt.10:32-33).**

1. A lot of men *profess* Christ but do not *confess* Christ. What is the difference? Why is confession necessary?
2. Is it asking too much of a person to believe that God actually raised Jesus Christ from the dead? Why or why not? What is so important about believing it?

6. GOD'S RIGHTEOUSNESS AND SALVATION DELIVER A PERSON FROM SHAME (v.11) (cp. Is.28:16).

Note two points.
1. Whoever believes in Christ is saved. The gospel is available to all, both Jew and Gentile. The gospel is the message of God's righteousness and salvation to the whole world. The gospel is universal.

> **"In the last day, that great day of the feast, Jesus stood and cried, saying, If <u>any man</u> thirst, let him come unto me, and drink" (Jn.7:37).**
> **"Ho, every one that thirsteth, come ye to the waters, and he that hath no money; come ye, buy, and eat; yea, come, buy wine and milk without money and without price" (Is.55:1).**

2. The true believer is not ashamed.
   a. He is not ashamed to face God, for he is covered with the righteousness of Christ.

   > **"But <u>put ye on the Lord Jesus Christ</u>, and make not provision for the flesh, to fulfil the lusts thereof" (Ro.13:14).**

   b. He is not ashamed to confess Christ before men. He readily confesses the glorious life and assurance God has given him in Christ Jesus the Lord.

   > **"But ye shall receive power, after that the Holy Ghost is come upon you: and ye shall be witnesses unto me both in Jerusalem, and in all Judaea, and in Samaria, and unto the uttermost part of the earth" (Acts 1:8).**

If you are a Christian believer, you have no reason to be ashamed of living for Christ before men. A lack of confidence in the power of the gospel will keep you from experiencing the victorious Christian life.

> *"On July 15, 1986, Roger Clemens, the sizzling right-hander for the Boston Red Sox, started his first All-Star Game. In the second inning he came to bat, something he hadn't done in years because of the American League's designated-hitter rule [pitchers were not usually allowed to bat]. He took a few uncertain practice swings and then looked out at his forbidding opponent, Dwight Gooden, who the previous year had won the Cy Young award.*
> *"Gooden wound up and threw a white-hot fastball past Clemens. With an embarrassed smile on his face, Clemens stepped out of the [batter's] box and asked catcher Gary Carter, 'Is that what my pitches look like?'*
> *"'You bet it is!' replied Carter. Although Clemens quickly struck out, he went on to pitch three perfect innings and be named the game's most valuable player. From that day on, he later said, with a fresh reminder of how overpowering a good fastball is, he pitched with far greater boldness.*

"Sometimes we forget the Holy Spirit within us and how powerful our witness can be. The gospel has supernatural power—when we speak it in confidence."[2]

QUESTIONS:

1. Can you explain in simple terms how the righteousness of Christ covers you in God's eyes? Why is it critical to grasp this concept?
2. Why are so many believers ashamed to share their faith? What can you do to increase your boldness in witnessing for Christ?

SUMMARY:

Every man without exception has sinned and come short of God's perfection. Mankind has turned from a relationship with God to a life poisoned by depravity, a life filled with sin. But thankfully, God has made a way for us to keep from missing God's righteousness. The way is the righteousness of Christ.

1. There was Paul's desire and Israel's mistake.
2. God's righteousness is Jesus Christ.
3. God's righteousness is opposed to man's righteousness, to man's way for reaching God.
4. God's righteousness does not have to seek out a Messiah or a Deliverer (utopia).
5. God's righteousness and salvation are right before a person.
6. God's righteousness and salvation deliver a person from shame.

PERSONAL JOURNAL NOTES:
(Reflection & Response)

1. The most important thing that I learned from this lesson was:

2. The thing that I need to work on the most is:

3. I can apply this lesson to my life by:

4. Closing Prayer of Commitment: (put your commitment down on paper).

---

[2]   Craig B. Larson. *Illustrations for Preaching and Teaching*, p.72.

	E. The Gospel (Righteousness by Faith) is Not for Israel Alone—It is Universal, 10:12-21	all obeyed the gospel. For Esaias saith, Lord, who hath believed our report? 17 So then faith cometh by hearing, and hearing by the	says the gospel is universal a. Proves some Jews did not believe b. Proves "believing the report" is the method of salvation
1. Proof 1: The Lord treats all men just alike a. He makes no distinction between men b. He is rich to all 2. Proof 2: All men are saved by the same promise	12 For there is no difference between the Jew and the Greek: for the same Lord over all is rich unto all that call upon him. 13 For whosoever shall call upon the name of the Lord shall be saved.	word of God. 18 But I say, Have they not heard? Yes verily, their sound went into all the earth, and their words unto the ends of the world. 19 But I say, Did not Israel know? First	for all (Is.53:1) 5. Proof 5: Israel's disobedience proves the gospel is universal a. Not because they did not hear, cp. Ps.19:4 b. Not because they did not know, cp. Dt.32:21; Is.65:1
3. Proof 3: The world cannot be saved apart from the gospel a. The world cannot call, nor believe, nor hear without a preacher, cp. Is.52:7 b. The preacher cannot preach unless he is sent	14 How then shall they call on him in whom they have not believed? and how shall they believe in him of whom they have not heard? and how shall they hear without a preacher? 15 And how shall they preach, except they be sent? as it is written, How beautiful are the feet of them that preach the gospel of peace, and bring glad tidings of good things!	Moses saith, I will provoke you to jealousy by them that are no people, and by a foolish nation I will anger you. 20 But Esaias is very bold, and saith, I was found of them that sought me not; I was made manifest unto them that asked not after me. 21 But to Israel he saith, All day long I have stretched forth my hands unto a	c. Because they were disobedient & obstinate (unbelieving), cp. Ro.9:33; Is.65:2
4. Proof 4: Scripture	16 But they have not	disobedient and gainsaying people.	

Section VII
ISRAEL AND THE GOSPEL OF RIGHTEOUSNESS
Romans 9:1-11:36

Study 5: The Gospel (Righteousness by Faith) Is Not for Israel Alone--It Is Universal

Text: Romans 10:12-21

Aim: To be an effective witness to this fact: the gospel is meant for all people and needed by all people.

Memory Verse:
"For whosoever shall call upon the name of the Lord shall be saved" (Romans 10:13).

INTRODUCTION:
The great majority of parents with more than one child will tell you this: "My kids are as different as night and day." And yet the same parents would testify (or should) that they love their children equally. Through most of the children's growing years, the parents are giving of themselves willingly and selflessly—to all children equally. Yet a

certain number of the children will choose to rebel and disobey while their siblings are enjoying peaceful and happy relationships with their parents. What is the difference? The same things are offered to every individual—but some accept and some reject. Some children, just like the Jews who rejected Christ, think their own way is better than what has been offered. And just like the Jews, their choice is harmful and potentially fatal.

Author Max Lucado speaks honestly and to the point when he says...

> *"If there are a thousand steps between us and God, He will take all but one. He will leave the final one for us. The choice is ours."*[1]

God loves the whole world and every person in it. His love is not limited to any one nation or people or type of person. The gospel is universal; it is for the whole world.

OUTLINE:
1. Proof 1: the Lord treats all men just alike (v.12).
2. Proof 2: all men are saved by the same promise (v.13).
3. Proof 3: the world cannot be saved apart from the gospel (v.14-15).
4. Proof 4: Scripture says the gospel is universal (v.16-17).
5. Proof 5: Israel's disobedience proves the gospel is universal (v.18-21).

1. PROOF 1: THE LORD TREATS ALL MEN JUST ALIKE (v.12).

1. There is no distinction between men, not in God's eyes. All men are related to God in the very same way. In God's eyes, all men...
- are His creatures
- are sinful and alienated from Him
- are loved by Him
- are saved only through the righteousness provided by His Son

God does not save one man a certain way and another man some other way; neither does God reject a man because he is a Jew or a Greek. God does not show partiality; He has no favorites. No person is favored over another person in being saved or condemned.

> **"But we are sure that the judgment of God is according to truth against them which commit such things" (Ro.2:2).**
> **"Is it fit to say to a king, Thou art wicked? and to princes, Ye are ungodly? How much less to him that accepteth not the persons of princes, nor regardeth the rich more than the poor? For they all are the work of his hands" (Job 34:18-19).**

2. The Lord God is *"rich* to all that call upon Him." Scripture clearly declares:

> **"The Lord, the Lord God, merciful and gracious, long-suffering, and abundant in goodness and truth" (Ex.34:6; cp. 2 Chron.30:9; Ps.103:8; 116:5; 145:8; Joel 2:13).**

The Lord God is rich in mercy and grace and in all else that is good and beneficial. He is so generous and so wealthy that every good gift and every perfect gift that exists in the world has flowed from His mercy and grace (Jas.1:17). Note two significant points.

---

[1] Edward K. Rowell, Editor. *Quotes & Idea Starters for Preaching & Teaching.* (Grand Rapids, MI: Baker Books, 1996), p.65.

a. God has enough supply to richly bless all who call upon Him. There is no limit to the riches of His grace.

> **"In whom we have redemption through his blood, the forgiveness of sins, according to the riches of his grace" (Eph.1:7).**
> **"But God, who is rich in mercy, for his great love wherewith he loved us, even when we were dead in sins, hath quickened us together with Christ, (by grace ye are saved;) and hath raised us up together, and made us sit together in heavenly places in Christ Jesus: that in the ages to come he might show the <u>exceeding riches</u> of his grace in his kindness toward us through Christ Jesus" (Eph.2:4-7).**

b. A man must call upon God to receive the riches of God's mercy and grace. (See note—Ro.10:13 for discussion.)

QUESTIONS:
1. Why does God refuse to play favorites? What would be the danger if He did play favorites?
2. Do you think God loves you more than someone who is practicing gross sin? Considering the sin in your own life, are you not glad that God is impartial?
3. Verse 12 tells us that God is rich to all who call upon Him. Does this necessarily mean materially? Which of God's blessings are most valuable to you as a believer? Do you ever miss out on God's blessings because you do not call on Him?

2. PROOF 2: ALL MEN ARE SAVED BY THE SAME PROMISE (v.13).

Note that this promise was foretold in the Old Testament (Joel 2:32). This verse is one of the great promises of God. God loves every person, no matter his nationality or race. God is not willing that any person should perish; He wants every person to be saved (2 Pt.3:9). In fact, God promises salvation to every man if the man will do just one thing: "Call upon the name of the Lord." Note what God says.

1. **"Whosoever shall call upon the name of the Lord shall be saved."** The word "whosoever" means anyone and everyone, no matter who they are.
    ⇒ It means any person, any nationality, any race, any color.
    ⇒ It means any person from any environment, condition, background, country, government, or family.
    ⇒ It means any person, whether immoral or moral, unjust or just, bad or good, poor or wealthy, mean or nice, lonely or befriended, unpopular or popular, deformed or attractive, diseased or healthy, needful or without need.

"Whosoever" means that any person can be saved no matter who he is. No matter how terrible a person and his circumstances may be, he can be saved. He may be in the depths of the inner city or in the depths of the jungle, and he may be enslaved by the most terrible spirit of sin and evil imaginable—God can still save him.

ILLUSTRATION:
Do you really believe that "whosoever" means *any person*? Too many people try to complicate the issue by adding to the interpretation of Scripture. The gospel is so simple, yet so profound. So available, yet so unacceptable by so many.

> *"A leading manufacturing company developed a new cake mix that required only water to be added. Tests were run, surveys were made, and the cake mix was found to be of superior quality to the other mixes available. It*

tasted good, it was easy to use, and it made a moist, tender cake. The company spent large sums of money on an advertising campaign and then released the cake mix to the general market. But few people bought the new cake mix.

"The company then spent more money on a survey to find out why the cake mix didn't sell. Based on the results of this survey, the company recalled the mix, reworked the formula, and released the revised cake mix. The new cake mix required that one add not only water, but also an egg. It sold like hot cakes and is now a leading product in the field. You see, the first cake mix was just too simple to be believable. People would not accept it. The same is true of salvation by grace."[2]

God's words are simple and clear: **"Whosoever shall call upon the name of the Lord shall be saved."** Nothing more. Nothing less.

"Whosoever believeth that Jesus is the Christ is born of God: and every one that loveth him that begat loveth him also that is begotten of him" (1 Jn.5:1).

2. "Whosoever shall call upon the name of the Lord shall be saved." To "call upon the name of the Lord" means at least two things.
   a. It means that a person *calls* upon the name of Lord Jesus Christ: he reaches out; he takes action; he believes Jesus Christ can and will save him. It means that the person looks upon and believes that Jesus Christ is the Savior of the world, that He is the Son of God who came to earth to save men. Very simply, it means that a person believes the message of John 3:16.

   "For God so loved the world, that he gave his only begotten Son, that whosoever believeth in him should not perish, but have everlasting life" (Jn.3:16).

   b. It means that a person calls Jesus Christ *Lord*, that he looks upon Jesus as the Lord God of the universe and upon himself as His servant. It means that a person surrenders and dedicates himself to serve Jesus Christ throughout life—in everything and through everything, no matter the cost. To "call upon the name of the *Lord*" means total surrender and dedication of all one is and has.

   "And he said to them all, If any man will come after me, let him deny himself, and take up his cross daily, and follow me" (Lk.9:23).

3. "Whosoever shall call...shall be *saved*"—delivered, made whole, preserved. From what does man need to be saved and delivered and preserved? From being lost, from sin, from enemies and dangers, from aging and wasting away (both physically and mentally), from deterioration and decay, from death and hell.

QUESTIONS:
1. God excludes no person from His offer of salvation. Is there any person with whom you would not be willing to share the gospel? What lesson should this teach you about prejudice?
2. Why is it important to *call* upon the name of the Lord?
3. Exactly what is it that God has saved you *from*?

---

2   Michael P. Green. *Illustrations for Biblical Preaching*, p.318-319.

3. PROOF 3: THE WORLD CANNOT BE SAVED APART FROM THE GOSPEL (v.14-15).

Remember what has just been said: "<u>Whosoever</u> shall call upon the name of the Lord shall be saved." "Whosoever" refers to the whole world. But note the critical point: a person has to "call" in order to be saved. A person cannot "call upon the name of the Lord" unless he has heard about the Lord. Therefore, the gospel has to be carried to the whole world. This is the point of the present two verses.

1. The world cannot call or believe or hear without a preacher. To prove the point, Scripture reverses the order of what actually happens.

    a. How can a person call on Jesus Christ if he has not believed in Him? It is impossible. Even in dealing with secular purposes, a person has to really believe in the purpose before he will give his life to it. Imagine giving all one is and has! No person is going to do that unless he really believes in something. The same is true in dealing with the Lord. No person is going to call upon the *Lord* to save him, nor is any person going to surrender and dedicate all he is and has to the Lord, unless he truly believes in the Lord.

    b. How can a person believe in Christ if he has not heard about Christ? How can a person know that Jesus Christ came to earth to die for his sins and that Jesus Christ arose from the dead conquering death so that he might live eternally? Is a person born with the knowledge about Jesus Christ?

      ⇒ Picture the native in the depths of the jungle. Does he know that God's Son died for his sins? Was he born with knowledge of Jesus Christ? The answer is obvious: No! The native in the depths of the jungle has to hear before he can believe and call upon the Lord to save him.

      ⇒ Picture the man in the depths of the inner city, the city dweller who has never been exposed to the gospel, who has interest only in the things of the city and the world. Does he know that God's Son died for his sins? The answer is obvious: No! Not if he has never heard. The city dweller has to hear before he can believe and call upon the Lord to save him.

      ⇒ Picture the religionist in the depths of religion, the religionist who has never been exposed to the clear-cut presentation of the gospel, who has only heard about the life of Jesus and the form, ceremony, and ritual of religion. Does the religionist know that God's Son died to set him free from sin, death, and hell so that he might not serve sin any more? The answer is obvious: No! Not if he has never heard a clear-cut presentation of the gospel. Even the religionist has to hear before he can truly believe and truly call upon the Lord to save him. (What an indictment and warning to Christian ministers and teachers—a warning to present the gospel in simple, clear-cut terms.)

    c. How can a person hear without a preacher? How can a person hear that Jesus Christ died for him if a preacher or some Christian does not tell him? To hear anything requires a person who either speaks or writes. To receive communication requires a communicator. To hear a message requires a messenger. The message of the Lord Jesus Christ must be carried to the world, but in order to be carried, a messenger is needed. Christian believers must preach the message if people are to hear the message.

2. Now note that the basis of missions and evangelism is the preacher or witness himself. In the present context the word "preacher" means any believer who bears witness to the Lord Jesus Christ. It takes a preacher to proclaim the message of the Lord Jesus so that people can hear and believe and call upon Him. However, note what this verse says: the preacher cannot preach unless he is sent.

    a. God is the One who sends forth preachers and witnesses of the Lord Jesus Christ. God is the One who commissions, qualifies, and instructs the preachers and witnesses of the gospel.

      "Ye have not chosen me, but I have chosen you, and ordained you, that ye should go and bring forth fruit, and that

your fruit should remain: that whatsoever ye shall ask of the Father in my name, he may give it you" (Jn.15:16).

b. Christian believers, as well as God, have a part in sending forth laborers. We are to pray for laborers (Mt.9:37).
⇒ We are to go forth ourselves.

"Go ye therefore, and teach all nations, baptizing them in the name of the Father, and of the Son, and of the Holy Ghost: teaching them to observe all things whatsoever I have commanded you: and, lo, I am with you alway, even unto the end of the world" (Mt.28:19-20).

⇒ We are to pray for laborers.

"Then saith he unto his disciples, The harvest truly is plenteous, but the labourers are few; pray ye therefore the Lord of the harvest, that he will send forth labourers into his harvest" (Mt.9:37-38).

c. We are to give to meet the needs of the world.

"But whoso hath this world's good, and seeth his brother have need, and shutteth up his bowels of compassion from him, how dwelleth the love of God in him?" (1 Jn.3:17).

3. The gospel is the message of peace and "glad tidings of good things." Note three points.
a. The message of the gospel is peace.

"Peace I leave with you, my peace I give unto you: not as the world giveth, give I unto you. Let not your heart be troubled, neither let it be afraid" (Jn.14:27).

b. The message of the gospel is "glad tidings of *good things.*"

"I am come that they might have life, and that they might have it more abundantly" (Jn.10:10).

c. The feet of the preacher and witness are beautiful; that is, they are a welcome sight to the world. The world desperately needs the message of peace and the glad tidings of good things.

"How beautiful upon the mountains are the feet of him that bringeth good tidings, that publisheth peace; that bringeth good tidings of good, that publisheth salvation; that saith unto Zion, Thy God reigneth!" (Is.52:7).

QUESTIONS:
1. Why is it so critically important for the gospel to be preached to every person, in every place?
2. What is your specific role in sharing the gospel with the world? How effective have you been in fulfilling your role? Could you do more?
3. How faithful have you been to pray for those who labor for Christ? What difference would it make in your church if everyone were committed to praying for world evangelization? Does God expect intercessory prayer for those who do His work?

4. The message of the gospel is peace and glad tidings of good things. Is this how you present the gospel? Do you bear a positive testimony that your message is truly "good news"?

4. PROOF 4: SCRIPTURE SAYS THE GOSPEL IS UNIVERSAL (v.16-17).

Isaiah says that many Jews did not "believe the report [message] of God" (cp. Is.53:1). Therefore, they prove that salvation is not by race, heritage, tradition, religion, institution, nor works established by the Jewish nation or any other people.

Note a second thing: Isaiah used the phrase, "believing our report." Isaiah was saying that *believing the message* is the way of salvation. The message was to stir faith.

There are three steps involved in faith.
1. The step of hearing. A man must *be willing to listen to the message of Christ.*

> **"But blessed are your eyes, for they see: and your ears, for they hear" (Mt.13:16).**

2. The step of mental assent. A man must *agree that the message is true*, that the facts of the case are thus and so. But this is not enough. Mere agreement does not lead to action. Many a person knows that something is true, but he does not change his behavior to match his knowledge. For example, a man knows that eating too much harms his body, but he may continue to eat too much. He is a double-minded man: he agrees to the truth and knows the truth, but he does nothing about it. This man still does not have faith, not the kind of faith that the Bible talks about.

> **"Of his own will begat he us with the word of truth, that we should be a kind of firstfruits of his creatures" (Jas.1:18).**

3. The step of commitment. A man must *make a personal commitment to the truth.* When the New Testament speaks of faith, it speaks of *commitment*. A man hears the truth, agrees that it is true, and does something about it. He commits and yields his life to the truth. The truth becomes a part of his very being, a part of his behavior and life.

Saving faith is believing in the name of Jesus Christ and committing your life to Him. It is trusting Jesus Christ, completely putting your trust in Him, who He is and what He has done. It is casting your life into His hands, believing He will take care of your past (sins), present (looking after), and future (delivering from death unto life eternal).

> **"That whosoever believeth in him should not perish, but have eternal life" (Jn.3:15).**

QUESTIONS:
1. What lessons can you learn from the mistakes of the Jews, from their unbelief? How are you to pray for the Jew who has not accepted Jesus Christ as the Messiah?
2. Many people have *heard* the gospel but still reject its message. What excuses have you heard from unbelievers? What excuses did you have before you came to Christ?
3. How would you explain the difference between *mental assent* (just acknowledging something is true) and "saving faith" to an unbeliever?

A CLOSER LOOK # 1

(10:16) **Faith—Obedience**: note that the gospel is to be obeyed. Obedience and belief are synonymous terms when dealing with the gospel. A person who truly believes in Jesus Christ will obey Him. There is no such thing...

- as true belief without obedience
- as truly believing in Jesus Christ and not following Him
- as truly believing Jesus Christ has forgiven your sin and continuing to live in sin
- as truly believing the gospel and living like the world

"Wherefore come out from among them, and be ye separate, saith the Lord, and touch not the unclean thing; and I will receive you, and will be a Father unto you, and ye shall be my sons and daughters, saith the Lord Almighty" (2 Cor.6:17-18).

"And being made perfect, he became the author of eternal salvation unto all them that <u>obey</u> him" (Heb.5:9).

QUESTIONS:

1. It was William Shakespeare who said that life is a stage. Claiming to be a believer places you on a stage. Those who observe you often make up their minds about Christianity—to accept it or to reject it—based upon your behavior. As non-Christians look at you, do they see...
   - a believer whose actions speak louder than words?
   - a believer who is faithful to serve his Lord?
   - a believer whose lifestyle is different from the rest of the world?
   - a believer who really cares about the needs of people—spiritual, emotional, and physical needs?
2. What is the impact of claiming to be a Christian and then refusing to obey the Lord?

5. PROOF 5: ISRAEL'S DISOBEDIENCE PROVES THE GOSPEL IS UNIVERSAL (v.18-21).

Why did Israel not obey the gospel?

1. Israel's disobedience was not because they did not hear the Word of God (v.18). The very opposite is true. Israel was the very custodian of the Scriptures, the very people whom God had chosen to bring salvation to the world. No matter where the Jewish people were scattered, they had the Word of God and heard it. (Note that Paul quotes Ps.19:4 as Scriptural proof of what he says.)

2. Israel's disobedience was not because the people did not know the truth (v.19). They knew the truth, and they had a dynamic example and demonstration of the truth. They had the example of the Gentiles who turned to the gospel in great numbers.

Note how Scripture words this: "I will provoke you to jealousy." Israel had the stirrings of jealousy and envy to help them turn to the gospel. They heard and knew. Their disobedience to the gospel was not because they were ignorant of the gospel. The gospel was actually lived out before their faces in the person of Jesus Christ and in the Gentiles turning to Christ for salvation. (Again, Paul supports his point from the Old Testament, Dt.32:21; Is.65:1.)

3. Israel's rejection was because they were a disobedient and obstinate people. Note how good God had been to Israel.

   a. God "stretched forth His hands": inviting; offering forgiveness, peace, and reconciliation; pleading and begging for Israel to return to Him.
   b. God pleaded "all day long": being patient, longsuffering, and forbearing; waiting until the last moment to turn away.

"Come, and let us return unto the Lord: for he hath torn, and he will heal us; he hath smitten, and he will bind us up" (Hos.6:1).

Nevertheless, Israel refused and rejected God's gracious invitations. Israel chose to remain disobedient and obstinate. They closed their minds despite the clear evidence and refused to consider the truth of Christ as the true Savior of the world.

ILLUSTRATION:

God is not at fault when a man or a nation rejects the offer of salvation. Instead, the fault lies solely with sinful men who refuse to heed and obey the Word of God.

> *"An unbeliever once ridiculed the power of the gospel of Jesus Christ by saying, 'If Jesus Christ is able to save to the uttermost, why is it that there are so many unbelievers?' The Christian to whom he was speaking stopped a very dirty little boy who was passing by and turning to the unbeliever said, 'Can you blame soap and water for the filth of this boy?' It was available to all, but only those who accept it experience its regeneration power."*[3]

Unfortunately, Israel is not alone in its disobedience. Throughout the generations, men have heard the truth proclaimed and still rejected it. But they have no one to blame but themselves.

"But exhort one another daily, while it is called To day; lest any of you be hardened through the deceitfulness of sin" (Heb.3:13).

QUESTIONS:

1. Why does anyone who has heard the Word of God and knows the truth fail to obey God? Is any excuse acceptable? How is Israel's failure a warning to you?
2. Do you ever push God to the limit with your disobedience—whether it be sins of commission or sins of omission?

SUMMARY:

The gospel is for everyone. The glorious love of God has not been reserved for only a select group of people. Just think about it for a moment: If God saved you, He can save anyone, can't He?

Proof 1: the Lord treats all men just alike.
Proof 2: all men are saved by the same promise.
Proof 3: the world cannot be saved apart from the gospel.
Proof 4: Scripture says the gospel is universal.
Proof 5: Israel's disobedience proves the gospel is universal.

---

[3]   Spiros Zodhiates, Th.D. *Illustrations of Bible Truths*, p.204.

ROMANS 10:12-21

1. The most important thing that I learned from this lesson was:

2. The thing that I need to work on the most is:

3. I can apply this lesson to my life by:

4. Closing Prayer of Commitment: (put your commitment down on paper).

	CHAPTER 11	present time also there is a remnant according to the election of grace.	remnant at this present time—a strong assertion
	F. The Callous on Israel's Heart is Not Total—There is a Remnant, 11:1-10		
		6 And if by grace, then is it no more of works: otherwise grace is no more grace. But if it be of works, then is it no more grace: otherwise work is no more work.	6. Proof 5: God's grace assures a remnant
1. Israel was disobedient (10:21) a. Is all Israel rejected? b. God forbid!	I say then, Hath God cast away his people? God forbid. For I also am an Israelite, of the seed of Abraham, of the tribe of Benjamin.		
2. Proof 1: Paul himself was part of the remnant			
3. Proof 2: God's foreknowledge guarantees a remnant	2 God hath not cast away his people which he foreknew. Wot ye not what the scripture saith of Elias? how he maketh intercession to God against Israel, saying,	7 What then? Israel hath not obtained that which he seeketh for; but the election hath obtained it, and the rest were blinded	a. Israel did not obtain righteousness, but the chosen few did
4. Proof 3: Elijah foresaw the remnant		8 (According as it is written, God hath given them the spirit of slumber, eyes that they should not see, and ears that they should not hear;) unto this day.	b. Israel is accused by Scripture 1) Of being drowsy
a. Elijah's mistake: He felt he was the only faithful believer in all Israel	3 Lord, they have killed thy prophets, and digged down thine altars; and I am left alone, and they seek my life.		
b. God's assurance to Elijah: There is a godly remnant	4 But what saith the answer of God unto him? I have reserved to myself seven thousand men, who have not bowed the knee to the image of Baal.	9 And David saith, Let their table be made a snare, and a trap, and a stumblingblock, and a recompence unto them:	2) Of being worthy of judgment
		10 Let their eyes be darkened, that they may not see, and bow down their back always.	3) Of being blinded
5. Proof 4: There is a	5 Even so then at this		

Section VII
ISRAEL AND THE GOSPEL OF RIGHTEOUSNESS
Romans 9:1-11:36

Study 6: **The Callous on Israel's Heart Is Not Total--There Is a Remnant**

Text: Romans 11:1-10

Aim: To gain the most comforting assurance: you are a part of God's true remnant, one of His true believers and followers.

Memory Verse:
> "Even so then at this present time also there is a remnant according to the election of grace" (Romans 11:5).

ROMANS 11:1-10

INTRODUCTION:
What would your life be like...
- if you were ignored by everyone around you?
- if your morals were seen by the public as "outdated convictions"?
- if right were called prudish and wrong were called acceptable and lawful?
- if your values were judged as being "politically incorrect"?
- if respect for God was removed by evil men from every visible domain (like schools, media, government, etc.)?
- if you felt like you were the only one who was trying to follow God?

If you have felt any of these, your experience is common with believers from every generation. But throughout the ages, one thing has remained true: God will always have a witness—a people called by Him and committed to Him. In spite of what you feel or have personally experienced, God remains faithful to His glorious promises...*all* of them!

There is a glorious hope both for Israel and for the world. God's promises are always fulfilled. The callous on *Israel's heart* is not total—there is a remnant, a small group of believers who have remained true to the faith, who have believed in the promise of the Messiah and Savior. The callous on *any people's heart* is not total—there can be a remnant. God will have His witnesses among all people. People everywhere can be saved if they will turn to God's Son, Jesus Christ.

OUTLINE:
1. Israel was disobedient (v.1).
2. Proof 1: Paul himself was part of the remnant (v.1).
3. Proof 2: God's foreknowledge guarantees a remnant (v.2).
4. Proof 3: Elijah foresaw the remnant (v.2-4).
5. Proof 4: there is a remnant at this present time—a strong assertion (v.5).
6. Proof 5: God's grace assures a remnant (v.6-10).

1. ISRAEL WAS DISOBEDIENT (v.1).

Israel was disobedient to God, gripped by an obstinate unbelief (cp. Ro.10:21). The nation as a whole did not believe or obey God. They even rejected God's own Son (Jn.1:11). How can this fact be reconciled with the fact that Israel is *God's people*? Note that even in this verse they are called "His people" (v.1).
- ⇒ God had given birth to Israel through Abraham and had made some great promises to the nation through Abraham.
- ⇒ "In Isaac shall thy seed be called" (v.7).
- ⇒ God had even promised that He would never cast off His people: "For the LORD will not cast off his people, neither will he forsake his inheritance" (Ps.94:14).

In light of this, is it not inconsistent and is it not denying God's Word to teach that Israel is not saved, that Israel is no longer the people of God? To ask the question as Paul asked: "Has God cast away His people?" The words "cast away" mean to push away, to thrust away, to repel, to repudiate. The idea is to *utterly, totally, and finally* cast away. Has God utterly cast away the Jews? Paul shouts: "God forbid." It is impossible! It must never be! It can never be! God has not broken and violated His Word to Israel. But God's promises to Israel did not mean that all Jews were *locked in* to salvation no matter how sinful and disobedient they were. It did not mean that an unbelieving and disobedient Jew was acceptable to God simply because he had been *born* a Jew. God's promises were intended for those who *believed and obeyed Him*. The people who believed and obeyed Him have always been "His people." Paul gives five proofs to show that God has not rejected every Jew. God accepts and fulfills His promises to all those who believe and obey Him.

1. Some people feel they will be saved because of their heritage, because they have a godly parent or spouse or someone else close. But what does the example of Israel show about this?
2. Who are the only ones who can legitimately claim God's promises?

2. PROOF 1: PAUL HIMSELF WAS PART OF THE REMNANT (v.1).

God had not totally rejected Israel. There was a remnant of godly and obedient believers in Israel. Paul himself is proof of the glorious fact.

1. Paul was a pure Jew, a true descendant of Abraham, not a mere proselyte; and he was of the elite, of the Benjaminite aristocracy.

2. Paul was part of the remnant of God. He was claiming to be a true child of God, a true son of Abraham, one of the sons whom God had not cast away. Therefore, he himself was proof that God had not cast away His people. (Cp. Acts 9:1-19; 22:1-6; 26:12-18 for Paul's conversion.)

> **"And he said, Who art thou, Lord? And the Lord said, I am Jesus whom thou persecutest: it is hard for thee to kick against the pricks. And he trembling and astonished said, Lord, what wilt thou have me to do? And the Lord said unto him, Arise, and go into the city, and it shall be told thee what thou must do" (Acts 9:5-6).**

QUESTIONS:
1. Paul claimed to be a part of God's remnant. Was his claim legitimate?
2. Does your family heritage have a part in keeping you out of God's kingdom? Does it have a part in getting you into God's kingdom?

3. PROOF 2: GOD'S FOREKNOWLEDGE GUARANTEES A REMNANT (v.2).

Very simply stated, God Himself guarantees a remnant; He saves those whom He foreknows. Remember, this is not saying that God chooses some for heaven and others for a terrible hell. What God wants believers to do is to take heart, for He has assured their salvation. God is going to complete His purpose for believers: "That Christ might be the firstborn [have the preeminence] among many brethren" (Ro.8:29).

> **"For whom he did foreknow, he also did predestinate to be conformed to the image of his Son, that he might be the firstborn among many brethren" (Ro.8:29).**
> **"Elect according to the foreknowledge of God the Father, through sanctification of the Spirit, unto obedience and sprinkling of the blood of Jesus Christ: Grace unto you, and peace, be multiplied" (1 Pt.1:2).**

ILLUSTRATION:
How can a believer have assurance, real assurance, that God will not save him today and lose him tomorrow? What circumstances would cause God to change his mind about you?

> *"The story is told of an elderly grandfather who was very wealthy. Because he was going deaf, he decided to buy a hearing aid. Two weeks later he stopped at the store where he had bought it and told the manager he could now pick up conversation quite easily, even in the next room. 'Your relatives must be happy to know that you can hear so much better,' beamed the delighted proprietor.'*

"'Oh, I haven't told them yet,' the man chuckled. 'I've just been sitting around listening—and you know what? I've changed my will twice!'

"God is not like a dear old grandfather who hears only when we speak clearly and directly to him. He always hears us. And his attitude toward us is not changed by what he hears, because we stand before him by grace."[1]

God has guaranteed a remnant. God has guaranteed to keep what He saved before time began. Have you taken the right steps toward being a part of His holy remnant?

QUESTIONS:
1. Why is a proper understanding of God's foreknowledge important in understanding your salvation?
2. Does God's guarantee of a remnant give you license to live as you please after you have been saved?
3. How would you explain God's foreknowledge to someone who worried about the future?

4. PROOF 3: ELIJAH FORESAW THE REMNANT (v.2-4).

This is proof from the very highest authority among men, the authority of Scripture itself. From the very beginning, Scripture clearly says that not all Israel was saved, but only a remnant truly followed God. This is clearly seen in Elijah's experience (1 Ki.19:9-18). His day was a terrible day of sin and apostasy, and he himself was being marked for death because he refused to stop his preaching of righteousness. In a moment of extreme pressure and uncertainty, he cried out to God in prayer wondering if he was the only godly person left in Israel. God assured Elijah by telling him there were still seven thousand godly believers in the nation. The point is this: in Elijah's day the vast majority of people were as they are today—disobedient and disloyal to God, rejecting and denying God, controlling their own lives and following after the man-made, humanistic gods of this earth. But there *was* a remnant, a few who were loyal and obedient to God. There were only seven thousand; nevertheless, there was a remnant, a few who were trusting God to fulfill His promises to them.

APPLICATION 1:
Note two revealing facts:
⇒ Many stray away from God and reject Him—many within a nation, a state, a city, a neighborhood, a family, a religious body!
⇒ God always has His few, His promised remnant, who do obey and remain loyal to Him!

> **"Wherefore seeing we also are compassed about with so great a cloud of witnesses, let us lay aside every weight, and the sin which doth so easily beset us, and let us run with patience the race that is set before us" (Heb.12:1).**

APPLICATION 2:
Note how the image of a nation is determined by the life-style of the majority. The wickedness of the majority in Israel overshadowed the godliness of the few. Even Elijah, the great prophet of God, was unaware of the seven thousand godly scattered throughout the nation. Yet they were there. God will never leave Himself without a witness, nor will He ever leave His people without fellow laborers throughout the world. We may not know about each other, but we can rest assured there are other witnesses scattered around, witnesses who are bearing testimony for the Lord Jesus. God has His remnant, His faithful few.

---

[1] Michael P. Green. *Illustrations for Biblical Preaching*, p.171.

"Righteousness exalteth a nation: but sin is a reproach to any people" (Pr.14:34).

QUESTIONS:
1. As a Christian believer, there are times when you might feel all alone in this world. When you feel this way, what are some specific things you need to do?
2. When the evil and depravity of this world get to you, how can the Scriptures bring you comfort?

A CLOSER LOOK # 1
(11:2) **Israel, Remnant**: Elijah foresaw the remnant in 1 Ki.19:9-18. Other prophets also saw the remnant: Isaiah (Is.1:9; 4:3; 11:16; 37:4), Jeremiah (Jer.6:9; 23:3; 3:7), Ezekiel (Ezk.14:14, 20, 22), Amos (Amos 9:8-12), Micah (Mic.2:12; 5:3), Zephaniah (Zeph.2:9; 3:12-13).

---

5. PROOF 4: THERE IS A REMNANT AT THIS PRESENT TIME—A STRONG ASSERTION (v.5).

"There is a remnant." There is no question about the fact. Note why: because of the "election of grace." What does this mean? If there were a remnant in Israel in the day of Elijah, there is bound to be a remnant of believers today. Why? Because of grace: the grace of God in Jesus Christ has now come to earth, and the Spirit of God is actively at work making God's grace known.

> "For the grace of God that bringeth salvation hath appeared to all men, teaching us that, denying ungodliness and worldly lusts, we should live soberly, righteously, and godly, in this present world; looking for that blessed hope, and the glorious appearing of the great God and our Saviour Jesus Christ; who gave himself for us, that he might redeem us from all iniquity, and purify unto himself a peculiar people, zealous of good works" (Tit.2:11-14).

QUESTIONS:
1. In a world that is under a cloud of darkness, full of sin, and given over to perversity, what proof could you offer that there is truly a remnant of people who love God?
2. Can the world ever be so evil that God would not be able to find a remnant? Why or why not?

6. PROOF 5: GOD'S GRACE ASSURES A REMNANT (v.6-10).

A person is not saved because he merits or works for salvation. No man deserves God's grace. No one deserves being chosen by God for anything. God does not bestow His grace upon a man because a man deserves or earns grace. A man does not secure God's acceptance because he wills or runs after God (Jn.1:12). God has mercy upon a man because He is a gracious God. If a man were saved because of works, then salvation...

- would not be by grace (of God) but by works (of man)
- would remove grace (God) from the picture and put works (man) in the forefront

Very simply, God would no longer be necessary, for man would be saving himself. If by some figment of the imagination and scientific work man could save himself by figuring out how to live eternally, then God Himself would not be needed. In fact, neither grace nor works would be necessary, for man would have reached perfection. The absurdity of such a possibility is clearly seen.

The point is this: it is God's grace that saves men. Therefore, God will see to it that there is always a remnant of believers in Israel. The vast majority of Jews stumbled and fell at the snare of works (v.6), but the callous on Israel's heart is not total. There is a remnant. Note two points.

1. The vast majority of Israel did not obtain righteousness, but the chosen few did.

   ⇒ Most sought after righteousness, but they failed to secure it because they sought it by works.

   ⇒ However, the elect have obtained righteousness. That is, the saved can know that they are accepted as righteous before God. How? Through the righteousness of Jesus Christ. "Christ is the end of the law for righteousness to every one that believeth."

2. Israel is accused and condemned by Scripture of three terrible things.

   ⇒ Of being drowsy and condemned to drowsiness (Is.29:10; 6:9).

   ⇒ Of being worthy of judgment and condemned to judgment (Ps.69:22).

   ⇒ Of being blind and condemned to blindness (Ps.69:23).

The picture is that of men's sitting and feasting comfortably at a banquet table. They are at ease, secure, and possessed with a sense of safety. In fact, they are so comfortable that their safety becomes their ruin. The enemy sneaks upon them unaware.

Note this: God is said to be the One who made Israel drowsy and blind and worthy of judgment. This is Scripture's way of stressing what can be called the *judicial blindness and rejection of men* (see A Closer Look # 2—Ro.11:7-10 for discussion).

ILLUSTRATION:

Let us state this fact again: it is the grace of God that saves a person. It is not a person's own works, religious traditions, or family heritage that save him. Every generation is full of people who try and try to gain eternal life outside of grace. Anyone who tries to "break into heaven" will be treated like a thief.

> "A Quaker had a bundle of hides stolen from his warehouse. He wondered what steps he should take to prevent a repetition of such an act. Instead of putting the machinery of the law in motion, he placed the following ad in the newspapers: 'Whoever stole a quantity of hides on the 5th of this month is hereby informed that the owner has a sincere wish to be his friend. If poverty tempted him to take this step, the owner will keep the whole transaction secret and will gladly help him to obtain money by means more likely to bring him peace of mind.'

> "A few nights later, when the family was about to retire to rest, a man knocked at the door of the Quaker's house, carrying with him a bundle of skins. 'I have brought them back,' he said. 'It is the first time I ever stole anything, and I have felt very bad about it.' 'Let it be the last, friend.' said the Quaker. 'The secret still lies between ourselves.'

> "He spoke to the man faithfully and affectionately about the folly of dishonesty and of the claims of the gospel. He also took him into his employment, and the man became a changed character, living an exemplary life from then on."[2]

Man does not deserve to be forgiven or saved, but God is gracious and gives man what he does not deserve!

---

[2] Spiros Zodhiates, Th.D. *Illustrations of Bible Truths*, p.109.

QUESTIONS:
1. In what ways does modern man attempt to save himself? Why is he doomed to failure?
2. What does Paul accuse Israel of doing wrong in these verses? Why should Israel's failures be a stern warning to every unbeliever?

A CLOSER LOOK # 2

(11:7-10) <u>Judgment—Judicial Blindness and Rejection—Spiritual Abandonment</u>: note the words "were blinded" and "God hath given them the spirit of slumber" (cp. Is.39:10; 6:9; Ps.69:22-23). The idea is that God is the One who blinded Israel. However, Scripture clearly says that God does not tempt people, much less cause them to sin (Jas.1:13). What does this mean then? It means at least two things.

1. The unbeliever's rejection is wilful, always deliberate. The unbeliever does see and hear, yet he refuses to really open his eyes and ears. He refuses to understand. But why does a person act so illogically by rebelling and refusing to understand? Christ answers this question by saying, "This people's heart is waxed gross" (Mt.13:15). The Greek is "this people's heart has grown fat [overweight]." Being fat indicates sensuality and senselessness. To eat and eat, adding weight upon weight, is living after the flesh; and living after the flesh makes no sense at all. Christ is therefore saying that the unbeliever has become so sensual and senseless that he rebels and refuses to understand the gospel of God.

⇒ His sensuality is due to worldliness and the lust for the things of the world.

> **"For they that are after the flesh do mind the things of the flesh; but they that are after the Spirit the things of the Spirit. For to be carnally minded is death; but to be spiritually minded is life and peace. Because the carnal mind is enmity against God: for it is not subject to the law of God, neither indeed can be. So then they that are in the flesh cannot please God" (Ro.8:5-8).**

⇒ His senselessness is due to being deceived by the evil one.

> **"But if our gospel be hid, it is hid to them that are lost: in whom the god of this world hath blinded the minds of them which believe not, lest the light of the glorious gospel of Christ, who is the image of God, should shine unto them" (2 Cor.4:3-4).**

2. The unbeliever experiences a judicial blindness and rejection by God. A person who *deliberately chooses* to be blind to the gospel and to reject Christ is given over to a *just punishment*. God offers His love and salvation of eternal life to a man, but a man has to choose to receive God's offer.

⇒ Man's unbelief is allowed to roam in the sphere of unbelief and to become obstinate unbelief—if the man continues to blind himself to the truth. God will not violate the will of a man.

⇒ Man's sin is allowed to roam in the sphere of sin and to become constant sin—if the man continues to blind himself to the truth. God does not violate the will of a man.

A person's rejection leads to *judicial blindness* and to being rejected by God.

> **"For with what judgment ye judge, ye shall be judged: and with what measure ye mete, it shall be measured to you again" (Mt.7:2).**

ROMANS 11:1-10

QUESTIONS:
1. Why is God not to be blamed for a person's spiritual blindness?
2. What causes an unbeliever to be spiritually blind?
3. How can a spiritually blind man gain his sight?

SUMMARY:

Heaven will not be an empty place. God's people will be there with Him and will live with Him forever. No one but God knows the number. But the important thing for you to settle today is this: Will you be in that number? God *will have* a remnant. The proof is in the Scriptures.

1. Israel was disobedient.
2. Proof 1: Paul himself was part of the remnant.
3. Proof 2: God's foreknowledge guarantees a remnant.
4. Proof 3: Elijah foresaw the remnant.
5. Proof 4: there is a remnant at this present time—a strong assertion.
6. Proof 5: God's grace assures a remnant.

PERSONAL JOURNAL NOTES:
(Reflection & Response)

1. The most important thing that I learned from this lesson was:

2. The thing that I need to work on the most is:

3. I can apply this lesson to my life by:

4. Closing Prayer of Commitment: (put your commitment down on paper).

	G. The Callous on Israel's Heart is Not Final— There is to be a Restoration, 11:11-16	you Gentiles, inasmuch as I am the apostle of the Gentiles, I magnify mine office:	**to stir the Jews to be saved**
1. Proof 1: God has overruled Israel's stumbling over Christ	11 I say then, Have they stumbled that they should fall? God forbid: but rather	14 If by any means I may provoke to emulation them which are my flesh, and might save some of them.	a. By magnifying his ministry to the Gentiles
a. God opens salvation to the Gentiles	through their fall salvation is come unto the Gentiles, for to	15 For if the casting away of them be the reconciling of the	b. Paul's purpose 1) To stir some to be saved
b. God stirs the Jews to be restored	provoke them to jealousy.	world, what shall the receiving of them be,	
c. God assures the glorious restoration of Israel & a rich blessing for the whole earth	12 Now if the fall of them be the riches of the world, and the diminishing of them	but life from the dead? 16 For if the first-fruit be holy, the	2) To bring about the restoration, the great climax of history **3. Proof 3: The forefathers, that is, the**
2. Proof 2: Paul tries	the riches of the Gentiles; how much more their fulness? 13 For I speak to	lump is also holy: and if the root be holy, so are the branches.	**patriarchs, give a heritage of holiness**

Section VII
ISRAEL AND THE GOSPEL OF RIGHTEOUSNESS
Romans 9:1-11:36

Study 7: **The Callous on Israel's Heart Is Not Final--There Is to Be a Restoration**

Text: **Romans 11:11-16**

Aim: To be aware of your role in reaching people for Christ.

Memory Verse:
> **"I say then, Have they stumbled that they should fall? God forbid: but rather through their fall salvation is come unto the Gentiles, for to provoke them to jealousy" (Romans 11:11).**

INTRODUCTION:

If you could sit on God's throne for one day and have the opportunity to rule the world, what would you do with...

- those who have made it a habit to mock your faith in God?
- those who have repeatedly rejected the claims of Christ?
- those who have not changed—in spite of your fervent prayers for them?
- those who use religion as an excuse to live as they please?
- those who continue to be vulgar, crude, and insulting toward the things of God?
- those who live evil and wicked lives?

Now, quickly snap back to reality—and thank God you do *not* have to make any of these decisions—it is up to God alone! We must always remember one clear fact: where we are quick to lose hope and give up on people, God is very patient with men. The grace of God allows those who have once rejected Him to come to Him, forgiven and restored. In fact, the overall theme of the Bible shows that God is a God of restoration.

The callous on a man's heart does not have to be final. Every man can repent and turn to Christ and be restored to God. This is the message of this passage. The callous on Israel's heart is not final. There is to be a restoration of Israel. Many in Israel are going to return to God and accept the Lord Jesus Christ as their Savior.

OUTLINE:
1. Proof 1: God has overruled Israel's stumbling over Christ (v.11-12).
2. Proof 2: Paul tries to stir the Jews to be saved (v.13-15).
3. Proof 3: the forefathers, that is, the patriarchs, give a heritage of holiness (v.16).

1. PROOF 1: GOD HAS OVERRULED ISRAEL'S STUMBLING OVER CHRIST (v.11-12).

> ⇒ Israel has stumbled over Christ.
> ⇒ Has Israel stumbled that they should fall?

The contrast between stumbling and falling is devastating. The idea is that of a permanent and final fall—spiritually. Is Israel's problem with Christ permanent and final? Will Israel never accept God's Son, Jesus Christ, as the true Messiah? Is the spiritual fall of Israel to be forever?

Paul's response is forceful: God forbid! Perish the thought! Let it never be! Such a thing is impossible in God's plan for the world. God has overruled Israel's stumble over Christ in three glorious ways.

1. God has opened the door of salvation to the whole world. The Lord's messengers went to Israel first, but Israel did not want to hear that Jesus Christ is the Messiah, the Son of God Himself. Very few received the gospel. In fact, so many rejected the message that it can be said that Israel, the nation as a whole, has stumbled over Christ. Israel, the Jews...

- have shut their eyes, lest they should see Christ (v.8)
- have closed their ears, lest they should hear Christ (v.8)
- have set themselves to bitterly oppose Christ (1 Th.2:15-16)

God had no other choice but to do the logical thing. The glorious message of His love and of His Son was at stake; therefore, God sent His messengers throughout the world (the Gentile world) in search of any person who would receive the message of His Son. God did what the Jews had always failed to do: God threw open the door of salvation to the whole world.

> **"Then saith he to his [God's] servants, The wedding is ready, but they which were bidden were not worthy. Go ye therefore into the highways, and as many as ye shall find, bid to the marriage" (Mt.22:8-9).**

APPLICATION 1:
Note two provoking thoughts.
1) Think how wonderful it would have been if the Jews had accepted Jesus Christ and had become God's missionary force to carry the message of Christ to the world! Would the world have been reached by now? It has been two thousand years since Christ came to earth, and the world still has not been reached with the gospel. If the Jews had accepted Christ, would the task now be complete? How many more people would have been saved?
2) Think how wonderful it would be if more of us (the Gentiles) would accept Christ! If we would dedicate our lives more sacrificially to carrying God's message of salvation to the world, how many more people would be saved and delivered from death?

APPLICATION 2:
Note how God "worked all things out for good." He took Israel's rejection of His Son and *enriched* the world. Why? Because God has determined that His Son Jesus Christ shall have many *brothers* who will worship and serve Him throughout all eternity. Therefore, if a people rejects the message of His Son, God will work it out to send the message to another people. (Cp. Ro.8:28-29.)

2. God stirs the Jews to be restored. God has not forsaken the Jews. The door of salvation is open to them as well as to the Gentiles. The Jews can look at true Christian believers and see the holiness, love, joy, and peace of their lives; and the Jews can be stirred to receive Christ. In fact, this is the very point of the present passage. God sees to it that some Jews are "provoked," that is, stirred to receive Christ and the glorious life of salvation which He offers.

> **"Nevertheless I tell you the truth; It is expedient for you that I go away: for if I go not away, the Comforter will not come unto you; but if I depart, I will send him unto you. And when he is come, he will reprove the world [both <u>Jew</u> and <u>Gentile</u>] of sin, and of righteousness, and of judgment: of sin, because they believe not on me; of righteousness, because I go to my Father, and ye see me no more; of judgment, because the prince of this world is judged" (Jn.16:7-11).**

QUESTIONS:
1. God will always find someone to be His messenger. Has God ever had to use someone else to share His Word with the lost because you refused to obey Him? How can you become more useful to God?
2. Note that it is God who stirs people to receive Christ. How did this "stirring" happen in your life? In what way can your testimony encourage a lost friend to accept Christ?

3. God assures the glorious restoration of Israel and a rich period for the whole earth. Note the sharp contrast...
- between "fall" and "riches"
- between "diminishing" and "riches"

The word "diminishing" means loss, defeat, injury. It means that Israel became impoverished spiritually. Israel was spiritually injured and defeated; the Jewish people lost the blessings of salvation. Now...
- if the spiritual fall of Israel led to the riches of salvation being carried to the world...
- if the spiritual diminishing of Israel led to the riches of salvation being carried to the Gentiles...

...how much more shall the fulness (the restoration of Israel) bring the blessings of God to earth?

Note the word "fulness," which means completion or that which is filled. The idea is that the day is coming when God's plan and purpose for Israel will be completed and perfectly fulfilled. That day, the day of Israel's restoration, will cause even a greater blessing to spread out across the world.

APPLICATION:
The spread of the gospel has had an enormous impact upon the world.
- ⇒ It has liberated millions from sin and shame.
- ⇒ It has saved millions from death and hell.
- ⇒ It has assured millions of life eternal with God.
- ⇒ It has liberated women and children from slavery.
- ⇒ It has proclaimed morality and purity world-wide.
- ⇒ It has stirred justice and the enactment of just laws among men.

However, when Israel is restored and large numbers of Jews begin to turn to Christ, then the world will experience unprecedented blessings from the hand of God. God promises such blessings to the world.

The point is clear: God has overruled and is going to continue overruling Israel's stumble and fall over Christ.

⇒ More and more Gentiles are going to be saved. The uttermost part of the earth is going to hear the gospel.

> **"And this gospel of the kingdom shall be preached in all the world for a witness unto all nations; and then shall the end come" (Mt.24:14).**

⇒ More and more Jews are going to be stirred to accept Christ and to be restored to God.

⇒ A glorious restoration of Israel is going to take place. Jews by the teeming thousands are going to turn to Christ someday out in the future. So many will turn to Christ that it can be said that the nation Israel has been restored. And when that day comes, the whole earth will be greatly blessed, blessed more fully than ever before.

> **"For I would not, brethren, that ye should be ignorant of this mystery, lest ye should be wise in your own conceits; that blindness in part is happened to Israel, until the fulness of the Gentiles be come in. And so all Israel shall be saved: as it is written, There shall come out of Sion the Deliverer, and shall turn away ungodliness from Jacob" (Ro.11:25-26).**

ILLUSTRATION:

One of the worst things we can do is make false assumptions. There are many people who believe that God will forever punish Israel for rejecting the call to be His chosen people. Before you make a wrong assumption, look closely at the facts.

> *"A traveler, between flights at an airport, went to a lounge and bought a small package of cookies. Then she sat down and began reading a newspaper. Gradually, she became aware of a rustling noise. From behind her paper, she was flabbergasted to see a neatly dressed man helping himself to her cookies. Not wanting to make a scene, she leaned over and took a cookie herself.*
>
> *"A minute or two passed, and then came more rustling. He was helping himself to another cookie! By this time, they had come to the end of the package, but she was so angry she didn't dare allow herself to say anything. Then, as if to add insult to injury, the man broke the remaining cookie in two, pushed half across to her, and ate the other half and left.*
>
> *"Still fuming some time later when her flight was announced, the woman opened her handbag to get her ticket. To her shock and embarrassment, there she found her pack of unopened cookies!*
>
> *"How wrong our assumptions can be."*[1]

QUESTIONS:

According to Scripture, God has promised to restore the Jewish people. In what way does this great promise assure you of God's...

- great power?
- great love?
- great sovereignty?
- great ability to work in the hearts of a stubborn people?

---

[1] Craig B. Larson. *Illustrations for Preaching and Teaching*, p.9.

2. PROOF 2: PAUL TRIES TO STIR THE JEWS TO BE SAVED (v.13-15).

Paul was God's primary minister to the Gentiles in the first century. Paul magnified the ministry and gloried in God's call, and he stressed the fact every chance he could. Why? Paul had two purposes.

1. He wanted to arouse the Jews to envy; that is, he wanted to stir them to look at Christ and to see what Christ had done for the Gentiles. He wanted to stir men to look at the lives of believers, to see the wonderful change Christ had brought about. Thereby, Paul hoped that some Jews would be saved.

2. Paul wanted to hasten the day of Israel's restoration. He knew there was to be a restoration; therefore, he knew that every time he was able to reach a Jew for Christ, the callous on Israel's heart would soften a little more. The more he could soften the callous, the sooner the restoration would take place. Note the question of Paul:

> **"If the casting away [that is, the rejection] of Israel led to the reconciliation of the world [to God], what shall the receiving [the restoration] of them be, but life from the dead?"**

    a. The *reconciliation* of the world has a twofold meaning. It means...
- that *all* men, both Jew and Gentile, can now be reconciled to God, can now have *peace with God* and possess the *peace of God*

> **"For if, when we were enemies, we were reconciled to God by the death of his Son, much more, being reconciled, we shall be saved by his life" (Ro.5:10).**

- that all men, both Jew and Gentile, can now be reconciled to each other

> **"And that he might reconcile both unto God in one body by the cross, having slain the enmity thereby" (Eph.2:16).**

    b. Paul believed strongly in the restoration of Israel. The very fact that he asked the question indicates his belief. He firmly expected Israel to be restored, and he expected their restoration to bring such a great revival to earth that it would be like the world's moving to "life from the dead."

    c. The phrase "life from the dead" is interpreted several ways.
    ⇒ Some Bible scholars say it refers to the resurrection of the dead, to the climax of human history when Jesus Christ shall return to deliver the whole creation from corruption, to rule and reign over the world (cp. Ro.8:21). This, of course, would mean that believers are not resurrected until the restoration of the Jews to God.
    ⇒ Other scholars say it is merely figurative language. When the Jews are restored, it will be like resurrection, like gaining life from the dead.

Whatever the interpretation, the restoration of Israel will be a most glorious event, an event so magnificent that it will be like a true resurrection. It will lead to a new world, a world of righteousness that will benefit all involved. The scene is that the most glorious blessings will be poured out upon the whole world and everyone in it.

> **"And I will give them a heart to know me, that I am the LORD: and they shall be my people, and I will be their God: for they shall return unto me with their whole heart" (Jer.24:7).**

3. PROOF 3: THE FOREFATHERS, THAT IS, THE PATRIARCHS, GIVE A HERITAGE OF HOLINESS (v.16).

This is an extremely important verse in dealing with the restoration of Israel. God gives two pictures to show that Israel can never be totally or finally rejected. Both pictures have to do with the first-fruits.

⇒ The Jew always dedicated the first fruit of his harvest to God. He gave the first part to God, and by giving the first part, the man was saying to God that he was dedicating all of his food to God. It was not necessary to offer every mouthful to God. The offering of the first part sanctified the whole.

⇒ The second picture is that of a little tree's being planted and the sapling's being offered to God. Every branch thereafter was looked upon as being sacred to God. It was not necessary to dedicate each branch separately.

What Paul is saying is that the root, the first part, refers to the patriarchs, that is, the fathers of Israel. Israel, by merit of its patriarchs, its fathers, holds a very special place in God's heart. The whole nation benefits from the dedicated lives of Abraham and the other godly fathers. The whole nation (masses of them) will be restored and saved, brought back to God because of the godliness of the forefathers and because of God's promise to the forefathers (cp. v.25).

Note this: to call Israel a holy nation does not mean that the Jewish people live holy lives in the sight of God. Scripture is not talking about practical, day-to-day holiness. There have been few Jews—just as there have always been few Gentiles—who have lived holy lives. But Israel was *initially* chosen by God to be His witness upon earth: chosen to be His *federal nation* or His *representative nation* to bear testimony for Him. The first fathers of the nation believed God and lived lives of faith, and a few Jews have continued to follow God down through the generations of every century. God very clearly says that because of the holiness of these few, He cares for the nation as a whole—for the whole lump. What this means is this: because of the holy lives of the few, God looks with favor upon the nation. It does not mean that He saves everyone in the nation; but rather, He blesses the nation, all those who live around the followers of God. Those who live holy lives bring godly blessings upon all who surround them and who succeed from them. Many of Israel will be blessed by God and restored because of the nation's godly patriarchs.

APPLICATION 1:

Note the influence of godly parents, forefathers, and nations upon children and succeeding generations. It is important for every parent and generation to live godly lives.

> **"The LORD God, merciful and gracious, long-suffering, and abundant in goodness and truth, keeping mercy for thousands, forgiving iniquity and transgression and sin, and that will by no means clear the guilty; visiting the iniquity of the fathers upon the children, and upon the children's children, unto the third and to the fourth generation" (Ex.34:6-7; cp. Lev.14:18).**

APPLICATION 2:
Note the influence of godly men upon nations.

> **"And ye shall be unto me a kingdom of priests, and a holy nation. These are the words which thou shalt speak unto the children of Israel" (Ex.19:6).**
> **"They are beloved for their father's sakes" (Ro.11:28).**
> **"And because he loved thy fathers, therefore he chose their seed after them, and brought thee out in his sight with his mighty power out of Egypt" (Dt.4:37).**

However, we must always remember that the people of a nation can be restored to God only through repentance, only by turning from sin back to God.

> **"If they shall confess their iniquity, and the iniquity of their fathers, with their trespass which they trespassed against me, and that also they have walked contrary unto me; and that I also have walked contrary unto them, and have brought them into the land of their enemies; if then their uncircumcised hearts be humbled, and they then accept of the punishment of their iniquity:** *then will I remember my covenant with Jacob, and also my covenant with Isaac, and also my covenant with Abraham will I remember; and I will remember the land"* **(Lev.26:40-42).**

ILLUSTRATION:
No true believer has ever regretted living a life of commitment to personal holiness. Material things will come and go during this life, but not spiritual things. A spiritual investment will last into eternity. We must never allow insignificant things to stand in the way of bringing the lost to Christ.

> *"A farmer had an only son whose conversion was the subject of daily thought and prayer. The time of the camp meeting came before it was possible to finish the seeding. When the opening day came the farmer hitched up the wagon and invited the family to go to the meeting. 'But, Dad,' said the boy, 'you aren't going to leave the field unseeded? It will never be in as good form again this season.'*
> *"'The field will have to take its chances,' replied the father. 'The meeting has first place.' The son was soundly converted. Less than a year later he lay dying, and as the father bent over him the boy's arms went around his neck, and, with shining face, he drew him close. 'Oh, Dad,' he whispered, 'I'm so glad you let the field wait.'"[2]*

What kind of heritage are you creating for your loved ones? One they will be ashamed of or one they will be thankful for?

QUESTIONS:
1. What advantages are given to the child who grows up in a home with godly parents?
2. Can you think of any godly leaders who have led their nations toward godliness? What was the impact? What would happen to your nation if more believers were totally committed to doing God's will? To your community? To your family?

---

[2] From *Life's Great Adventure--Prayer*, by Solomon Cleaver. As quoted in *Knight's Master Book of 4,000 Illustrations* by Walter B. Knight, p.453-454.

SUMMARY:

The great hope of the gospel, the *good news*, is that men *can* repent of their evil hearts. When you get discouraged about sharing the life-changing message of Jesus Christ, be patient and remember: God has already given you convincing proof that men can be changed.

Proof 1: God has overruled Israel's stumbling over Christ.
Proof 2: Paul tries to stir the Jews to be saved.
Proof 3: the forefathers, that is, the patriarchs, give a heritage of holiness.

PERSONAL JOURNAL NOTES:
(Reflection & Response)

1. The most important thing that I learned from this lesson was:

2. The thing that I need to work on the most is:

3. I can apply this lesson to my life by:

4. Closing Prayer of Commitment: (put your commitment down on paper).

	H. The Callous on Israel's Heart is a Warning to Other Nations, 11:17-24	not the natural branches, take heed lest he also spare not thee.	to spare unnatural branches
		22 Behold therefore the goodness and severity of God: on them which fell, severity; but toward thee, goodness, if thou continue in his goodness: otherwise thou also shalt be cut off.	4. Warning 3: Take a sharp look at the goodness & severity of God a. God was severe to those who fell b. God is good to the steadfast
1. A parable of the olive tree a. Some branches are broken off: Jews b. Some wild branches are grafted in: Gentiles	17 And if some of the branches be broken off, and thou, being a wild olive tree, wert graffed in among them, and with them partakest of the root and fatness of the olive tree;		
2. Warning 1: Do not be arrogant a. You are wild & grafted in b. You are not the root	18 Boast not against the branches. But if thou boast, thou bearest not the root, but the root thee.		
3. Warning 2: Fear complacency & unbelief a. Israel was not rejected for the Gentiles but because of unbelief b. The Gentiles stand by faith— not by any merit c. God is less likely	19 Thou wilt say then, The branches were broken off, that I might be graffed in. 20 Well; because of unbelief they were broken off, and thou standest by faith. Be not highminded, but fear: 21 For if God spared	23 And they also, if they abide not still in unbelief, shall be graffed in: for God is able to graff them in again. 24 For it thou wert cut out of the olive tree which is wild by nature, and wert graffed contrary to nature into a good olive tree: how much more shall these, which be the natural branches, be graffed into their own olive tree?	5. Warning 4: Be alert, for the restoration is a probable event a. If unbelief is removed b. "God is able..." c. The grafting of a natural branch (the Jews) is more likely than the calling of the Gentiles

Section VII
ISRAEL AND THE GOSPEL OF RIGHTEOUSNESS
Romans 9:1-11:36

Study 8: **The Callous on Israel's Heart Is a Warning to Other Nations**

Text: **Romans 11:17-24**

Aim: To be aroused more and more against complacency; to become more and more alert in following God

Memory Verse:
> "Behold therefore the goodness and severity of God: on them which fell, severity; but toward thee, goodness, if thou continue in his goodness: otherwise thou also shalt be cut off" (Romans 11:22).

INTRODUCTION:
One of the great traps every believer faces is taking people, things, and even God for granted.

⇒ A marriage will quickly become stale when romance is replaced by routine.
⇒ A job will be put at risk if productivity is replaced by passivity.
⇒ Faith will become lukewarm if commitment is replaced by convenience.

The Bible is very clear about God's commitment to those who are truly His. But do you ever take God for granted? There are some people who feel as if God "owes" them because of...
- their good deeds
- their godly parents and spouses
- their religious acts and traditions

God owes no man anything—not ever. We are forever in God's debt. How do we prove our love for God? We must keep a tender and spiritually sensitive heart and never—no never—take God and His glorious salvation for granted.

People can harden their hearts against God. People can become so callous against God that the conviction of the Holy Spirit is never felt. Hardness of heart can doom people to an eternity of separation from God. The callous on Israel's heart is a warning to all people everywhere, a warning to the nations of the world.

OUTLINE:
1. A parable of the olive tree (v.17).
2. Warning 1: do not be arrogant (v.18).
3. Warning 2: fear complacency and unbelief (v.19-21).
4. Warning 3: take a sharp look at the goodness and severity of God (v.22).
5. Warning 4: be alert, for the restoration is a probable event (v.23-24).

1. A PARABLE OF THE OLIVE TREE (v.17).

The olive tree was the most useful, productive, and valuable tree in Israel; therefore, it was precious to the economy and welfare of the nation. Because of this, the nation's relationship to God was sometimes pictured as an olive tree (cp. Ps.52:8; Jer.11:16; Hos.14:6).

Now note the exact picture given. The natural branches refer to Israel, and the wild olive branches refer to Gentile believers. The olive tree refers to God and a right relationship with Him.

1. Some natural branches were broken off the olive tree and rejected. Some Jews did not and do not believe in Christ; therefore, they are not attached to God. They do not have a right relationship with God. But note: only some of the branches were broken off. Some Jews did accept Christ as the Messiah and did maintain a right relationship with God.

> **"Therefore say I unto you, The kingdom of God shall be taken from you, and given to a nation bringing forth the fruits thereof" (Mt.21:43).**

2. Some wild olive branches were grafted into the tree. Note that the words "and thou" or "you" is singular. Paul is not speaking to Gentiles as a whole but to the individual Gentile. Note two things.

a. The Gentile believer is said to have been a *wild olive branch*. The word "wild" means that the Gentile was not part of the olive tree (God); he was outside and estranged and alienated from the olive tree (God). Therefore, he was...
- part of the wilderness and desert and uncultivated world
- growing loose and uncontrolled
- useless and worthless
- uncared for and unprotected
- insect-infested, sour, and inferior

b. The Gentile believer is now said to have been grafted into the olive tree. He is now attached to God, that is, in a right relationship with God; therefore, he now partakes of the root and fatness of the olive tree. Very simply, this means that the believer is fed and nourished by God.

APPLICATION:
The glorious privilege of being nourished by God becomes as much the right of the Gentile as it is of the Jews.

> **"And in thy seed shall all the nations of the earth be blessed; because thou hast obeyed my voice" (Gen.22:18).**
> **"All the ends of the world shall remember and turn unto the Lord: and all the kindreds of the nations shall worship before thee" (Ps.22:27).**
> **"And when the Gentiles heard this, they were glad, and glorified the word of the Lord: and as many as were ordained to eternal life believed" (Acts 13:48).**

c. Note the words "with them." The Gentile believer is grafted into the olive tree *with the natural branches*. This is important to note, for it means there is *only* one family of God, not two. Both the natural branches and the wild branches are part of the same olive tree. The only difference is that the natural branches were the first branches that grew on the olive tree. The wild branches had to be brought or grafted into the tree.

APPLICATION:
Note that some natural branches are broken off because they did not bear fruit.

> **"If a man abide not in me, he is cast forth as a branch, and is withered; and men gather them, and cast them into the fire, and they are burned" (Jn.15:6).**

QUESTIONS:
1. Throughout Scripture, God uses pictures to help us better understand what He is saying to us. As a Christian believer, whether Jew or Gentile, where do you fit into this picture?
2. Is your place on the tree (with God) a guaranteed one or is it subject to change? What is your role in assuring that you will never be cut off from the tree (from God)?

2. WARNING 1: DO NOT BE ARROGANT (v.18).

The Gentile believer must not be arrogant and prideful over the Jews. The idea is that...

- we must not treat them as inferior beings because they deny Christ
- we must not insult and ridicule them because they differ from us as Christian believers
- we must not trample them underfoot because they refuse to believe and be like us
- we must not boast that we know the truth about the Messiah and they do not
- we must not glory in our knowledge of Christ, conveying the idea that we are better than the Jews

The Gentile believer has no right to elevate himself over the Jews nor over anyone else. The reason is clearly seen. We were once wild branches, very wild. We did not bear the root (Judaism); the root bore us (Christianity). If it had not been for Judaism, there would be no Christianity. If it had not been for Jewish believers, there would be no Christian believers. If Peter and Paul and the others had not surrendered their lives to preach Christ, then the message of Christ would never have reached us. We must never forget that "salvation is of the Jews" (Jn.4:22).

APPLICATION 1:

Every Gentile believer owes a debt to Jewish people. We must carry the gospel to the Jews even as some of the earliest Christian Jews brought the gospel to us.

"For I am not ashamed of the gospel of Christ: for it is the power of God unto salvation to every one that believeth; to the Jew first, and also to the Greek" (Ro.1:16).

APPLICATION 2:

All boasting and arrogance, pride and conceit against the Jews is wrong. It is wrong to elevate ourselves above others; in fact, it is even wrong to *think* that we are better or higher than anyone else.

"For I say, through the grace given unto me, to every man that is among you, not to think of himself more highly than he ought to think; but to think soberly, according as God hath dealt to every man the measure of faith" (Ro.12:3).

ILLUSTRATION:

Some people believe that their social position, economic status, or *spirituality* makes them more important than their fellow man. But as Scripture says:

"Pride *goeth* before destruction, and an haughty spirit before a fall" (Pr.16:18).

"A minister, a Boy Scout, and a computer expert were the only passengers on a small plane. The pilot came back to the cabin and said that the plane was going down but there were only three parachutes and four people. The pilot added, 'I should have one of the parachutes because I have a wife and three small children.' So he took one and jumped.

"The computer whiz said, 'I should have one of the parachutes because I am the smartest man in the world and everyone needs me.' So he took one and jumped.

"The minister turned to the Boy Scout and with a sad smile said, 'You are young and I have lived a rich life, so you take the remaining parachute, and I'll go down with the plane.'

"The Boy Scout said, 'Relax, Reverend, the smartest man in the world just picked up my knapsack and jumped out!'"[1]

As you walk through this life, make sure the baggage you are carrying is humility and not pride!

QUESTIONS:

1. There is often a temptation to become proud of your salvation. What elements of pride do you struggle with?
2. It has been said that all the ground at the foot of the cross is level. There is absolutely no spiritual *hierarchy* among fallen sinners. In light of this, what should your attitude be toward...
   - the Jew?
   - the Muslim?
   - the Buddhist?
   - the secular humanist?

---

[1] Michael P. Green. *Illustrations for Biblical Preaching*, p.287-288.

3. WARNING 2: FEAR COMPLACENCY AND UNBELIEF (v.19-21).

There is the danger of Gentile believers thinking...
- they are more *acceptable* to God because they have replaced the Jews as the true followers of God
- they are safe and secure in Christianity because Christianity is the religion that acknowledges God's Son

However, we must always remember what this Scripture is saying: Israel was not rejected by God so that we, the Gentiles, might be saved. Israel was rejected by God because of unbelief. God did not and does not reject one people in order to save another people. God reaches out to every nation of people, longing for all to be grafted into (to be a part of) Him.

God accepts a person because the person believes in His Son Jesus Christ. The Jews did not believe; some Gentiles did believe. A Gentile believer stands attached to the olive tree by faith, not because of any goodness or merit or value within himself.

Now note: the Gentile believer must guard against complacency, against feeling safe and secure and more acceptable because he stands in Christianity, the religion that acknowledges God's Son. The Gentile believer must not be high-minded, but rather fear. He must fear, for God is less likely to spare the unnatural branches than He was the natural branches. The warning is strong: "Take heed lest He also spare thee not" (v.21).

APPLICATION:

If God did not spare the Jews because of their unbelief, how much more will He not spare us. The Jews were the natural branches; we are the unnatural branches.
- ⇒ The Jews had the godly heritage; we had the wild, ungodly heritage.
- ⇒ The Jews had the fathers, the followers of the only living and true God; we had heathen, polytheistic fathers, fathers who created humanistic gods to suit their own fancies.
- ⇒ The Jews had the Word of God and the Savior; we had neither.
- ⇒ The Jews had the prophets of God; we had the false humanistic priests of the world.

In light of this and of so much more depravity, we must guard against self-complacency and conceit. We must walk in humility and in the fear of God, fearing unbelief lest we too be *broken off* (v.17).

"He that believeth on the Son hath everlasting life: and he that believeth not the Son shall not see life: but the wrath of God abideth on him" (Jn.3:36).

QUESTIONS:
1. On what basis did God save you from your sins? Why does He treat all sinners the same?
2. In what areas of your life do you struggle with complacency?

4. WARNING 3: TAKE A SHARP LOOK AT THE GOODNESS AND SEVERITY OF GOD (v.22).

The Gentile believer must take a sharp look at the goodness and severity of God.

1. The severity of God is seen in the spiritual fall of Israel. In this sense, the word "severity" means abrupt, sharp, rough, cut off. The Jews had committed the very sins the Gentiles are being warned about in this passage.
- The Jews had developed an attitude of arrogance and boasting toward other people, refusing to carry the Word of God to them.

- The Jews had felt high-minded and complacent, feeling safe and secure, thinking themselves to be more acceptable to God than other people.

In addition to these gross sins, the Jews had rejected God's prophets down through the centuries until they eventually killed God's very own Son. In one brief word, their sin was *unbelief*. The vast majority of the Jews never did believe God, not to the point that they loved God supremely. As a result, the judgment and severity of God fell upon them.

> "You only have I known of all the families of the earth: there-
> fore I will punish you for all your iniquities" (Amos 3:2).

2. The goodness of God is seen in the grafting in and acceptance of the Gentiles by God. But note the stress of this point: the goodness of God is given only to those who continue in God's goodness. A person who knows about the love of God must walk and live in God's goodness. The word "continue" means to remain, be steadfast, abide, persevere, endure. The idea is both *position* and *relationship*. The believer...
- is positioned in the goodness of God
- is related to the goodness of God

It is the picture of a person who is remaining and abiding in the house of God's goodness. A Gentile believer must continue and abide, endure and persevere in the goodness of God, or else he too will be cut off just as the Jews were cut off (v.17).

> "Or despisest thou the riches of his goodness and forbearance
> and longsuffering; not knowing that the goodness of God leadeth
> thee to repentance?" (Ro.2:4).

QUESTIONS:
1. When you picture God, do you see Him as...
   - a benevolent grandfather type?
   - a deity who is out of touch with the world's problems?
   - an insane tyrant who rules with an unforgiving iron fist?
   - a holy and righteous God who grants both mercy and judgment?
   What is the only way to get an accurate view of God's true nature and character?
2. No person or nation of people is above committing the same sins as Israel: un-belief, complacency, and pride. What can you do to keep yourself from re-peating their mistakes?
3. What does it mean to continue in God's goodness? What are some things in your life that could prevent you from doing this?

5. WARNING 4: BE ALERT, FOR THE RESTORATION IS A PROBABLE EVENT (v.23-24).

The Gentile believer must know that Israel's restoration is a probable event.
   1. The restoration of Israel is conditional. Note the word "if"—"if they abide not still in unbelief." Genuine belief is the condition for salvation. A person has to turn from his unbelief to belief in order to be grafted in and accepted by God. No person comes to God unless he believes in His Son Jesus Christ.

> "For God so loved the world, that he gave his only begotten
> Son, that whosoever believeth in him should not perish,
> but have everlasting life" (Jn.3:16).

2. God is able to graft the Jews back into the olive tree. Two things are meant by this.

a. God is *able* because of His enormous love. God loves everyone and will forgive any person for anything if that person will turn from his life of sin and unbelief. God will accept any person who approaches Him through His Son Jesus Christ.

"Who is a God like unto thee, that pardoneth iniquity, and passeth by the transgression of the remnant of his heritage? he retaineth not his anger for ever, because he delighteth in mercy" (Mic. 7:18).

b. God is *able* because of His enormous knowledge and power. God is God; therefore, He has unlimited knowledge and power. He knows when a man's heart is subject to Him and moving toward Him. He knows just when to move upon a person's heart, and He can arrange circumstances that will cause the person to turn to Him. Therefore, when the time comes, He has the power to stir Jewish hearts to turn to Him in large numbers. The valley of dry bones can be resurrected by the power of God (Ezk.37:1f).

"Now to him that is of power to stablish you according to my gospel, and the preaching of Jesus Christ, according to the revelation of the mystery, which was kept secret since the world began" (Ro.16:25).
"For with God nothing shall be impossible" (Lk.1:37).

ILLUSTRATION:

We often forget what kind of God we need to save us. We need a God who is *able* to save and who *wants* to save. We need a God who is all-knowing and all-powerful.

"Some years ago in a little western town, a crowd of men gathered about a store window through which they saw a large American eagle. It was fastened by one of its feet to a chain which was secured at the other end by a ring in the floor. Held captive this way for some months, it had become seemingly indifferent to its condition. While the men were looking at the huge bird, a tall, young mountaineer pushed his way through the crowd and entered the store. He asked the proprietor [owner] what he would take for the eagle, and the owner said, 'Two dollars.'

"When the young man took the money from his pocket and paid the price, the keeper of the store unfastened the chain and handed the eagle to his new owner. Followed by the crowd, he carried the great bird down the street until he came to a signboard, and on top of this, he placed the one-time child of the skies. But the great bird remained motionless and the crowd was disappointed. It had been bound so long to this earth that it did not seem to care to fly any longer.

"Suddenly, high above the mountain, the sun struck its eyes, and the eagle seemed to remember that it was an eagle and that its home was up yonder among the crags and the cliffs. It lifted first one foot and then the other. With a shriek and a bound, it flew away, and higher and higher it ascended until it was lost in the face of the sun. The crowd cheered."[2]

In the same way, our Lord and Savior Jesus Christ has set His people free. As He offers us a glimpse of Himself and of Heaven, we have no other choice but to leave behind our chains and soar with Him.

---

[2] Ted Kyle & John Todd. *A Treasury of Bible Illustrations*. (Chattanooga, TN: AMG Publishers, 1995), p.296-297.

3. The grafting in of the natural branches (the Jews) is much more likely than the calling of the Gentiles was. Note the words "much more." Paul is confident that God is not only able, but God will graft the Jews back into the olive tree. Paul proclaims that the Jews will turn to Christ and be restored into a right relationship with God.

"Esaias also crieth concerning Israel, Though the number of the children of Israel be as the sand of the sea, a remnant shall be saved" (Ro.9:27).

QUESTIONS:
1. Israel's restoration is conditional. What is that specific condition? Is that condition any different than what is required of you?
2. Why is God willing to graft the Jews back into the olive tree? What does this tell you about the character of God?

SUMMARY:

A careful study of Scripture reveals a very telling fact: no man, Jew or Gentile, is ever to take his salvation for granted. The challenge for every believer is to live each day with a spirit of gratitude to the Lord. Why? Because salvation is much too precious and costly a gift to abuse by ignoring the One who willingly gave up His life for us. A life committed to Christ is a life that testifies to the truth, acknowledging Christ as Lord, Judge, and Savior. Paul reminds us of this very thing in the parable of the olive tree:

Warning 1: do not be arrogant.
Warning 2: fear complacency and unbelief.
Warning 3: take a sharp look at the goodness and severity of God.
Warning 4: be alert, for the restoration is a probable event.

PERSONAL JOURNAL NOTES:
(Reflection & Response)

1. The most important thing that I learned from this lesson was:

2. The thing that I need to work on the most is:

3. I can apply this lesson to my life by:

4. Closing Prayer of Commitment: (put your commitment down on paper).

	I. The Restoration of Israel & Its Surety, 11:25-36	past have not believed God, yet have now obtained mercy through their unbelief:	liever's mercy & witness to the Jews
1. Surety 1: God's great revelation about the Jews	25 For I would not, brethren, that ye should be ignorant of this mystery, lest ye should be wise in your own conceits;	31 Even so have these also now not believed, that through your mercy they also may obtain mercy.	
a. It was a mystery			
b. Israel's blindness is only partial: "In part"			
c. Israel's blindness is only temporary	that blindness in part is happened to Israel, until the fulness of the Gentiles be come in.	32 For God hath concluded them all in unbelief, that he might have mercy upon all.	5. Surety 5: God's holiness & mercy
1) Until the fulness of the Gentiles is come			
2) All Israel shall be saved	26 And so all Israel shall be saved: as it is written, There shall come out of Sion the Deliverer, and shall turn away ungodliness from Jacob:	33 O the depth of the riches both of the wisdom and knowledge of God! how unsearchable are his judgments, and his ways past finding out!	6. Surety 6: God's glorious plan for the world
2. Surety 2: God's promise in Scripture—God's Deliverer, Jesus Christ, shall turn Israel			a. His plan includes His wisdom & knowledge, His judgments & ways
3. Surety 3: God's pleasure with Israel's forefathers	27 For this is my covenant unto them, when I shall take away their sins. 28 As concerning the gospel, they are enemies for your sakes: but as touching the election, they are beloved for the fathers' sakes.	34 For who hath known the mind of the Lord? or who hath been his counsellor? 35 Or who hath first given to him, and it shall be recompensed unto him again?	b. No man can grasp God's plan
a. God loves Israel because of the great faith of their forefathers			c. No man can earn God's gift
b. God is unchangeable: He shall fulfill His will for Israel	29 For the gifts and calling of God are without repentance.	36 For of him, and through him, and to him, are all things: to whom be glory for ever. Amen.	d. God alone is the source, the channel, & the end of all things
4. Surety 4: The be-	30 For as ye in times		

Section VII
ISRAEL AND THE GOSPEL OF RIGHTEOUSNESS
Romans 9:1-11:36

Study 9: **The Restoration of Israel and Its Surety**

Text: **Romans 11:25-36**

Aim: To gain one unshakable assurance: God has a firm grip on your life

Memory Verse:
> "**O the depth of the riches both of the wisdom and knowledge of God! how unsearchable are his judgments, and his ways past finding out!**" (Romans 11:33).

INTRODUCTION:

You might be familiar with the old spiritual, "He's Got the Whole World In His Hands." The title reminds us of this great fact: God is in complete control of our lives. A small child feels very secure in a large crowd of people if his hand is in the firm grip of his parent. The size of the crowd nor the place where they are does not matter to the child—if his hand is in the right place. In like fashion, there is no better feeling than for you to know that God will never lose His grip on your life. Even when...

- you fall into sin for a period of time
- the political boundaries of nations change
- world leaders are rushing nations into climactic wars
- the carnality of the world becomes even more blatant, deceiving the naive
- all hope seems to be forever lost

In spite of all of these and endless other circumstances, God is sovereign and good, and He remains firmly positioned upon His throne. From His throne, God will rule and reign, fulfilling His will—all of His will—to the most minute detail.

Israel's history is a surety. God loves man with an infinite love, and God's love is unchangeable. Therefore, any person can be restored to God if the person will call upon the name of the Lord Jesus Christ, asking Christ to save him. This is clearly seen in the history of Israel. Israel's restoration is a surety, and as such, Israel stands as a prime example of the unchangeable love of God toward man.

OUTLINE:
1. Surety 1: God's great revelation about the Jews (v.25-26).
2. Surety 2: God's promise in Scripture—God's Deliverer, Jesus Christ, shall turn Israel (v.26-27).
3. Surety 3: God's pleasure with Israel's forefathers (v.28-29).
4. Surety 4: the believer's mercy and witness to the Jews (v.30-31).
5. Surety 5: God's holiness and mercy (v.32).
6. Surety 6: God's glorious plan for the world (v.33-36).

1. SURETY 1: GOD'S GREAT REVELATION ABOUT THE JEWS (v.25-26).

The revelation comes from Paul. Note three significant facts.

1. The revelation had been an unknown mystery until Paul. The word "mystery" in the Bible is not used as most men use the word, as something mysterious or difficult to understand. *A Biblical mystery means that...*
- something that was unknown is now revealed
- something that was hidden is now made known
- something that was a secret is now told

The future of Israel is now revealed and made known to men. Note exactly why God revealed the future of Israel: so we would not be ignorant of Israel's future; so we would not be wise in our own conceits or imaginations. This last reason can mean two things.

⇒ Gentiles become guilty of looking down upon the Jews because the Jews are so different from the rest of us. They have rejected Jesus Christ and are opposed to Christianity to such a degree that they remain almost exclusively among themselves. Gentiles face the danger of becoming puffed up, of thinking that they are more acceptable to God because they look with favor upon Jesus Christ and are more open in professing Him. There is the danger of being prideful and arrogant, of lording it over the Jews.

⇒ A Gentile, especially a Gentile believer, can begin to think that his idea of Israel's destiny is the correct idea and that he and the followers of his position are the persons who have a full understanding of the truth. All other understandings are incorrect. There is the danger of becoming "wise in [our] own conceits."

2. Israel's blindness is only partial, only "in part." There were Jewish believers who followed Christ in His day and there have been Jewish believers who have followed

Christ down through the centuries. The blindness and hardness of Israel to the gospel is not total; it is only partial. Granted, just as Scripture says, so many Jews have rejected and still do reject Christ that it is as though *all Israel as a nation* has stumbled and fallen over Him (cp. v.8-9). However, there have been and always will be some Jews who believe. Israel's blindness is only partial.

3. Israel's blindness is only temporary. Two statements clearly show this.
   a. Israel's blindness is only "until the fulness of the Gentiles be come in." Just what "the fulness of the Gentiles" means is open to different interpretations, but it does not change what is to happen to Israel. It only affects *when* the blindness is to be removed from Israel. Israel's blindness is to continue *only* until the fulness of the Gentiles comes. Now what does this event mean? The fulness of the Gentiles can mean...
      * a certain number of Gentile converts are to be saved, to fill up the "cut off branches of Israel" (v.17-21).
      * the end of the Gentile age, a time when the emphasis of salvation will no longer be upon the Gentiles but upon the Jews.
      * the end of the Gentile age, a time when God will rapture the church (all believers) and cause a revival among the Jews who will then become the primary witnesses for Him.

      The point is worth repeating. No matter what the phrase "the fulness of the Gentiles" means, it does not change the event of Israel's revival. The blindness of Israel will be removed.
   b. "All Israel shall be saved." The fact could be stated no clearer:
      ⇒ Israel's blindness is only temporary.
      ⇒ The restoration of Israel is a surety.
      ⇒ Israel shall experience a revival.
      ⇒ Israel shall turn to God's Son, the Lord Jesus Christ.

APPLICATION:
There is hope for every person. Note two critical facts:
1) A person's blindness to the Lord Jesus Christ is only partial. As long as a person is alive, he can still turn to Christ.
2) A person's blindness is temporary *only* if the person turns to the Lord Jesus Christ. Unless a person believes and commits his life to Christ, his blindness becomes permanent, and he is lost forever.

> **"And this is the condemnation, that light is come into the world, and men loved darkness rather than light, because their deeds were evil" (Jn.3:19).**

QUESTIONS:
1. Paul says that Israel's blindness is only partial. How should this impact your perception of Jews?
3. At what point is it acceptable to stop witnessing to lost souls, whether Jew or Gentile? Are you ready to give up on somebody? (Think where you might be if someone had given up on you!)

A CLOSER LOOK # 1

(11:25-26) **Israel, Restoration**: there are many reasons for taking this passage at its face value, that is, as a prediction of the Jewish people's conversion as a nation.

1. The whole context favors this view. The conversion of the Jews as a probable event has been described in the plainest and simplest of terms.

2. The nation was rejected, not as individuals but as a community or nation. Therefore, it is only natural to say that when God speaks of a restoration, He is speaking not

---

only of individuals' being restored, but of the community or nation as being restored (v.11, 15).

3. Paul speaks of a great event, something that will attract universal attention.

4. Paul says this is a "mystery." The gradual conversion of a few Jews would be no mystery. When speaking of the mystery of the Gentiles (Eph.1:9; 3:4), Paul is speaking of the Gentiles as a community being admitted into the church of God. Therefore, it is only natural to assume that when Paul speaks of the mystery of the Jews, he is speaking of a great event, of a great movement of Jews toward Christ.

5. The words "all Israel" (v.26) cannot mean the spiritual Israel. Such an interpretation would do violence to the use of the word "Israel" throughout this whole context. It simply means Israel as a nation, as a community of people. This is also clear from the warnings that are given throughout this passage to both Gentile and Jew.

However, "all Israel" looks at the nation en masse. It does not necessarily have to mean every single individual. Note a very significant fact: when the nation became hardened, Scripture speaks of the nation, that is, of all Israel, being rejected. However, not every single person was rejected. There were a few individuals who still believed and who comprised a remnant (cp. Ro.11:1-10). Every single individual was not lost, so the same is probably true when the nation is restored. There will be a large number of Jews who will become open and tender to the gospel, but not necessarily every individual. In one simple statement: Israel will be open to the gospel just as the Gentiles are open to the gospel. Many Jews will begin to be saved just as many Gentiles are now saved.

> "That then the LORD thy God will turn thy captivity, and have compassion upon thee, and will return and gather thee from all the nations, whither the LORD thy God hath scattered thee" (Dt.30:3).
>
> "And it shall come to pass in that day, that the great trumpet shall be blown, and they shall come which were ready to perish in the land of Assyria, and the outcasts in the land of Egypt, and shall worship the LORD in the holy mount at Jerusalem" (Is.27:13).
>
> "I will surely assemble, O Jacob, all of thee; I will surely gather the remnant of Israel" (Mic.2:12).

2. SURETY 2: GOD'S PROMISE IN SCRIPTURE—GOD'S DELIVERER, JESUS CHRIST, SHALL TURN ISRAEL (v.26-27).

Scripture gives a glimpse into the future of Israel's restoration in this verse, but note that it is only a glimpse. Just how Israel will be restored is not discussed in this passage. Only two major things are given.

1. Some great manifestation of Christ the Deliverer will cause Israel to turn to the gospel.

> "For I say unto you [Israel], Ye shall not see me henceforth, till ye shall say, Blessed is he that cometh in the name of the Lord" (Mt.23:39).
>
> "But their minds [Israel] were blinded: for until this day remaineth the same veil untaken away in the reading of the old testament; which veil is done away in Christ. But even unto this day, when Moses is read, the veil is upon their heart. Nevertheless when it [Israel] shall turn to the Lord, the veil shall be taken away" (2 Cor.3:14-16).

2. The great Deliverer, Jesus Christ, will do two things for Israel.
   a. Jesus Christ will turn away ungodliness from Israel (cp. Is.27:9).
   b. Jesus Christ will fulfill God's covenant with Israel: He will take away their sins (cp. Is.59:21; 27:9).

"Then Peter said unto them, Repent, and be baptized every one of you in the name of Jesus Christ for the remission of sins, and ye shall receive the gift of the Holy Ghost" (Acts 2:38).

ILLUSTRATION:

Jesus Christ will do for Israel what He has done for anyone who has ever placed his faith in the work of Christ. When a person believes in Christ, God promises *through Christ* to forgive his sins and place within his heart a desire to live a godly life. This defines what a Christian is: one who has believed in Jesus Christ. It is a promise that must be claimed by every man in order to be saved. Sadly, there are many who do not know what it means to be a Christian.

"A small boy sat in church with his mother and listened to a sermon entitled 'What is a Christian?' Every time the minister asked the question, he banged his fist on the pulpit for emphasis.

"The tension produced by the sermon built up in the boy and he finally whispered to his mother, 'Mama, do you know? Do you know what a Christian is?'

"'Yes, dear,' she replied. 'Now sit still and be quiet.'

"Finally, as the minister was winding up the sermon, he again thundered, 'What is a Christian?' and banged especially hard on the pulpit. This time it was too much for the little boy, so he jumped up and cried out, 'Tell him, Momma, tell him!'" [1]

Being a Christian does not mean...
- doing good deeds for the poor
- going to every church service
- knowing all the religious terms
- being better than other people
- not cursing, not drinking, not robbing a bank

None of these has anything to do with becoming a Christian. Becoming a Christian is believing in Christ and trusting Him to forgive your sins. Have *you* trusted in Christ? Are *you* a Christian?

QUESTIONS:
1. All of God's promises, like the restoration of Israel, are found in the Bible. How ambitious are you when it comes to claiming God's promises for your life? Which of His promises do you claim the most? The least?
2. The promise of Christ to restore Israel should be an exciting thing for Christian believers? Why? Do you understand and pray for it like you should?

3. SURETY 3: GOD'S PLEASURE WITH ISRAEL'S FOREFATHERS (v.28-29).

1. The statement "they [the Jews] are enemies for your sakes" sounds as though God predestinated Israel's rejection. However, God does not cause sin (Jas.1:13-14); God does not cause people to reject His Son and His will. What the statement means is this: the word "enemy" has both an active and a passive meaning. It means either hostile or hated by, and it means either hating or being hated. It is possible that in this particular passage it is to be read both ways. The Jews were hostile to God; they had refused the offer of God's righteousness in Jesus Christ, and they had refused to be the missionary force for God's Son. Therefore, they had aroused God's displeasure. They hated God; consequently, God was displeased with them.

Note that God did what He had to do. He turned to the Gentiles. Israel had refused to be the missionary force for God's Son, so God had to turn to the Gentiles. Among

---

[1] Michael P. Green. *Illustrations for Biblical Preaching*, p.56.

the Gentiles, God found a receptive people. The Gentiles accepted the offer of God's righteousness in Jesus Christ, and they have become the missionary force for Christ to the world. It is critical to remember something, however: this does not mean that every Gentile is saved. Most are not, but a fair number of them have accepted and still do accept Jesus Christ. We must remember this: in this passage God is speaking *nationally not individually*.

⇒ A few Jews do accept Christ as the Messiah, but the number is small. The number is so small that God can say that Israel as a nation has rejected Christ.

⇒ A far greater number of Gentiles accept Christ as their Savior. However, as is clearly evidenced by the unholy lives of most Gentiles, the majority reject Him. But the number is large enough for God to say that the Gentiles as a *community* do accept His offer of salvation in Christ.

APPLICATION:

The point is that God is speaking *nationally not individually*. And we must remember this, for it is absolutely essential that every individual make a *personal decision* to receive Christ and follow Him by living a pure life.

"For the grace of God that bringeth salvation hath appeared to all men, teaching us that, denying ungodliness and worldly lusts, we should live soberly, righteously, and godly, in this present world; looking for that blessed hope, and the glorious appearing of the great God and our Saviour Jesus Christ; who gave himself for us, that he might redeem us from all iniquity, and purify unto himself a peculiar people, zealous of good works" (Tit.2:11-14).

2. The statement "they [the Jews] are beloved for the fathers' sakes" shows that God still loves Israel. As a people, they are still very precious to Him. How can this be when they have been so hostile to God's Son, Jesus Christ, and toward the missionary force of God's Son? There are two reasons why God still loves Israel:

a. The forefathers of Israel were a godly people, a people of unusual faith in God. There were people such as Abraham, Isaac, Jacob, Moses, Joshua, Deborah, Ruth, Elijah—the list could go on and on. As Scripture says:

"And what shall I more say? for the time would fail me to tell of Gedeon, and of Barak, and of Samson, and of Jephthae; of David also, and Samuel, and of the prophets: who through faith subdued kingdoms, wrought righteousness, obtained promises, stopped the mouths of lions, quenched the violence of fire, escaped the edge of the sword, out of weakness were made strong, waxed valiant in fight, turned to flight the armies of the aliens. Women received their dead raised to life again: and others were tortured, not accepting deliverance; that they might obtain a better resurrection: and others had trial of cruel mockings and scourgings, yea, moreover of bonds and imprisonment: they were stoned, they were sawn asunder, were tempted, were slain with the sword: they wandered about in sheepskins and goatskins; being destitute, afflicted, tormented; (of whom the world was not worthy:) they wandered in deserts, and in mountains, and in dens and caves of the earth" (Heb.11:32-38).

Such godly men and women knew God—knew Him personally and intimately—and God would never forget a people who loved Him so greatly. Keep this in mind as well: godly people are a praying people, a people who pray for their families and neighbors, for their nation and world. And God hears and answers the prayers of His people. God would never turn His back upon Israel for this reason alone.

b. There is a second reason why God still loves Israel: God Himself is *unchangeable in His gifts and calling*. God called and promised some very special gifts to the forefathers of Israel, and God is unchangeable; therefore...

- every purpose for which God called Israel shall be fulfilled in the lives of many Jews
- every gift God promised Israel shall be given to many Jews

The point is striking. God does not change His mind. He is constant, immutable, unchangeable. He shall perfectly fulfill His calling and gifts to Israel.

"**The counsel of the LORD standeth for ever, the thoughts of his heart to all generations**" (**Ps.33:11**).

"**But thou art the same, and thy years shall have no end**" (**Ps.102:27**).

"**Thy name, O LORD, endureth for ever; and thy memorial, O LORD, throughout all generations**" (**Ps.135:13**).

"**For I am the LORD, I change not**" (**Mal.3:6**).

"**Thou art the same, and thy years shall not fail**" (**Heb.1:12**).

"**Jesus Christ the same yesterday, and to day, and for ever**" (**Heb.13:8**).

QUESTIONS:
1. What does it mean that the Jews "are enemies for your sakes"? How did God use the Jews' rejection of Christ to bring about a blessing to you?
2. How can you know for sure that God still loves Israel? What does this tell you about God's character? How can you use this scenario to witness to an unbeliever?

4. SURETY 4: THE BELIEVER'S MERCY AND WITNESS TO THE JEWS (v.30-31).

These two verses are speaking historically. Very simply, history shall be repeated.
⇒ In times past—before Christ ever came—the Gentiles did not know and obey God, but the Jews did.
⇒ Eventually the Jews rejected God, which is ultimately seen in their killing God's Son, Jesus Christ. They, too, failed to believe (obey God).
⇒ Therefore, God turned to the Gentiles.

Now note: if we came to know God through the unbelief of the Jews, how much more shall the Jews be shown mercy through the mercy of the Gentiles!

The point seems to be this: we truly know the mercy of God through Jesus Christ our Lord; therefore, we want the world to experience the same mercy and forgiveness of sins. In particular, we feel indebted to the Jews, the people through whom God gave us His Word, His Son, and His promises. Therefore, Scripture predicts that the evangelistic efforts to reach the Jews will someday bear fruit. The Jews will be reached by the mercy of God; they shall believe and obey Jesus Christ as Lord. The Jews shall be restored into the favor of God.

APPLICATION:
Every believer who knows the mercy of God should share the mercy of God. God hates exclusiveness, prejudice, partiality. The world desperately needs the gospel, the Jew as well as the Gentile, and God demands that His mercy be shared with the world.

"Then said Jesus to them again, Peace be unto you: *as my Father hath sent me*, **even so send I you" (Jn.20:21).**

1. God will show you how to be merciful to Jews whom you know personally. Are you open and available to His leading? How would you go about sharing Christ with a Jew?
2. Has your own salvation caused you to reach out with a passion to the lost? If not, why not? Who needs to be added to your prayer list today?

5. SURETY 5: GOD'S HOLINESS AND MERCY (v.32).

The word "concluded" means to shut up in a place, to close up, to lock up. This is an unusual idea: God has taken men, both Jews and Gentiles, and shut them up to unbelief or disobedience. This is the judicial judgment of God. It is the picture of God's using sin and events for good. God takes sin and works it out for the good of the world. Man has chosen sin, choosing to go his own way in life, so God allows man to do his own thing. God locks man up in his own world of selfishness, allowing man to roam around in his world of sin. Why? So that man's true nature of sinfulness will be clearly seen, thereby causing the honest and thinking man to seek God. God will have mercy upon all, both Jew and Gentile; but before men can come to God, they must confess two things:
⇒ that they are sinful and dying creatures in desperate need of God.
⇒ that God exists, that He will have mercy upon the person who diligently seeks Him.

Now note: all men, both Jew and Gentile, are shut up in their world of sin. Why? That God may have mercy upon both. The holiness and love of God assure that the Jews will be saved and restored to the mercy of God. All that is needed is for the Jews to begin seeking God. God will have mercy upon any who genuinely seek Him.

> **"But without faith it is impossible to please him: for he that cometh to God must believe that he is, and that he is a rewarder of them that diligently seek him" (Heb.11:6).**
> **"Who is a God like unto thee, that pardoneth iniquity, and passeth by the transgression of the remnant of his heritage? he retaineth not his anger for ever, because he delighteth in mercy" (Mic.7:18).**

1. In what ways have you personally seen God take sin and work it out for good?
2. How have God's holiness and mercy worked in your own life?

6. SURETY 6: GOD'S GLORIOUS PLAN FOR THE WORLD (v.33-36).

Note four points.
1. God's glorious plan for the world involves four great acts of God.
   a. His infinite wisdom and knowledge: knowing how to do everything perfectly; knowing how to create and arrange, order and govern everything so that all things work out perfectly. Note how God's wisdom and knowledge are said to be deep and rich: **"O the depth of the riches both of the wisdom and knowledge of God."** God's wisdom and knowledge are so deep and rich...
   - that angels desire to look into them (1 Pt.1:13)
   - that they are infinite (Eph.3:18)
   - that they are too wonderful for man (Ps.139:6. This one verse alone shows just how great God's mercy is toward us.)
   - that they include thoughts more numerous than the grains of sand in the world (Ps.139:17-18)

b. His infinite judgments and ways: His judgment in planning and deciding every-thing, and His ways in executing His purposes and decisions. Note that His judgments and ways are said to be unsearchable and past finding out.
⇒ Secret things belong to God (Dt.29:29).
⇒ God is glorified by His infinite judgments and ways (Pr.25:2).
⇒ The great things of God are unsearchable and without number (Job 5:9; 9:10).
⇒ Man cannot discover God by searching (Job 11:7).
⇒ There is no searching of God's understanding (Is.40:28).

2. No man can grasp God's plan. No man can know the mind of the Lord; no man can be a counsellor to God. Look at two significant points.
a. No man can grasp God's plan. Scripture makes this abundantly clear.

"[Jesus Christ] who only hath immortality, dwelling in the light which no man can approach unto; whom no man hath seen, nor can see: to whom be honour and power everlasting" (1 Tim.6:16).

b. Believers do, however, have *the mind of Christ*. This does not mean that be-lievers understand God and His ways perfectly, but it does mean that God re-veals Himself and the truth to believers—enough of Himself and His ways to save them from sin, death, judgment, and hell.

"For who hath known the mind of the Lord, that he may in-struct him? But we have the mind of Christ" (1 Cor.2:16).
"Now we have received, not the spirit of the world, but the spirit which is of God; that we might know the things that are freely given to us of God" (1 Cor.2:12).

3. No man can earn God's gift. Notice two facts about this verse.
a. No man can put God in debt to him. No man can give anything to God and claim that God owes him something in return. God owes man nothing. Man has rejected and rebelled against following God, choosing to go his own way. Man is committing high treason against God. Man does not deserve nor can he earn any favor from God. If man is to receive a favor from God, God has to freely give the favor.

"Many will say to me in that day, Lord, Lord, have we not prophesied in thy name? and in thy name have cast out devils? and in thy name done many wonderful works? And then will I profess unto them, I never knew you: depart from me, ye that work iniquity" (Mt.7:22-23).

b. Man's depravity should silence his boasting. It does not, but it should.

4. God alone is the source, the means, and the end of all things. Therefore, God is to be glorified forever and ever.
⇒ All things are *of God*: all things were created by and find their source in God.
⇒ All things are *through God*: all things come through His wisdom and knowl-edge, His judgments and ways.
⇒ All things are *to God*: all things exist for God, for His goodness and pleasure.

"Thou art worthy, O Lord, to receive glory and honour and power: for thou hast created all things, and for thy pleas-ure they are and were created" (Rev.4:11).

"All thy works shall praise thee, O LORD; and thy saints shall bless thee" (Ps.145:10).

"For ye are bought with a price: therefore glorify God in your body, and in your spirit, which are God's" (1 Cor.6:20).

ILLUSTRATION:

What a glorious conclusion to this section of Romans: God alone is the source, the channel, and the end of all things. If you faithfully believe this and live it out in your everyday life, then you will be a powerful testimony to God's glorious plan for man.

"One Sunday on their way home from church, a little girl turned to her mother and said, 'Mommy, the preacher's sermon this morning confused me. The mother said, 'Oh? Why is that?' The little girl replied, 'Well, he said that God is bigger than we are. Is that true?' The mother replied, 'Yes, that's true, honey.' "And he also said that God lives in us? Is that true Mommy?' Again the mother replied, 'Yes.' 'Well,' said the little girl, 'if God is bigger than us and he lives in us, wouldn't He show through?'"[2]

Out of the mouths of babes come some of the most profound statements of life! If you are allowing God to take control of your life, it will shine forth in a way that is impossible to hide!

QUESTIONS:

1. When are you most aware that God is still in control of the world's events? When are you least aware? What makes the difference?
2. Oftentimes, we are prone to give God a little advice on how or why something should be done. Does God need our counsel? Why is it impossible for man to fully grasp God's plan?

SUMMARY:

There are a lot of things in this world that are not sure any more. Nations, leaders, the economy, morals, character, and values seem to come and go with the winds of popular opinion. But through it all, one thing has remained stable, strong, and sure: God. God is in complete control of this world, ruling in the lives and events of every man who has ever lived. How can you be completely sure that God is in control? He has said so.

Surety 1: God's great revelation about the Jews.
Surety 2: God's promise in Scripture—God's Deliverer, Jesus Christ, shall turn Israel.
Surety 3: God's pleasure with Israel's forefathers.
Surety 4: the believer's mercy and witness to the Jews.
Surety 5: God's holiness and mercy.
Surety 6: God's glorious plan for the world.

---

[2] James S. Hewett. *Illustrations Unlimited.* (Wheaton, IL: Tyndale House Publishers, Inc., 1988), p. 303.

ROMANS 11:25-36

1. The most important thing that I learned from this lesson was:

2. The thing that I need to work on the most is:

3. I can apply this lesson to my life by:

4. Closing Prayer of Commitment: (put your commitment down on paper).

OUTLINE & SUBJECT INDEX

ROMANS
Volume 2, Chapters 6-11

ROMANS
Volume 2, Chapters 6-11

REMEMBER: When you look up a subject and turn to the Scripture reference, you have not only the Scripture, you have *an outline and a discussion* (commentary) of the Scripture and subject.

This is one of the *GREAT VALUES* of the Teacher's Outline & Study Bible. Once you have all the volumes, you will have not only what all other Bible indexes give you, that is, a list of all the subjects and their Scripture references, *BUT* you will also have...

- An outline of *every* Scripture and subject in the Bible.
- A discussion (commentary) on every Scripture and subject.
- Every subject supported by other Scriptures or cross references.

DISCOVER THE GREAT VALUE for yourself. Quickly glance below to the very first subject of the Index of Romans, Volume 2. It is:

ABIDE - ABIDING
    Meaning. "In" Christ.   Ro.8:1

Turn to the reference. Glance at the Scripture and outline of the Scripture, then read the commentary. You will immediately see the GREAT VALUE of the INDEX of the Teacher's Outline & Study Bible.

OUTLINE & SUBJECT INDEX

OUTLINE & SUBJECT INDEX

Sinful, depraved. Discussed. 7:14-17; 7:18-20

Struggles for deliverance. 8:28-39

Problem.

Human nature cannot solve sin problem. 7:14-17

Human will cannot solve sin problem. 7:18-20

Relationship with God. Ways all men are r. to God. 10:12

Spirit of. Can live forever. 8:10-11

MERCY

Duty. To seek God for m. 9:15-18

MIND

Law of. Meaning. 7:21-23

New m. Renewed by Jesus Christ. Discussed. 7:25

Of believer.

Pulled to spiritual things by Holy Spirit. 8:5-8

Renewed. 8:5-8

Verses. List of. 8:5-8

Vs. carnal m. Discussed. 8:5-8

MINISTERS (See BELIEVERS; DISCIPLES)

Commission - Mission.

Is important in God's plans. 10:14-15

To be enslaved by the gospel. 8:15

MISERY

Cause. Seeking God by law. 6:14-15

MISSION - MISSIONS (See EVANGELISM)

Duty. To reach city-dwellers & religionists. 10:14-15

Essentials. Fourfold. 10:14-15

MORTIFY

Meaning. 8:12-13

NATURE

Deliverance from. Shall be delivered from corruption. 8:19-22

Discussed. 8:19-22

State of. Is corruptible; suffering under corruption. 8:19-22

NEEDS - NECESSITIES

Verses. List of. 8:34

NEGLECT

Of duty. Knowing, but not doing. 9:4

NEW LIFE (See NEW MAN)

How to receive. By the resurrection of Christ. 6:3-5

Results.

Changes masters. 6:17-18

Frees from the law. 7:4

NEW MAN

Duty. To put on, to be clothed with Christ. 10:11

Law of. Discussed. 7:21-23

Result.

Changes masters. 6:17-18

Swaps sin for God. 6:17-18

Source - Cause. A decision for Christ. 6:17-18

NEWNESS OF SPIRIT

Meaning. 7:6

OBEY - OBEDIENCE

A Closer Look. Meaning. Synonymous with belief. 10:16

OLD MAN

Discussed. 6:6-7

Of believer. Old m. has been crucified with Christ. 6:6-7

OLIVE TREE

Discussed. 11:17

PARTIALITY

And God.

Treats all men just alike. 10:12

Ways all men are related to God. Four w. 10:12

PAUL

Accusations against. A false prophet & a liar. 9:1-3

Conversion & call.

Life of. Is proof of a Jewish remnant. 11:1

Life of.

Love for Israel, for his own people. 9:1-3; 11:13-15

Spiritual struggle. 7:14-25

Ministry. Love for Israel, for his own people. 9:1-3

PHARAOH

Nature. Evil, harsh, stubborn man. 9:15-18

Purpose. Raised up by God for God's purposes. 9:15-18

OUTLINE & SUBJECT INDEX

ILLUSTRATION INDEX

ROMANS
Volume 2, Chapters 6-11

ILLUSTRATION INDEX

ILLUSTRATION INDEX

ILLUSTRATION INDEX

PURPOSE STATEMENT

LEADERSHIP MINISTRIES WORLDWIDE

exists to equip ministers, teachers, and laymen in their
understanding, preaching, and teaching of God's Word
by publishing and distributing worldwide
The Preacher's Outline & Sermon Bible®
and related *Outline* Bible materials,
to reach & disciple men, women, boys, and girls for Jesus Christ.

•MISSION STATEMENT•

1. To make the Bible so understandable - its truth so clear and plain - that men
   and women everywhere, whether teacher or student, preacher or hearer,
   can grasp its Message and receive Jesus Christ as Savior; and…
2. To place the Bible in the hands of all who will preach and teach God's Holy
   Word, verse by verse, precept by precept, regardless of the individual's
   ability to purchase it.

The *Outline* Bible materials have been given to LMW for printing and especially
distribution worldwide at/below cost, by those who remain anonymous. One fact,
however, is as true today as it was in the time of Christ:

• The Gospel is free, but the cost of taking it is not •

LMW depends on the generous gifts of Believers with a heart for Him and a love and
burden for the lost. They help pay for the printing, translating, and placing *Outline*
Bible materials in the hands and hearts of those worldwide who will present God's
message with clarity, authority and understanding beyond their own.

LMW was incorporated in the state of Tennessee in July 1992 and received IRS 501(c) 3 nonprofit status in March 1994. LMW is an international, nondenominational mission organization.
All proceeds from USA sales, along with donations from donor partners, go 100% into under-
writing our translation and distribution projects of *Outline* Bible materials to preachers,
church & lay leaders, and Bible students around the world.

PO Box 21310 - Chattanooga, TN 37424 • (423) 855-2181 • FAX (423) 855-8616
• E-Mail - outlinebible@compuserve.com — Web site: www.outlinebible.org •

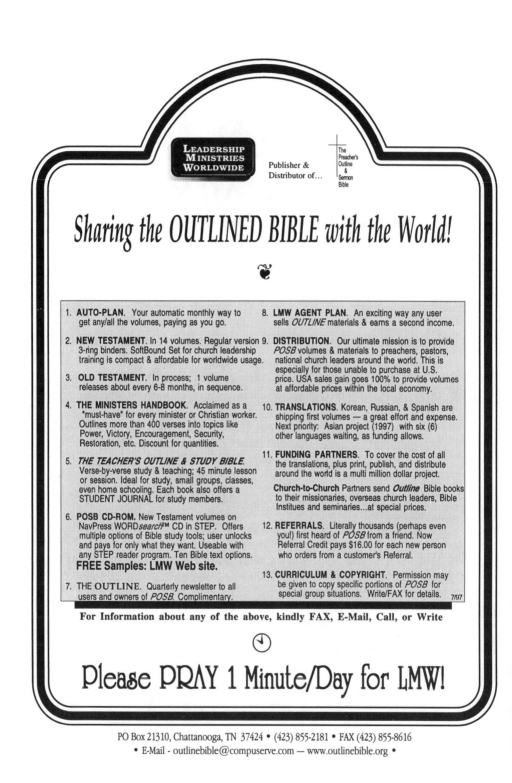